More
CLASSICS

FROM THE FILES OF

TODD WILBUR

Illustrated by the Author

A PLUME BOOK

PLUME
Published by the Penguin Group
Penguin Group (USA) Inc., 375 Hudson Street, New York, New York 10014, U.S.A.
Penguin Books Ltd, 80 Strand, London WC2R 0RL, England
Penguin Books Australia Ltd, 250 Camberwell Road, Camberwell, Victoria 3124, Australia
Penguin Books Canada Ltd, 10 Alcorn Avenue, Toronto, Ontario, Canada M4V 3B2
Penguin Books India (P) Ltd, 11 Community Centre, Panchsheel Park, New Delhi –
110 017, India
Penguin Books (N.Z.) Ltd, Cnr Rosedale and Airborne Roads, Albany, Auckland 1310,
New Zealand
Penguin Books (South Africa) (Pty) Ltd, 24 Sturdee Avenue, Rosebank, Johannesburg
2196, South Africa

Penguin Books Ltd, Registered Offices: 80 Strand, London WC2R 0RL, England

First published by Plume, a member of Penguin Group (USA) Inc.

First Printing, October 2005
10 9 8 7 6 5 4 3 2 1

Most of the recipes in this edition are selected from *Top Secret Recipes, More Top Secret Recipes, Even More Top Secret Recipes, Top Secret Restaurant Recipes, Low-Fat Top Secret Recipes, Top Secret Recipes Lite!,* and *Top Secret Recipes: Sodas, Smoothies, Spirits, & Shakes,* all published by Plume.

 REGISTERED TRADEMARK—MARCA REGISTRADA

ISBN: 0-452-28724-3

Manufactured in China.

CONTENTS

Restaurants

BEVERAGES: SODAS, SIPS, SMOOTHIES, AND SHAKES

Lite: Conversions

A LITTLE FOREWORD

As with the first *Top Secret Recipes,* each of these recipes was subjected to an array of bakings and mixings, batch after batch, until the closest representation of the actual commercial product was finally achieved. I did not swipe, heist, bribe, or otherwise obtain any formulas through coercion or illegal means. I'd like to think that many of these recipes are the actual formulas for their counterparts, but there's no way of knowing for sure. In such cases of closely guarded secret recipes, the closer one gets to matching a real product's contents, the less likely it is that the protective manufacturer will say so.

The objective here is to match the taste and texture of our favorite products with everyday ingredients. In most cases, obtaining the exact ingredients for these mass-produced foods is nearly impossible. For the sake of security and convenience, many of the companies have contracted confidentially with vendors for the specialized production and packaging of each of their products' ingredients. These prepackaged mixes and ingredients are then sent directly to the company for final preparation.

Debbi Fields of Mrs. Fields Cookies, for example, arranged with several individual companies to custom manufacture many of her cookies' ingredients. Her vanilla alone is specially blended from a variety of beans grown in various places around the world. The other ingredients—the chocolate, the eggs, the sugars, the flour—all get specialized attention specifically for the Mrs. Fields company. The same holds true for McDonald's, Wendy's, KFC, and most of the big-volume companies.

Even if you could bypass all the security measures and somehow get your hands on the secret formulas, you'd have a hard time executing the recipes without locating many ingredients usually impossible to find at the corner market. Therefore, with taste in mind, substitution of ingredients other than those that may be used in the actual products is necessary to achieve a closely cloned end result. Happy cloning!

INTRODUCTION

When a popular, ex–NBA basketball player was recently in Las Vegas, he was having a wild night at the roulette table. Tens of thousands of dollars had changed hands and he was getting mighty hungry. Recognizing this, the pit boss insisted on setting up a complimentary spread of food for the athlete and his entourage. The casino was braced to serve anything and everything the wealthy players desired. A dining room was set up; waiters and chefs stood by anxiously awaiting the order. Would the fancy feast include piles of imported Russian beluga caviar? Broiled fresh Maine lobster? Roquefort-encrusted corn-fed filet mignon? What do a large hungry man and his large hungry friends order when money isn't an issue? To the casino's delight the request was a simple one: It required only one person to make a quick trip to a drive-thru window just off the strip. Within twenty minutes the private dining room featured a fabulous spread of hot, juicy Fatburgers with cheese, thick milkshakes, and french fries. The hungry gamblers were in hamburger hog heaven.

I know that feeling well. Although I've never been "comped" for more than the $5.99 buffet while gambling in Las Vegas, I do know what it's like to crave that special sinful something, when nothing else matters. You lock on hard to the thought of a particular favorite food—one of your edible guilty pleasures—knowing for certain that you just won't be as deeply satisfied by anything else. When craving a drippy Taco Bell Burrito Supreme, a plateful of Peking duck—as good as Peking duck is at the right moment—isn't going to do the job. Sure, when it's all over your stomach's full just the same, but the road you mowed getting there wasn't the most delicious route.

For years now I've been sharing my secret recipes for clone cuisine, both here in these *Top Secret Recipes* books and on the

Web site at TopSecretRecipes.com. I've cloned recipes for drinks and for appetizers and entrees from well-known restaurant chains across the country, such as Chili's and T.G.I. Friday's. I've even created lite clone recipes for favorite sweet-tooth munchables such as Hostess Twinkies and Olive Garden Tiramisu.

Much has changed in the food industry since the first *Top Secret Recipes* book came out in 1993. In the Introduction of that book I included a list of the top-grossing fast food chains in America based on 1991 sales. Now, years later, it's interesting to glance back at how much has changed in this volatile industry in just a decade (and then again, how much hasn't).

CHAIN	U.S. UNITS	'91 U.S. SALES (IN MILLIONS)
1. McDonald's	12,418	19,928.2
2. Burger King	6,409	6,200.0
3. KFC	8,480	6,200.0
4. Pizza Hut	9,000	5,300.0
5. Hardee's	3,727	3,431.0

CHAIN	U.S. UNITS	'91 U.S. SALES (IN MILLIONS)
6. Wendy's	3,804	3,223.6
7. Taco Bell	3,670	2,800.0
8. Domino's Pizza	5,500	2,400.0
9. Dairy Queen	5,329	2,352.4
10. Little Caesar	3,650	1,725.0
11. Arby's	2,500	1,450.0
12. Subway	6,106	1,400.0
13. Dunkin' Donuts	2,203	990.8
14. Jack in the Box	1,089	978.0
15. Baskin-Robbins	3,533	829.7
16. Carl's Jr.	630	614.0
17. Long John Silver's	1,450	555.0
18. Popeye's Chicken	808	540.2
19. Sonic Drive-Ins	1,112	518.0
20. Church's Chicken	1,136	506.6
21. Captain D's	636	420.8
22. Chick-fil-A	460	324.6

23. TCBY	1,850	321.0
24. Round Table Pizza	575	320.0
25. Whataburger	475	318.4

Source: *Nation's Restaurant News*

Since 1991, the planet's largest restaurant chain has focused almost all of its growth on McDonald's hamburger outlets overseas, with restaurants now located in 120 countries. Over 4000 of those stores are in Asia, including five of the world's busiest McDonald's. Even though the chain hasn't flexed its domestic hamburger muscle much, Ronald has been busy dotting the globe.

Along the way McDonald's scooped up the faltering Boston Market chain (a new addition to the top 25 fast food chains list in the last 10 years), with an initial plan to gut 1000 of the Boston Market units and crown them with the Golden Arches.

Mickey D's has diversified with other brands as well, including ownership in Donatos Pizza and Chipotle Mexican Grill. And don't be surprised if one day you're ordering a Grande McLatte at McDonald's new McCafe coffeehouse. This Starbucks-like coffee chain has already seen success in other countries, and will now be grinding the beans here on our shores with test units opening in select cities. Just when you thought you'd seen it all, if you're looking for a place to stay in Switzerland some day you may find rooms in one of

CHAIN	U.S. UNITS	'00 U.S. SALES (IN MILLIONS)
1. McDonald's	12,804	19,573.0
2. Burger King	8,064	8,695.0
3. Wendy's	5,095	5,813.4
4. Taco Bell	6,746	5,100.0
5. Pizza Hut	7,927	5,000.0
6. KFC	5,364	4,400.0
7. Subway	12,254	3,788.0
8. Domino's Pizza	4,818	2,647.2
9. Arby's	3,153	2,410.0
10. Dairy Queen	5,058	2,225.0
11. Dunkin' Donuts	3,641	2,178.0
12. Hardee's	2,526	2,027.6

13. Jack in the Box	1,634	1,921.3
14. Starbucks	2,700	1,785.0
15. Sonic Drive-Ins	2,175	1,778.8
16. Papa John's	2,533	1,669.0
17. Little Caesar's Pizza	3,290	1,110.0
18. Chick-fil-A	958	1,082.1
19. Popeye's Chicken	1,248	1,076.8
20. Carl's Jr.	945	1,002.8
21. Long John Silver's	1,195	761.6
22. Church's Chicken	1,217	698.7
23. Boston Market	712	685.0
24. Whataburger	550	559.0
25. Baskin-Robbins	2,435	554.0

Source: *Nation's Restaurant News*

two Golden Arch Hotels opened by the Swiss arm of McDonald's Corp. (French fries on the pillows at night?)

Years later Burger King still holds its position at second place with nearly 2000 units added since 1991. The King is closing the gap with McDonald's and has challenged the Golden Arches not only with the Big King, a burger that looks and tastes similar to the Big Mac, but has altered its french fry formula twice in the last four years in the hopes of gaining some ground on the spud front. Unfortunately the Big King burger didn't catch on, and reviews for the first round of new fries came up soggy.

Wendy's moved up to number three from 1991, filling KFC's old slot. It seems burgers and sandwiches continue to thrive over fried chicken products. Hoping to ride the sandwich wave, KFC continues to develop new chicken sandwiches, despite some less than popular selections. Sure, the sandwiches are tasty, but not tasty enough to keep KFC's market share from shrinking. In the last decade the chain shuttered over 3000 domestic units, while converting many outlets into dual- or triple-brand multiconcept locations with parent company Tricon's other two brands, Taco Bell and Pizza Hut.

Taco Bell, however, nearly doubled its number of units since 1991 and moved up the ladder into fourth place. New products have bolstered the chain, as a talking Chihuahua coaxed us into munching on the occasional Gordita and Chalupa. The Bell has more recently been adding five-thousand-dollar grills to each restaurant to introduce a line of new grilled products that kicked off with the Grilled Stuft Burrito. Expect to see mucho other grilled offerings from the Bell in the future.

New product development was also important for Pizza Hut over the last decade. The Stuffed Crust Pizza, The Edge Pizza, and the Twisted Crust Pizza are several reasons why Pizza Hut remains the number-one pizza chain in the country, although competition from other chains (such as newcomer Papa John's) forced the Hut to close nearly 1000 units over the last decade, causing its overall fast food rank to fall from fourth to fifth place.

Subway was a big mover over the years, doubling its units from 6000 to over 12,000. That number of units is up in McDonald's territory, but since total sales per store is low compared to McDonald's, Subway ranks down at seventh on the list. Still, that's up from twelfth a decade ago, helped in part by a promotional campaign with a weight loss angle. Perhaps you've seen the spots with Jared, the young man who melted the pounds away on a diet of Subway sandwiches. Okay, whatever. Personally, I'm still waiting for the diet of french fries and beer.

Arby's, Dairy Queen, and Jack in the Box maintained their same approximate positions in the list. But Hardee's, a struggling hamburger joint with units throughout the South, Midwest, and Eastern United States, slipped way down, from fifth to twelfth place with the closure of over 1000 stores.

Even though Dairy Queen stayed strong, losing only around 200 units, it looks like we don't do ice cream and frozen yogurt like we did ten years ago. Have creamy frozen confections been replaced by coffee drinks and donuts? TCBY is off the list and Baskin-Robbins dropped seven places, losing over 1000 units. Dunkin' Donuts continues to thrive, and farther down (just off the list at number 27) Krispy Kreme is quickly approaching with "hot donuts now" signs a-flashing.

Take note of the newcomers to the top 25, most impressive of which is the Papa John's pizza chain. In 1999, Papa John's breezed right past Little Caesar's. Now Papa John's is over 2500 units strong and is raking in almost two billion dollars in sales. That's impressive stuff from a guy who, 18 years ago, was baking pizzas out of an old oven in a converted broom closet. If you're a big Papa John's fan, I've got clones of John's sauces on page 52.

Starbucks is another new success story on the list. This huge coffee house chain started in 1987, and in only 13 years has grown to 2700 units—remarkable numbers when you consider that in 1991, there were only 116 of the now-famous coffee houses, and in the year 2000, Starbucks added more than 700 new stores! That's a lot of hot milk foam.

Boston Market, our third new addition to the list, reached its peak somewhere in the middle of the last decade right around the time it changed its name from Boston Chicken. Despite slipping from a total of over 1200 units to the current 700, the chain still hangs on to a position on the list at twenty-third place. Once on the move in a big way, Boston Market made its mark selling home-style chicken and side dishes. But in 1995, when the chain added other meat products to the menu such as turkey and meatloaf (check out the meatloaf clone recipe on page 5), the company changed its name. Once the sweetheart of the stock market, Boston Market's aggressive growth plus increased competition in what they call the "home meal replacement" category led to a 1998 bankruptcy. Ouch. Hungry McDonald's swooped in to score the company at a bargain price and quickly closed many of the underperforming units. The remaining 700 Boston Market stores are now a profitable business, and McDonald's has scrapped plans to convert them to more McDonald's.

It's not hard to see that the food industry is an extremely competitive one. That's bad news for restaurants, but good news for *Top Secret Recipes* fans. Stiff competition means a constant flow of new products for us to clone at home. In fact, as I write this, a jingle just came on the radio advertising a new McDonald's breakfast sandwich with a hollandaise-like sauce: The Benedict McMuffin. The spot also mentions a new hot ham and cheese sandwich. Bingo! This goes on all the time. And as these new products catch on, the old ones are moved aside to clog the big artery in the sky. These "Dead Foods," as I call them, might be missing from menus, but I believe these products deserve a place to live here in this book. If you're one of the 12 fans of the Arch Deluxe, the only way you can take a little trip back in time to enjoy that same taste is to clone one of your own at home.

In addition to cloning dead foods, we can also clone the products that are only available at certain times of the year. Spring may be months away, but with the recipes in this book, you can now enjoy the taste of Thin Mints any time you want. And the cloned cookies will be even fresher than those you get in a box.

And what if you live in parts of the country where many of these products are unavailable? It's nearly impossible to find a fresh box of Drake's Devil Dogs on the west coast. And just forget about wolfing down a hot Wienerschnitzel chili dog if you live back east. Ah, but never fear, a clone recipe is here!

If you're new to these *Top Secret Recipes* books, and even if you aren't, let me now take some time to give you a few basic pointers that I've picked up along the way to help make your top secret cooking experience a dandy one. The recipes are designed with common ingredients and with as simple a process as I could muster, but since kitchen cloning is an inexact science, some thoughts come to mind:

• **Measure your ingredients very carefully.** These recipes copy products that are produced under highly controlled conditions. Although no two of you making these recipes at home will measure the ingredients exactly the same, you should still take the time to make accurate measurements with good measuring tools. Use liquid measuring cups (with the spouts) for the liquids, and dry measuring cups (no spouts) for the dry ingredients. Take time in measuring, never estimate, and resist the urge to make these recipes in a Winnebago kitchen while speeding down a dirt road in Tijuana.

• **Don't worry if your clone doesn't look exactly like the real thing.** Since many of these products are made by machines in custom molds and may include coloring or thickening additives that we won't use, your clone may look different from the real thing. That's okay. I usually try to include tricks to duplicate a product's appearance whenever possible (such as the foil mold for the Zingers clone, and various food colorings and consumer thickeners in other recipes). But my primary goal is to design a recipe that makes a finished product taste just like the real thing. Taste is job #1.

- **Use brand-name ingredients.** When I create these recipes I'm sure to use popular brands such as Best Foods Mayonnaise (or Hellmann's in the East), and Schilling, McCormick, and Spice Island spices. Generic brands may not be of the same quality and the final taste could be affected. For staple ingredients such as sugar, flour, and milk, you can use any old brand.

- **Don't be afraid to experiment.** The beauty of making Snickers Munch bars at home is that we can make them twice as big! Tweak your recipes to suit your tastes. Use ground turkey in your hamburgers and top 'em with soy American cheese if you want. That's the best part of home clone cuisine. If you like to customize your food to create something you can't get in the stores, no one can stop you.

- **Have fun, man!** Cloning your own brand-name food at home is some of the most fun you'll have in the kitchen. Kids love it, adults dig it. And it's even more of a kick when you genuinely fool somebody with a food that they thought could only be bought in a restaurant or store. That's what makes cleaning up that big mess you just made worth all the trouble!

I hope you enjoy cooking from this book as much as I've enjoyed writing it. If you want more recipes like these, check out the other books in the *Top Secret Recipes* series. You'll also find plenty of recipes and handy cooking tips on the *Top Secret Recipes* Web site at: *www.TopSecretRecipes.com.*

If you have any suggestions for other recipes to clone, I'd love to see your e-mail:

Todd@TopSecretRecipes.com

Enjoy the book, and happy cloning!

SOME COOKING TIPS
FROM A GUY WHO CARES

Sometimes I can be a real idiot in the kitchen. I've wasted as many as four eggs when separating the whites by accidentally dropping in specks of yolk. I've often burned chocolate when melting it for dipping candy, and I've squandered hours on making dough for a simple recipe just because I forgot to look at the date on the package of yeast.

It was on these days that I determined there is a hard way to pick up little cooking hints, and there's an easy way. The hard way is by doing what I did—screwing up, then having to throw away your mistakes and run to the store in the pouring rain with a fistful of change to buy more ingredients so you can start the whole thing over again.

Then there is the easy way, which is to get cooking tips from somebody who learned the hard way.

SOME WORDS ABOUT CHOCOLATE

First off, some words about that delicate substance we call chocolate. Everybody's eaten it, but if you've cooked with it, you know it can be a pain—especially when the recipe requires that you melt it, as some of the recipes in this book do.

There are several different types of chocolate: sweet, semisweet, bittersweet, unsweetened, milk chocolate, and white chocolate (which actually isn't chocolate at all).

You will be using only semisweet and milk chocolate. Both are called for in the form of chocolate chips, which you buy by the bag. The most common are Nestlé and Hershey. Each company makes both milk chocolate and semisweet, and each works equally well.

I have found that the best place to melt chocolate is in the microwave. Semisweet chocolate is much easier to work with than milk chocolate, because it contains more chocolate liquor and no milk solids. Semisweet will melt to a much smoother, thinner consistency, and will not scorch as easily. This means that semisweet lends itself much more readily to dipping.

When melting either type of chocolate, use a microwave-safe glass or ceramic bowl that will retain heat. Set your microwave on half power and melt the chips for 1 minute. Stir. Rotate the bowl and microwave for another minute. Stir again. After 2 minutes, if the chocolate needs to melt more, heat it in 30-second intervals.

With milk chocolate, you have to find a delicate balance between microwaving and stirring. If you heat the chips too much, the chocolate will scorch. If you stir too much, the chocolate won't set up properly when you dip. Perfectly melted milk chocolate should set nearly as firm as it was in its original form at room temperature (68 to 70°F).

If you can't use a microwave to melt your chocolate, use a double boiler. You want to set the heat very low so that the water in the double boiler is only simmering and not boiling. Boiling water will scorch chocolate. Grease the inside of your double boiler lightly before you put the chocolate in and you'll be able to get practically all melted chocolate out of the pan.

For some of the recipes in this book, you may feel like substituting dark, semisweet chocolate instead of milk chocolate or even using white chocolate. It may be worth a try. How about a white-chocolate–covered Milky Way? Hmm.

And here's another tip to remember when making anything with chocolate. You can intensify the chocolate flavor by adding some vanilla to the recipe. You'll notice that this is what I've done with the recipes in the book for chocolate icings.

SOME WORDS ABOUT YEAST DOUGH

There are some recipes in this book that call for yeast dough, and I thought it was important to supply you with some pointers that will help you here and in the rest of your dough-making life.

The only yeast you'll need to use with this book is Fleischmann's—the type that comes in the three-envelope packages. That's the only kind I ever use. Always check to be sure the yeast you're using has not expired. Every package of yeast is stamped with an expiration date—usually eight to twelve months from the date you purchased it. Store your unopened yeast packages in the refrigerator.

When kneading dough, use your hands. This is much better than a wooden or plastic spoon because the warmth of your hands will help the yeast start rising (and it brings you back to those carefree Play-Doh days). When the dough pulls away from your hands easily, it has been kneaded enough.

One good way to get the dough rising is to put it in its bowl, uncovered, in the oven (the oven should be off) with a pan of boiling water. The hot water will start the dough rising right away, and the moisture from the water will keep the dough's surface from getting hard and dry.

You can tell when the dough has risen enough by sticking your finger into it up to the first knuckle. If the dough does not bounce back, it's ready. If it giggles, you're in a Pillsbury commercial.

SOME WORDS ABOUT SEPARATING EGGS

For the recipes that require egg whites, I've found that one of the easiest ways to separate the white from the yolk is to crack the egg with one hand into the other hand cupped over a small bowl. The egg whites will run out between your fingers, and you will be holding just the yolk in your hand. You can also use a small funnel. Just crack the egg into the funnel, and the egg white will run through, leaving the yolk. Use a container other than the bowl you will be beating the whites in. You don't want to risk ruining all the whites if some yolk should fall through.

If an accident should happen and you do get some yolk into the whites, use one of the egg shells to scoop out the yolk. Strangely, the shells act like a magnet for the specks of stray yolk.

To save your yolks for another recipe, slide them into a small bowl or cup, pour some cold water over them, and store them in the refrigerator. When you want to use the yolks, just pour off the water and slide the yolks into your recipe.

By the way, as a general rule in this book and any other cookbook, when a recipe calls for eggs and does not specify size, always use large eggs. Medium or extra-large eggs could throw off your measurements.

SOME WORDS ABOUT BAKING

Every once in a while, you should check your oven thermostat with an oven thermometer. I did and found out that my oven was off by twenty-five degrees. That's normal. It can be off by twenty-five degrees in either direction, but if it's any more than that, you should make adjustments when cooking, and get it fixed.

When baking, allow at least fifteen minutes for your oven to preheat. This is especially important if you do not have an indicator light that tells you when your oven is ready.

Several recipes in this book call for baking on cookie sheets. I highly recommend using two cookie sheets and alternating them, putting one sheet in the oven at a time. This will allow you to let one sheet cool before loading it up for the next run. If you don't let the sheet cool, your cooking time may be inaccurate because the dough will start to heat before you put the sheet into the oven.

If you absolutely must bake more than one cookie sheet at a time, you'll have to extend the cooking time. It will take the oven longer to reach the proper temperature with more dough to heat.

If you're baking cookies, you can very easily make them all uniform in size by rolling the dough into a tube with the diameter you need, then slicing it with a very sharp knife.

Keep in mind, especially with cookies, that baked goods will continue to cook for a while even after they've come out of the oven unless you remove them to a rack. The cookie sheet or baking pan will still be hot, and the sugar in the recipe will retain heat. This is why many people tend to overcook their cookies. I know the feeling. When you follow suggested cooking times, it sometimes seems as though the cookies aren't done when they come out of the oven—and they probably aren't. But they'll be fine after sitting for some time on the cookie sheet.

SOME WORDS ABOUT HAMBURGER PATTIES

Just about every backyard hamburger cookout I've attended included hamburger patties that tipped the scale in size and weight.
Most homemade burgers are way too thick to cook properly, and
the added thickness doesn't add anything to the taste of the sandwich. In fact, if we cut the amount of beef we use in the hamburger
patties, we're cutting out excess fat and calories, decreasing the
chance that the burgers may not cook thoroughly, while not com-
promising anything in overall taste. At the same time, thicker patties
tend to shrink up as they cook into unmanageable mutant forms,
bulging in the middle, and stacking poorly onto buns and lettuce.

You'll notice that every hamburger recipe in this book requires
a very thin patty. This is the way the experts in the business do it—
the Dave Thomases, the Carl Karchers, the McDonald Brothers—
for concerns over cost, taste and a thorough, bacteria-free cooking
process. But just how do we get our patties so thin like the big boys,
and still make them easy to cook without breaking? We freeze 'em,
folks.

Plan ahead. Hours, even days, before you expect to make your
hamburgers, pat the patties out onto wax paper on a cookie sheet
with a diameter slightly larger than the buns you are using, and about
1/8 to 1/4 inch thick (with consistent thickness from center to edge).
Thickness depends on the burger: If you're making a small hamburger, like the one at McDonald's, which is only about 1/8 ounce before cooking, make the patties 1/8 inch thick. If you're going for the
Quarter Pounder, make your patty 1/4 inch thick—never more than
that. Lay wax paper over the top of your patties and put them in the
freezer.

When your patties are completely frozen, it's time to cook.
You can cook them straight out of the freezer on a hot grill or
frying pan for 3 to 7 minutes per side, without worrying about
thorough cooking. And the patties will flip easily without falling
apart.

INTRODUCTION TO
TOP SECRET RECIPES ®
MORE CLASSICS

Just about every person with taste buds wonders on some occasion after savoring a delicious restaurant dish or an addictive mass-produced convenience food if it's possible to re-create the taste in a home kitchen. I call it "kitchen cloning," and with this book, not only will you see that it is possible, but you'll also find out, first-hand, what a kick it is to duplicate the most famous brand-name foods in your own home using common ingredients.

My mission over the last decade—as I have chosen to accept it—is to develop secret formulas and simple techniques to help you produce home versions of the food on which America most loves to nosh. Throughout the seven previous *Top Secret Recipes* books are hundreds of kitchen clones for famous brand-name foods, often with deep histories and cult followings. These are foods that have made millionaires of their creators, and that trigger a reaction in our salivary glands upon a mere mention. These are foods that have satiated generations before us, and will continue to satisfy long after we are gone.

The mission is not often a simple one, since reverse-engineering foods can be a tedious and time-consuming task. Trial and error is the play of the day, and many of the results take a fateful trip into the garbage disposal or into the super-fat Chow Chow dog, Zebu. But when the finished product hits the mark, all the work is rewarded, and the successful results are passed along to you.

Here is a collection of my favorite recipes culled from all of my books produced over the last decade, arranged in one easy-to-use volume. These are my all-time favorites—my go-to recipes when I'm cooking from the *Top Secret Recipes* books, and the recipes I recommend when a friend asks, "What should I make?"

Special in this book are 22 new recipes that have never been available in stores. These recipes are truly special since they come from hundreds of reader requests, and have been on the *Top Secret* back burner for a long time. I'm talking about recipes such as Taco Bell Mexican Pizza, Tastycake Butterscotch Krimpets and McDonald's Biscuits. Oh, there go the salivary glands.

So have fun with this unique collection. And beware of other so-called copycat recipes floating around out there. My culinary assignment guarantees these *Top Secret Recipes* to be original creations that are thoroughly tested before I share them with you. That's the only way I can consider this a "mission accomplished."

—Todd Wilbur

AUNTIE ANNE'S PRETZELS

☆   ✌   💣   ✏   ☯   ✂   ☞

The first Auntie Anne's pretzel store opened in 1988 in the heart of pretzel country—a Pennsylvania Amish farmers' market. Over 500 stores later, Auntie Anne's is one of the most requested secret clone recipes around, especially on the Internet. Many of the recipes passed around the Web require bread flour, and some use honey as a sweetener. But by analyzing the Auntie Anne's home pretzel-making kit in the secret underground laboratory, I've discovered a better solution for re-creating the delicious mall treats than any clone recipe out there. For the best-quality dough, you just need all-purpose flour. And powdered sugar works great to perfectly sweeten the dough. Now you just have to decide if you want to make the more traditional salted pretzels, or the sweet cinnamon sugar–coated kind. Decisions, decisions.

1 ¼ cups warm water
1 tablespoon plus ¼ teaspoon yeast
3¾ cups all-purpose flour
¾ cup plus 2 tablespoons powdered
    sugar
1 ½ teaspoons salt
2 teaspoons vegetable oil

BATH
4 cups warm water

½ cup baking soda

¼ cup butter, melted

SALTED
kosher or pretzel salt

CINNAMON TOPPING
½ cup granulated sugar
2 teaspoons cinnamon

1. Dissolve the yeast in the warm water in a small bowl or cup. Let it sit for a few minutes.

2. Combine flour, powdered sugar, and salt in a large mixing bowl. Add water with yeast and vegetable oil. Stir with a spoon and then use your hands to form the dough into a ball. Knead the dough for 5 minutes on a lightly floured surface. Dough will be nice and smooth when it's ready. Place the dough into a lightly oiled bowl, cover it, and store it in a warm place for about 45 minutes or until the dough doubles in size.
3. When dough has risen, preheat oven to 425°F.
4. Make a bath for the pretzels by combining the baking soda with the warm water and stir until baking soda is mostly dissolved.
5. Remove the dough from the bowl and divide it into eight even portions. Roll each portion on a flat non-floured surface until it is about 3 feet long. Pick up both ends of the dough and give it a little spin so the middle of the dough spins around once. Lay the dough down with the loop nearest to you. Fold the ends down toward you and pinch to attach them to the bottom of the loop. The twist should be in the middle.
6. Holding the pinched ends, dip each pretzel into the bath solution. Put each pretzel on a paper towel for a moment to blot the excess liquid. Arrange the pretzels on a baking sheet sprayed with non-stick spray. If you want salt, sprinkle pretzels with kosher salt or pretzel salt. Don't salt any pretzels you plan to coat with cinnamon sugar. You will likely have to use two baking sheets, and be sure to bake them separately. Bake the pretzels for 4 minutes, then spin the pan halfway around and bake for another 4 to 5 minutes or until the pretzels are golden brown.
7. Remove the pretzels from the oven, and let them cool for a couple of minutes. If you want to eat some now, brush 'em with melted butter first, if desired, before serving. If you want the cinnamon sugar coating, make it by combining the ½ cup sugar and 2 teaspoons cinnamon in a small bowl. Brush the unsalted pretzels you plan to coat with a generous amount of melted butter. Sprinkle a heavy coating of the cinnamon sugar onto the entire surface of the pretzels over a plate. Munch out.

• MAKES 8 PRETZELS.

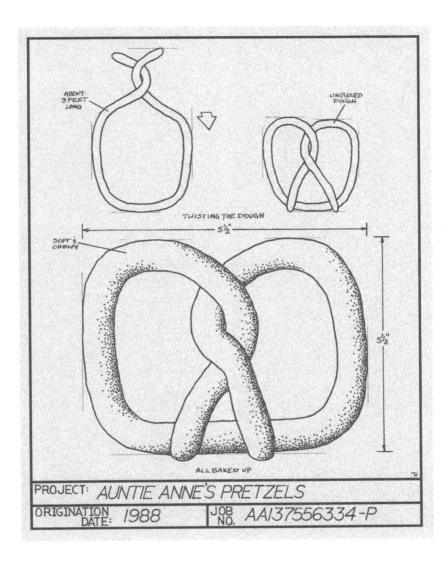

ABOUT 3 FEET LONG

UNBAKED DOUGH

TWISTING THE DOUGH

5½"

SOFT & CHEWY

5½"

ALL BAKED UP

PROJECT: *AUNTIE ANNE'S PRETZELS*

ORIGINATION DATE: *1988*

JOB NO. *AA137556334-P*

ARBY'S SAUCE

In 1964, when the Arby's concept was created by brothers Leroy and Forrest Raffel, the name was supposed to be R.B., for Raffel Brothers, but that was expanded to the more familiar Arby's. Having marked its 30th year in 1994, Arby's is celebrating more than $1.5 billion in sales from 2,603 outlets. Arby's Miami headquarters took a bit hit in 1992 from Hurricane Andrew, the most damaging hurricane to hit Florida in decades, but the company bounced back and continued growing.

The company's unique sliced beef sandwiches offer customers a departure from hamburgers made of ground beef. This special barbecue sauce enhances a roast beef sandwich, as well as many other homemade and store-bought creations.

1 cup catsup	1/4 teaspoon pepper
2 teaspoons water	1/4 teaspoon salt
1/4 teaspoon garlic powder	1/2 teaspoon hot pepper sauce
1/4 teaspoon onion powder	(Tabasco is best)

1. Combine all the ingredients in a small saucepan and cook over medium heat, stirring constantly, until the sauce begins to boil, 5 to 10 minutes.
2. Remove the sauce from the heat. Cover and allow to cool.
3. Pour into a covered container for storage in your refrigerator. Keeps for a month or two.

• MAKES 1 CUP.

• • • •

BOSTON MARKET
MEATLOAF

In the early 90s Boston Chicken was on a roll. The home meal replacement chain's stock was soaring and the lines were filled with hungry customers waiting to sink their teeth into a serving of the chain's delicious rotisserie chicken. So successful was the chain with chicken, that the company quickly decided it was time to introduce other entrée selections, the first of which was a delicious barbecue sauce–covered ground sirloin meatloaf. But offering other entrées presented the company with a dilemma: what to do about the name. The bigwigs decided it was time to change the name to Boston Market, to reflect a wider menu. That meant replacing signs on hundreds of units and retooling the marketing campaigns. That name change, plus rapid expansion of the chain and growth of other similar home-style meal concepts sent the company into a tailspin. By 1998, Boston Market's goose was cooked: the company filed for bankruptcy. Soon McDonald's stepped in to purchase the company, with the idea of closing many of the stores for good, and slapping Golden Arches on the rest. But that plan was scrapped when, after selling off many of the under-performing Boston Markets, the chain began to fly once again. Within a year of the acquisition Boston Market was profitable, and those meals with the home-cooked taste are still being served at over 700 Boston Market restaurants across the country.

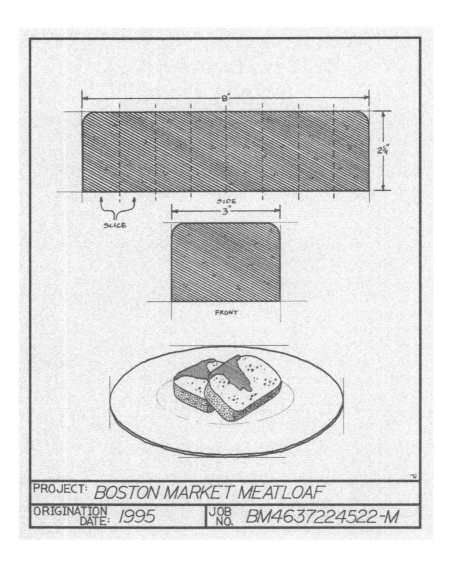

8"

2 1/4"

SLICE

SIDE
3"

FRONT

PROJECT: *BOSTON MARKET MEATLOAF*

ORIGINATION DATE: *1995*

JOB NO. *BM4637224522-M*

1 cup tomato sauce
1 ½ tablespoons Kraft original
    barbecue sauce
1 tablespoon granulated sugar
1 ½ pounds ground sirloin
    (10 percent fat)

6 tablespoons all-purpose flour
¾ teaspoon salt
½ teaspoon onion powder
¼ teaspoon ground black pepper
dash garlic powder

1. Preheat oven to 400ºF.
2. Combine the tomato sauce, barbecue sauce, and sugar in a small saucepan over medium heat. Heat the mixture until it begins to bubble, stirring often, then remove it from the heat.
3. In a large bowl, add all but 2 tablespoons of the tomato sauce to the meat. Use a large wooden spoon or your hands to work the sauce into the meat until it is very well combined.
4. Combine the remaining ingredients with the ground sirloin—flour, salt, onion powder, ground pepper, and garlic powder. Use the wooden spoon or your hands to work the spices and flour into the meat.
5. Load the meat into a loaf pan (preferably a meatloaf pan with two sections that allows the fat to drain, but if you don't have one of those a regular loaf pan will work). Wrap foil over the pan and place it into the oven for 30 minutes.
6. After 30 minutes, take the meatloaf from the oven, remove the foil and, if you aren't using a meatloaf pan, drain the fat.
7. Using a knife, slice the meatloaf all the way through into 8 slices while it is still in the pan. This will help to cook the center of the meatloaf. Pour the remaining 2 tablespoons of sauce over the top of the meatloaf, in a stream down the center. Don't spread the sauce.
8. Place the meatloaf back into the oven, uncovered, for 25 to 30 minutes or until it is done. Remove and allow it to cool for a few minutes before serving.

- SERVES 4.

•   •   •   •

CARL'S JR.
THE SIX DOLLAR BURGER

☆ ✌ ● ✐ ☯ ✂ ☞

This West Coast chain came up with a great idea: clone the type of burger you'd get at Chili's or T.G.I. Friday's for around six bucks, but sell it for just $3.95. It's ⅓-pound of ground beef stacked on top of plenty of fixings, including red onion and those sweet-tasting bread-and-butter pickle slices. And check this out: cloning your own six-dollar burger at home will cost you less than two bucks. And the product certainly paid off for Carl's Jr., as it quickly became the chain's bestselling new item.

⅓ pound ground beef
salt
pepper
1 large sesame-seed bun
3 teaspoons mayonnaise
1 teaspoon mustard

2 teaspoons ketchup
3 to 4 bread-and-butter pickle slices
iceberg lettuce
2 large tomato slices
4 to 5 red onion rings
2 slices American cheese

1. Preheat barbecue or indoor grill to medium heat.
2. Form the ground beef into a patty with a slightly larger di-ameter than the sesame-seed bun.
3. Grill the burger on the grill for 3 to 4 minutes per side or until done. Be sure to generously salt and pepper each side of the patty.
4. While the patty grills, brown the faces of the bun in a hot skillet over medium heat.
5. After the buns have browned, spread about 1½ teaspoons of

mayonnaise on the face of the top bun, as well as on the bottom bun.

6. Spread 1 teaspoon of mustard on the face of the top bun, followed by 2 teaspoons of ketchup.

7. Arrange 3 or 4 bread-and-butter pickle slices on the bottom bun.

8. Arrange lettuce on pickles followed by the tomato slices and red onion.

9. When the beef is cooked, arrange two slices of American cheese on the patty, let it melt a bit, then place the top bun on the cheese and scoop up the whole thing with a spatula and place it on the bottom half of the burger. Include a big napkin when serving.

• MAKES 1 HAMBURGER.

•   •   •   •

CARL'S JR.
CHICKEN CLUB

The first day's receipts at Carl Karcher's just-purchased hot-dog cart in 1941 totaled $14.75. Peanuts, right? But Karcher was determined to make it big. So during the next two years he purchased several more stands throughout the Los Angeles area, later expanding into restaurants and diversifying the menu. In 1993, what had once been a business of one tiny hot-dog cart had become a multimillion-dollar company with 642 outlets. From $14.75 on the first day to today's $1.6 million in daily receipts, old Carl was on the right track.

2 whole chicken breasts, skinned,
   boned, and halved
1 cup teriyaki marinade
   (Lawry's is best)
4 whole-wheat hamburger buns
8 slices bacon

1/4 cup mayonnaise
1 cup alfalfa sprouts, loosely packed
4 lettuce leaves
4 large tomato slices
4 slices Kraft Swiss Cheese Singles

1. Marinate the chicken in the teriyaki marinade in a shallow bowl for 30 minutes.
2. Preheat a clean barbecue to medium grilling heat.
3. Brown the faces of each bun in a frying pan on the stove. Keep the pan hot.
4. Cook the bacon in the pan until crisp, then set aside.
5. Grill the chicken breasts 5 to 8 minutes per side, or until cooked through.

6. Spread about ¹/2 tablespoon of mayonnaise on the face of each bun, top and bottom.
7. Divide the sprouts into 4 portions and mound on each bottom bun.
8. On the sprouts, stack a lettuce leaf, then a slice of tomato.
9. Place one chicken breast half on each of the sandwiches, atop the tomato.

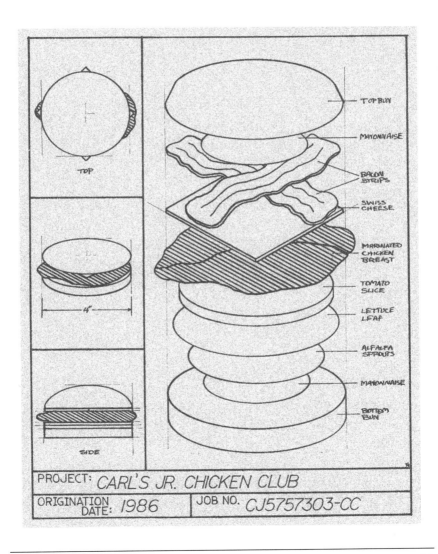

TOP

SIDE

4"

TOP BUN

MAYONNAISE

BACON STRIPS

SWISS CHEESE

MARINATED CHICKEN BREAST

TOMATO SLICE

LETTUCE LEAF

ALFALFA SPROUTS

MAYONNAISE

BOTTOM BUN

PROJECT: CARL'S JR. CHICKEN CLUB

ORIGINATION DATE: 1986   JOB NO. CJ5757303-CC

10. Next, stack a slice of Swiss cheese on the chicken, and then the 2 pieces of bacon, crossed over each other.
11. Top off the sandwich with the top bun.
12. Microwave for 15 seconds on high.

• MAKES 4 SANDWICHES.

•   •   •   •

DUNKIN' DONUTS

☆   ✌   💣   ✏   ☯   ✂   ☞

As he worked long, hard days at a shipyard in Hingham, Massachusetts, during World War II, William Rosenberg was struck with an idea for a new kind of food service. As soon as the war ended, Rosenberg started Industrial Luncheon Services, a company that delivered fresh meals and snacks to factory workers. When Rosenberg realized that most of his business was in coffee and donuts, he quit offering his original service. He found an old awning store and converted it into a coffee-and-donut shop called The Open Kettle. This name was soon changed to the more familiar Dunkin' Donuts, and between 1950 and 1955 five more shops opened and thrived. The company later spread beyond the Boston area and has become the largest coffee-and-donut chain in the world.

Today, Dunkin' Donuts offers fifty-two varieties of donuts in each shop, but the most popular have always been the plain glazed and chocolate-glazed yeast donuts.

DONUTS
One ¼-ounce package active dry
    yeast
2 tablespoons warm water (98°F)
¾ cup warm milk (30 seconds in the
    microwave does the trick)

GLAZE
5⅓ tablespoons (⅓ cup) margarine
    or butter

FOR CHOCOLATE GLAZE
1 cup semisweet chocolate chips

2½ tablespoons margarine or butter
1 egg
⅓ cup granulated sugar
1 teaspoon salt
2¾ cups all-purpose flour
3 cups vegetable oil

2 cups powdered sugar
½ teaspoon vanilla extract
⅓ cup hot water

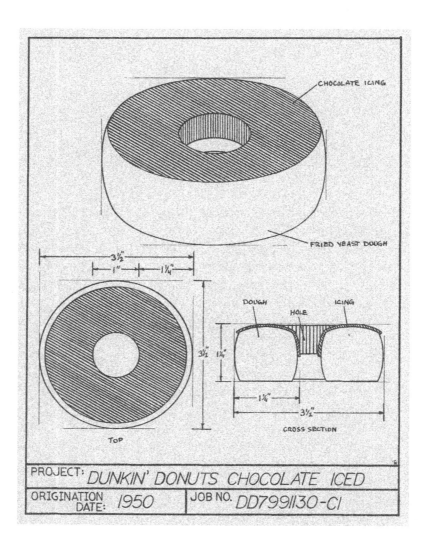

CHOCOLATE ICING

FRIED YEAST DOUGH

3½"
1"
1¼"
3½"

TOP

DOUGH
HOLE
ICING

1¼"
1¼"
3½"

CROSS SECTION

PROJECT: DUNKIN' DONUTS CHOCOLATE ICED

ORIGINATION DATE: 1950

JOB NO. DD7991130-C1

1. In a medium bowl, dissolve the yeast in the warm water.
2. Add the milk, margarine or butter, egg, sugar, and salt, and blend with an electric mixer until smooth.
3. Add half the flour and mix for 30 seconds.
4. Add the remaining flour and knead the dough with flour-dusted hands until smooth.
5. Cover the bowl of dough and leave it in a comfy, warm place until the dough doubles in size, about 1 hour. You can tell that the dough has risen enough when you poke it with your finger and the indentation stays.
6. Roll out the dough on a heavily floured surface until it's about $1/2$ inch thick.
7. If you don't have a donut cutter, and don't intend to buy one, here's a way to punch out your dough: Empty a standard 15-ounce can of whatever you can find—vegetables, refried beans, even dog food. Be sure to wash out the can very well, and punch a hole in the opposite end so that the dough won't be held inside the can by a vacuum.
8. When you've punched out all the dough (you should have about a dozen unholed donuts), it's time for the holes. Find the cap to a bottle of lemon juice or Worcestershire sauce, or any other small cap with a diameter of about $1 1/4$ inches. Use this to punch out holes in the center of each of your donuts.
9. Place the donuts on plates or cookie sheets, cover, and let stand in the same warm, comfy place until they nearly double in size. This will take 30 to 45 minutes.
10. Heat the vegetable oil in a large frying pan over medium heat. Bring the oil to about 350°F. It is easily tested with scrap dough left over from punching out the donuts. The dough should bubble rapidly.
11. Fry each donut for about 30 seconds per side, or until light golden brown. Cool 5 minutes on paper towels.
12. For either the plain or the chocolate glaze, combine the margarine or butter with the powdered sugar in a medium bowl and blend with an electric mixer.
13. Add the vanilla and hot water. Mix until smooth.
14. If you're making the chocolate glaze, melt the chocolate chips in a microwave-safe bowl in the microwave for 30 to 40 seconds.

Stir, then microwave another 30 seconds and stir again until completely melted. Add to the plain glaze mixture. Blend until smooth.

15. When the donuts have cooled, dip each top surface into the glaze and then flip over and cool on a plate until the glaze firms up, about 15 minutes.

• MAKES 1 DOZEN DONUTS.

TIDBITS

You can also make "donut holes" as they do at Dunkin' Donuts by cooking and glazing the holes you've punched out the same way you prepared the donuts.

•   •   •   •

EL POLLO LOCO
FLAME-BROILED
CHICKEN

☆　　　✌　　　💣　　　✏　　　☯　　　✂　　　☞

Okay, time to brush up on your Spanish.

El Pollo Loco, or "The Crazy Chicken," has been growing like mad since it crossed over the border into the United States from Mexico. Francisco Ochoa unknowingly started a food phenomenon *internacional* in 1975 when he took a family recipe for chicken marinade and opened a small roadside *restaurante* in Gusave, Mexico. He soon had 90 stores in 20 cities throughout Mexico. The first El Pollo Loco in the United States opened in Los Angeles in December of 1980 and was an immediate success. It was only three years later that Ochoa got the attention of bigwigs at Denny's, Inc., who offered him $11.3 million for his U.S. operations. Ochoa took the deal, and El Pollo Loco grew from 17 to more than 200 outlets over the following decade. *¡Muy bien!*

2 cups water
4 teaspoons salt
2 teaspoons pepper
1 garlic clove

1 teaspoon yellow food coloring (or a
　　pinch of ground saffron)
2 tablespoons pineapple juice
1 teaspoon lime juice
1 whole frying chicken with skin,
　　halved or quartered

1. In a blender, combine the water, salt, pepper, garlic, and food coloring (or saffron). Blend on high speed for 15 seconds. Add pineapple juice and lime juice to marinade blend for 5 seconds.
2. Marinate the chicken in the liquid in a bowl or pan for 45 minutes. Turn and marinate for 30 minutes more.

3. Preheat a clean barbecue to medium-low grilling heat.
4. Cook the chicken on the open grill for 45 minutes to 1 hour, or until the skin is golden brown and crispy. Be sure the flames are not scorching the chicken, or the skin may turn black before the center is done. Lower the heat if necessary. (If you do not have a gas grill, you can spray a little water on the charcoal to keep the flames at bay.) Turn the chicken often as it cooks.
5. Cut the chicken into 8 pieces, with a large, sharp knife, cutting the breast in half and cutting the thighs from the legs.

- MAKES 8 PIECES.

• • • •

EL POLLO LOCO
AVOCADO SALSA

☆ ✌ 💣 ✏ ☯ ✂ ☞

This creamy green sauce is available at the salsa bar at each of the more than 300 El Pollo Loco outlets located throughout the western U.S., and folks are going crazy over it. The problem is, you can only get it at the restaurants in small quantities. So you know what that means: time to put on our crafty kitchen cloning hats. You'll want to use a food processor to mix this one up (everything but the cilantro and onion goes in there). When it's all done, you'll have a delicious, spicy concoction that you can pour over your favorite homemade Mexican-style dishes, from tacos salads to fajitas. A big thanks goes out to Pancho Ochoa, who opened his first roadside chicken stand in Guasave, Mexico, in 1975. Today, Pancho's El Pollo Loco is the number one quick-service, flame-broiled chicken chain in America.

I ripe avocado
I jalapeño, stemmed and quartered
I cup water
I tablespoon white distilled vinegar

¾ teaspoon salt
2 tablespoons minced fresh cilantro
2 tablespoons diced onion

1. Combine avocado, jalapeño, water, vinegar, and salt in a food processor. Puree the mixture for several seconds on high speed, or until jalapeño is finely minced.

2. Pour mixture into a medium bowl. Stir in cilantro and onion. Cover and chill until ready to serve.

• MAKES 1 1/2 CUPS.

•   •   •   •

EL POLLO LOCO
SALSA

El Pollo Loco's success is based on its unique approach to fast food. The marinated, flame-broiled chicken is served with flour or corn tortillas and a fresh tomato salsa, so that hungry customers can strip the chicken from the bones and make their own soft tacos, smothered in spicy salsa. It's actually a very low-fat, low-calorie version of the fried chicken you normally find at a fast-food chain.

Use this salsa with the marinated chicken from the previous recipe wrapped in tortillas, or with other dishes.

2 medium tomatoes
1 fresh jalapeño pepper, stemmed, or
    10 slices canned jalapeños,
    or "Nacho Slices"

1/2 teaspoon salt

1. Chop the tomatoes and jalapeños together until they have the consistency of a coarse puree. You can use a food processor, but stop chopping when the mixture is still quite coarse. There will be a lot of liquid, which you want to use as well. Pour everything into a medium bowl.
2. Add the salt to the mixture and stir.
3. Pour the salsa into a covered container and let it sit for several hours to allow the flavor to develop. Overnight is best.

*   MAKES ABOUT 2 CUPS.

• • • •

FATBURGER
ORIGINAL BURGER

☆   ✌   💣   ✐   ☯   ✂   ☞

Southern California—the birthplace of famous hamburgers from McDonald's to Carl's Jr. and In-n-Out Burger—is home to another thriving burger chain that opened its first outlet in 1952. Lovie Yancey thought of the perfect name for the ⅓-pound bur-gers she sold at her Los Angeles burger joint: Fatburger. Now with over 41 units in California, Nevada, and moving into Washington and Arizona, Fatburger has become the food critics' favorite, winning "best burger in town" honors with regularity. The secret is the seasoned salt used on a big 'ol lean beef patty. And there's no ketchup on the stock version, just mayo, mustard, and relish. Replace the ground beef with ground turkey and you've got Fatburger's Turkeyburger all up and cloned.

⅓ pound lean ground beef
seasoned salt
ground black pepper
1 plain hamburger bun
½ tablespoon mayonnaise
¼ cup chopped iceberg lettuce
1 tomato slice
½ tablespoon mustard

½ tablespoon sweet pickle relish
1 tablespoon chopped onion
3 dill pickle slices (hamburger slices)

OPTIONAL
1 slice American cheese

1. Form the ground beef into a patty that is about 1 inch wider than the circumference of the hamburger bun.
2. Preheat a non-stick frying pan to medium/high heat. Fry the patty in the pan for 3 to 4 minutes per side or until done.

Season both sides of the beef with seasoned salt and ground black pepper.

3. As the meat cooks prepare the bun by spreading approximately ½ tablespoon of mayonnaise on the face of the top bun.
4. Place the lettuce on the mayonnaise, followed by the tomato slice.
5. When the beef is done place the patty on the bottom bun.
6. Spread about ½ tablespoon of mustard over the top of the beef patty.
7. Spoon about ½ tablespoon of relish over the mustard.
8. Sprinkle the chopped onion onto the relish.
9. Arrange the pickles on the chopped onion.
10. Bring the two halves of the burger together and serve with gumption.

- MAKES 1 BURGER.

TIDBITS

If you want cheese on your burger, put a slice of American cheese on the face of the bottom bun before adding the beef patty. The heat from the meat will melt the cheese.

•   •   •   •

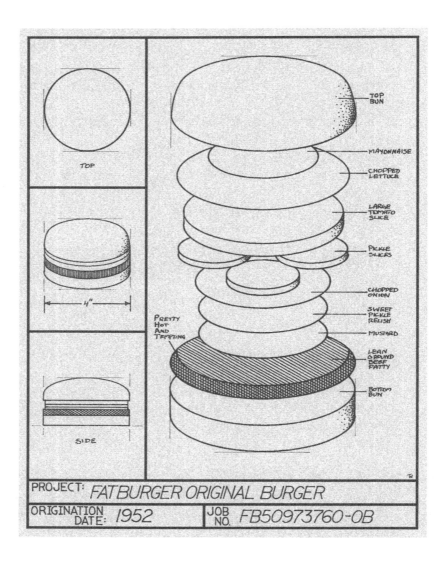

TOP

4"

SIDE

TOP BUN

MAYONNAISE

CHOPPED LETTUCE

LARGE TOMATO SLICE

PICKLE SLICES

CHOPPED ONION

SWEET PICKLE RELISH

MUSTARD

LEAN GROUND BEEF PATTY

BOTTOM BUN

PRETTY HOT AND TEMPTING

PROJECT: FATBURGER ORIGINAL BURGER

ORIGINATION DATE: 1952

JOB NO. FB50973760-OB

HONEYBAKED HAM GLAZE

☆ ✌ 💣 ✏ ☯ ✂ ☞

TSR has discovered that the tender hams are delivered to each of the 300 HoneyBaked outlets already smoked, but without the glaze. It is only when the ham gets to your local HoneyBaked store that a special machine thin-slices the tender meat in a spiral fashion around the bone. One at a time, each ham is then coated with the glaze—a blend that is similar to what might be used to make pumpkin pie. This sweet coating is then caramelized with a blowtorch by hand until the glaze bubbles and melts, turning golden brown. If needed, more of the coating is added, and the blowtorch is fired up until the glaze is just right. It's this careful process that turns the same size ham that costs 10 dollars in a supermarket into one that customers gladly shell out 3 to 4 times as much to share during the holiday season.

For this clone recipe, we will re-create the glaze that you can apply to a smoked/cooked bone-in ham of your choice. Look for a ham that's presliced. Otherwise you'll have to slice it yourself with a sharp knife, then the glaze will be applied. To get the coating just right you must use a blowtorch. If you don't have one, you can find a small one in hardware stores for around 10 to 15 bucks. And don't worry—I didn't leave out an ingredient. No honey is necessary to re-create this favorite holiday glaze.

1 fully cooked shank half ham, bone-
    in (presliced)
1 cup sugar
¼ teaspoon ground cinnamon
¼ teaspoon ground nutmeg

¼ teaspoon ground clove
⅛ teaspoon paprika
dash ground ginger
dash ground allspice

1. If you couldn't find a presliced ham, the first thing you must do
    is slice it. Use a very sharp knife to cut the ham into very thin
    slices around the bone. Do not cut all the way down to the
    bone or the meat may not hold together properly as it is being
    glazed. You want the slices to be quite thin, but not so thin that
    they begin to fall apart or off the bone. You may wish to turn
    the ham onto its flat end and cut around it starting at the
    bottom. You can then spin the ham as you slice around and
    work your way up.
2. Mix the remaining ingredients together in a small bowl.
3. Lay down a couple sheets of wax paper onto a flat surface,
    such as your kitchen counter. Pour the sugar mixture onto the
    wax paper and spread it around evenly.
4. Pick up the ham and roll it over the sugar mixture so that it is
    well coated. Do not coat the flat end of the ham, just the outer,
    presliced surface.
5. Turn the ham onto its flat end on a plate. Use a blowtorch with
    a medium-size flame to caramelize the sugar. Wave the torch
    over the sugar with rapid movement, so that the sugar bubbles
    and browns, but does not burn. Spin the plate so that you can
    torch the entire surface of the ham. Repeat the coating and
    caramelizing process until the ham has been well glazed (don't
    expect to use all of the sugar mixture). Serve the ham cold or
    reheated, just like the real thing.

• MAKES 1 HOLIDAY HAM.

•   •   •   •

HOT DOG
ON A STICK
HOT DOG

☆   ✌   💣   ✏   ☯   ✂   ☞

One hot summer day in 1946 Dave Barham was inspired to dip a hot dog into his mother's cornbread batter, then deep fry it to a golden brown. Dave soon found a quaint Santa Monica, California, location near the beach to sell his new creation with mustard on the side and a tall glass of ice-cold lemonade. Be sure you find the shorter dogs, not "bun-length." In this case size does matter. Snag some of the disposable wood chopsticks from a local Chinese or Japanese restaurant next time you're there and start dipping.

8 to 10 cups vegetable oil
2 cups flour
¾ cup cornmeal
½ cup sugar
1¾ teaspoons salt

1 teaspoon baking soda
1¾ cups fat-free milk
2 egg yolks, slightly beaten
8 to 10 turkey hot dogs
5 pairs chopsticks

1. Preheat oil in a deep pan or fryer to 375ºF.
2. Combine the flour, cornmeal, sugar, salt, and baking soda in a large bowl.
3. Add the milk and egg yolks to the dry ingredients and mix with an electric mixer on high speed until batter is smooth.
4. Dry off the hot dogs with a paper towel. Jab the thin end of a single chopstick about halfway into the end of each hot dog.
5. When the oil is hot, tip the bowl of batter so that you can completely coat each hot dog. Roll the hot dog in the batter until it is entirely covered.
6. Hold the hot dog up by the stick and let some of the batter drip off. Quickly submerge the hot dog in the oil and spin it

slowly so that the coating cooks evenly. After about 20 seconds you can use a lid to the deep fryer or pan to put weight on the stick, keeping the hot dog fully immersed in the oil. You can cook a couple dogs at a time this way. Cook for 5 to 6 minutes or until coating is dark brown. Turn them once or twice as they cook. Drain on paper towels while cooling, and repeat with the remaining hot dogs.

• MAKES 8 TO 10 HOT DOGS.

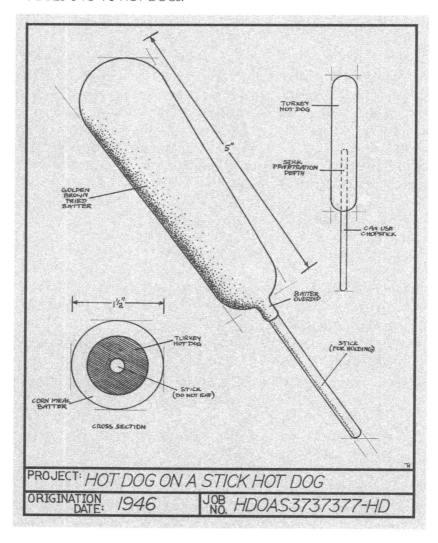

KENNY ROGERS ROASTERS CORN MUFFINS

☆　　✌　　💣　　✏　　☯　　✂　　☞

He knows when to hold 'em, he knows when to fold 'em. And lately he's been folding 'em quite a bit as Kenny Rogers Roasters restaurants across the country have bolted their doors for lack of interest. Looks like that whole "home meal replacement" thing hasn't worked out too well for this fire-roasted–chicken chain. But that doesn't mean that Kenny didn't know how to make awesome corn muffins that are served with every meal. And since it's becoming harder and harder to find a Kenny Rogers Roasters outlet, we have no choice but to duplicate these at home if we want to re-create this part of the Kenny experience.

½ cup butter
⅔ cup sugar
¼ cup honey
2 eggs
½ teaspoon salt

1 ½ cups all-purpose flour
¾ cup yellow cornmeal
½ teaspoon baking powder
½ cup milk
¾ cup frozen yellow corn

1. Preheat oven to 400°F.
2. Cream together butter, sugar, honey, eggs, and salt in a large bowl.
3. Add flour, cornmeal, and baking powder and blend thoroughly. Add milk while mixing.
4. Add corn to mixture and combine by hand until corn is worked in.

5. Grease a 12-cup muffin pan and fill each cup with batter. Bake for 20 to 25 minutes or until muffins begin to turn brown on top.

• MAKES 12 MUFFINS.

•   •   •   •

KRISPY KREME ORIGINAL GLAZED DOUGHNUTS

☆ ✌ 💣 ✏ ☯ ✂ ☞

The specifics of the well-guarded, 65-year-old secret recipe for Krispy Kreme doughnuts may be securely locked away in a safe at the Winston-Salem, North Carolina, headquarters, but discovering the basic ingredients in these puffy, fried cakes of joy was far from impossible. Simply asking to see the ingredients listed on the dry doughnut mix was all it took. Still, knowing the exact ingredients in a Krispy Kreme glazed doughnut is hardly all the information we need to clone one. There's an important cooking technique at work here that's a big part of the secret.

  The automated process for creating Krispy Kremes, developed in the 1950s, took the company many years to perfect. When you drive by your local Krispy Kreme store between 5:00 and 11:00 each day (both A.M. and P.M.) and see the "Hot Doughnuts Now" sign lit up, inside the store custom-made stainless steel machines are rolling. Doughnut batter is extruded into little doughnut shapes that ride up and down through a temperature- and humidity-controlled booth to activate the yeast. This creates the perfect amount of air pockets in the dough that will make a fluffy final product. When the doughnuts are swollen with air, they're gently dumped into hot vegetable shortening, where they float on one side until golden brown, then the machine flips them over to cook the other side. As the doughnuts finish frying, they ride up a mesh conveyer belt and through a ribbon of white sugar glaze. If you're lucky enough to taste some of these doughnuts just as they come around the corner from the glazing, you're in for a real treat. The warm circle of glazed goodness practically melts in your mouth. It's this secret process that has helped Krispy Kreme become the fastest-growing doughnut chain in the country.

As for the secret ingredients in a Krispy Kreme, you can probably guess that they are made mostly of basic wheat flour. That part's obvious. But there's also some soy flour in there, plus egg yolk, wheat gluten, non-fat milk, yeast, malted barley flour, modified food starch, ascorbic acid, salt, sugar, corn syrup solids, and natural flavors. For this clone recipe, I decided that some of the ingredients used in the real thing wouldn't be necessary for a home-grown duplicate. After numerous experiments over several weeks, I concluded that we could still create a finished product that's extremely close to the original without some of the harder-to-get ingredients such as soy flour, wheat gluten, malted barley, and modified food starch.

The recipe here requires only commonly found ingredients, since it is truly the process of raising the doughnuts carefully that's going to make them fluffy and tender like the real thing. In this case, the most important step is the one in which you transfer the doughnuts (after they have risen) from the baking sheet into the shortening. You must do this very gently so that the dough does not deflate. The fluffier the doughnuts are when they go into the shortening, the more tender and Krispy Kreme–like they'll be when they come out.

This clone recipe creates doughnuts that are probably very much like the original Krispy Kreme recipe, which founder Vernon Rudolph purchased from a New Orleans chef in 1937. That's long before machines took over the process.

1 pkg. (2¼ teaspoons) yeast
1½ teaspoons granulated sugar
¾ cup warm water (100 degrees to
    110 degrees)
1¾ cups all-purpose flour
½ teaspoon salt

1 egg yolk
1 tablespoon fat-free milk
¼ teaspoon vanilla extract

GLAZE

1¾ cups plus 2 tablespoons
   powdered sugar

¼ cup boiling water

6 to 12 cups vegetable shortening (as
   required by your fryer)

1. Dissolve yeast and sugar in warm water. Let solution stand for 5 minutes or until it becomes foamy on top. Make sure the water isn't too hot, or you may kill the yeast.
2. Combine flour and salt in a large bowl with an electric mixer. Add yeast solution, egg yolk, milk, and vanilla extract and mix well with electric mixer for 30 seconds or just until all ingredients are combined.
3. Form dough into a ball, then let it sit in a bowl, covered, in a warm place for approximately one hour, or until the dough doubles in size.
4. Gently roll out the dough until it's about ½-inch thick on a floured surface. Use a well-floured 3-inch biscuit cutter to cut out circles of dough. Then use a well-floured lid from a plastic soda bottle (about 1⅛-inch diameter) to cut the holes. You can also use a 3-inch doughnut cutter if you have one. Arrange the doughnuts on a couple of lightly floured cookie sheets, cover them with plastic wrap, and let them sit for one hour in a warm place. After about an hour, the doughnuts should have doubled in size.
5. While the doughnuts rest, make the glaze by combining powdered sugar and boiling water. Whisk glaze until smooth, then cover with plastic wrap until you're ready to use it.
6. As doughnuts rise, heat vegetable shortening in fryer to 375°F.
7. When doughnuts have doubled in size, carefully transfer 2 to 3 doughnuts at a time to the shortening. You must lift the doughnuts very gently or they will collapse and not turn out as fluffy as the real thing. Fry doughnuts for 1½ to 2 minutes per side, then remove them to a cooling rack.
8. After a minute or so on the cooling rack, spoon glaze generously over the top of each doughnut. You want the entire

surface of each doughnut well-coated with glaze. You can also recycle the glaze that falls through the rack by spooning it back into the bowl and stirring it up. Let the doughnuts cool for a few minutes, and they're ready to eat.

• MAKES 10 DOUGHNUTS.

• • • •

McDONALD'S
LOBSTER SANDWICH

☆   ✌   ●   ✏   ☯   ✂   ☞

On an excursion through Maine I practically drove off the road when I first saw a sign advertising a lobster sandwich at the world's most famous hamburger chain. I just had to get a closer look. That's when I discovered that this unique sandwich is served only at select McDonald's locations, mostly in New England, for a limited time only during the summer months. It turns out this is a lobster salad served on a hoagie roll with some lettuce. Simple enough. Since this sandwich is so limited in its availability, it's a perfect candidate for home cloning.

½ cup cooked Maine lobster, chilled
½ tablespoon mayonnaise

pinch salt
small hoagie roll
1 lettuce leaf

1. Mix together lobster, mayonnaise, and salt.
2. Slice the hoagie roll lengthwise, and spread the lettuce leaf on the bottom half.
3. Spread lobster over lettuce. Top off sandwich with the top half of the roll.

• MAKES 1 SANDWICH.

TIDBITS

If you don't want to use fresh lobster, you can use canned Maine lobster that can often be found in many supermarkets.

• • • •

MCDONALD'S
ARCH DELUXE

☆ ✌ 💣 ✏ ☯ ✄ ☞

In 1996, McDonald's set out to target more educated tastebuds in a massive advertising campaign for its newest burger creation. We watched while Ronald McDonald golfed, danced, and leisurely hung out with real-life grown-up humans, instead of the puffy Mayor Mc-Cheese and that bunch of wacko puppets. Supposedly the Arch Deluxe, with the "Adult Taste," would appeal to those golfers and dancers and anyone else with a sophisticated palate. But let's face it, we're not talking Beef Wellington here. The Arch Deluxe was just a hamburger, after all, with only a couple of elements that set it apart from the other menu items. The big difference was the creamy brown mustard spread on the sandwich right next to the ketchup. And the burger was assembled on a sesame seed potato roll (which actually tasted very much like your common hamburger bun). Also, you could order the burger with the optional thick-sliced peppered bacon, for an extra bit of ka-ching.

Okay, so the plan didn't quite work out the way Mickey D's had hoped. Sales of the Arch Deluxe were disappointing, to say the least. And shortly after the Arch Deluxe was unveiled it was but a figment of our drive-thru memory. That's why I thought this would be a good recipe to clone. You know, for all of you who have been struggling to get by without the Arch Deluxe in your lives. The Arch Deluxe may have gone on to join the McD.L.T. and the McLean Deluxe on the great list of fast food duds from our past. But you can now create a delicious kitchen facsimile of your own with this recipe. And hopefully, in the meantime, Ronald has gone back to work.

1 tablespoon mayonnaise
½ teaspoon brown mustard (French's
* "Hearty Deli" is good)*
1 sesame seed hamburger bun
¼ pound ground beef

1 slice American cheese
1 to 2 tomato slices
1 to 2 lettuce leaves, chopped
½ tablespoon ketchup
2 tablespoons chopped onion

1. In a small bowl, mix together the mayonnaise and the brown mustard. Set aside.
2. Grill the face of each of the buns on a griddle or frying pan over medium heat.
3. Roll the ground beef into a ball and pat it out until it's approximately the same diameter as the bun.
4. Cook meat on hot griddle or frying pan for about 5 minutes per side or until done. Be sure to lightly salt and pepper each side of the patty.
5. Build the burger in the following order, from the bottom up:

ON BOTTOM BUN
beef patty
American cheese slice
1 to 2 tomato slices
lettuce

ON TOP BUN
mayo/mustard
ketchup
onions

6. Slap the top onto the bottom and serve hot.

- MAKES ONE BURGER.

TIDBITS

If you can find thick-sliced pepper bacon in your supermarket, you can add it to the burger just as you could at the restaurant chain. Cut one slice in half after cooking and place the slices next to each other onto the bottom bun before adding the beef patty.

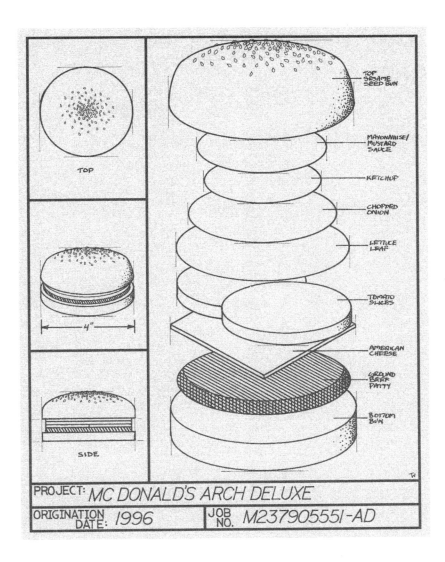

TOP

SIDE

4"

TOP SESAME SEED BUN

MAYONNAISE/ MUSTARD SAUCE

KETCHUP

CHOPPED ONION

LETTUCE LEAF

TOMATO SLICES

AMERICAN CHEESE

GROUND BEEF PATTY

BOTTOM BUN

PROJECT: MC DONALD'S ARCH DELUXE

ORIGINATION DATE: 1996

JOB NO. M23790555I-AD

39

MCDONALD'S BIGXTRA!

McDonald's roll-out of the BigXtra! is another bomb dropped on the battlefield of the latest burger war. Burger King took the first shot by introducing the Big King—a pretty good clone of McDonald's signature Big Mac, with a bit more meat and no middle bun. Then Mickey D's fired back with a clone of Burger King's popular Whopper hamburger, with, you guessed it, a bigger beef patty—20 percent bigger than the Whopper, to be exact. That's just under 5 ounces of ground beef, stacked on a huge sesame seed bun, with the same ingredients you would find piled on the Whopper—lettuce, onion, tomato, ketchup, mayo, and pickles. Plus McDonald's addition of a special spice sprinkled on the beef as it cooks. It's all very tasty. Especially if you like Whoppers.

Today the BigXtra! is less extra, having been shrunk down and renamed Big 'N Tasty.

1 large sesame seed bun (4¾-inch diameter)	1 tablespoon mayonnaise
5 ounces ground beef	1 tablespoon chopped onion
seasoned salt	3 pickle slices (hamburger style)
ground black pepper	½ cup chopped lettuce
2 teaspoons ketchup	1 large tomato slice
	non-stick cooking spray

1. Form the ground beef into a very large patty on wax paper. Make it approximately 5½ to 6 inches in diameter (the meat should shrink to the perfect size for the buns when cooked). Freeze this patty for a couple hours before cooking.

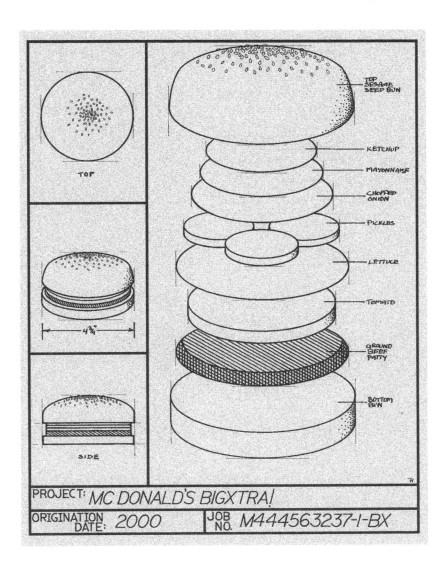

TOP

SIDE

4¾"

TOP
SESAME
SEED BUN

KETCHUP

MAYONNAISE

CHOPPED
ONION

PICKLES

LETTUCE

TOMATO

GROUND
BEEF
PATTY

BOTTOM
BUN

PROJECT: *MC DONALD'S BIGXTRA!*

ORIGINATION DATE: *2000*

JOB NO. *M444563237-I-BX*

2. Grill the faces of the hamburger bun in a hot skillet over medium heat. Grill until the buns are golden brown. Leave pan hot.
3. Grill the frozen patty in the pan for 2 to 3 minutes per side. Sprinkle one side with seasoned salt and ground black pepper.
4. Prepare the rest of the burger by first spreading the 2 teaspoons of ketchup on the face of the top bun. Follow the ketchup with the tablespoon of mayonnaise.
5. Stack the onion onto the top bun next, followed by the pickles and lettuce. Add the tomato slice to the top of the stack.
6. When the beef patty is done cooking, use a spatula to arrange it on the bottom bun. Turn the top of the burger over onto the bottom and serve.

• MAKES 1 HAMBURGER.

TIDBITS

If you want to add a slice of American cheese to your burger, it goes between the beef patty and bottom bun.

•   •   •   •

MCDONALD'S BISCUITS

Them's the biscuits served at America's most popular stop for breakfast, partners—simple to make and gosh darn tasty. Get yourself some Bisquick and buttermilk and crank up the oven for a clone that's become one very frequent request.

2 cups Bisquick baking mix
⅔ cup buttermilk
2 teaspoons sugar

¼ teaspoon salt
2 tablespoons margarine, melted and
   divided

1. Preheat oven to 450⁰F.
2. Combine the baking mix, 7buttermilk, sugar, salt, and half of the melted margarine in a medium bowl. Mix until well blended.
3. Turn dough out onto a floured surface and knead for about 30 seconds, or until dough becomes elastic.
4. Roll dough to about ¾ inch thick and punch out biscuits using a 3-inch cutter. Arrange the punched-out dough on an ungreased baking sheet, and bake for 10 to 12 minutes or until the biscuits are golden on top and have doubled in height.
5. Remove the biscuits from the oven and immediately brush each one with a light coating of the remaining melted margarine. Serve warm.

• MAKES 8 BISCUITS.

• • • •

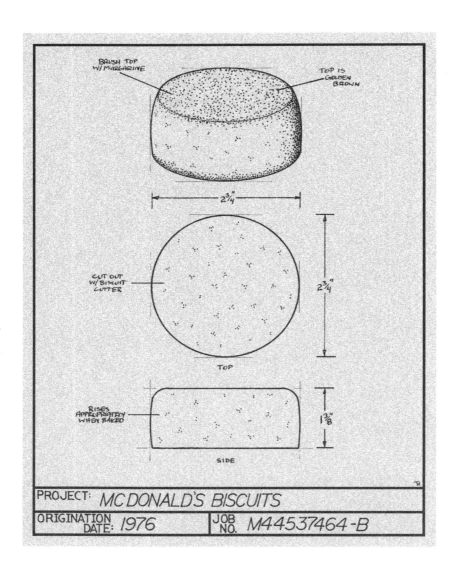

BRUSH TOP W/ MARGARINE

TOP IS GOLDEN BROWN

$2\frac{3}{4}''$

CUT OUT W/ BISCUIT CUTTER

$2\frac{3}{4}''$

TOP

RISES APPROPRIATELY WHEN BAKED

$1\frac{3}{8}''$

SIDE

PROJECT: *MC DONALD'S BISCUITS*

ORIGINATION DATE: *1976*

JOB NO. *M44537464-B*

MCDONALD'S HAMBURGER

Yes, Ronald McDonald is truly an international hero and celebrity. In Japan, since the "R" sound is not part of the Japanese language, everyone knows the burger-peddling clown as "Donald McDonald." And in Hong Kong, where people place a high value on family relationships, he is called Uncle McDonald, or in their language, "Mc-Donald Suk Suk."

These burgers were the original hallmark of the world's largest fast-food chain. In 1948, when brothers Dick and Mac Mc-Donald opened their first drive-in restaurant in San Bernardino, California, it was this simple sandwich that had hundreds of people driving in from miles around to pick up a sackful for just 15 cents a burger.

$1/8$ pound ground beef
1 plain hamburger bun
Salt to taste
1 tablespoon catsup

$1/2$ teaspoon prepared mustard
$1/2$ teaspoon finely minced onion
1 dill pickle slice

1. Roll the ground beef into a ball and then press flat on wax paper until about $1/8$ inch thick. You can also prepare the burger ahead of time and freeze it for easier cooking. The burger need not be defrosted before cooking.
2. Brown the faces of the bun in a frying pan over medium heat.
3. Remove the bun and cook the burger in the same pan for 2 minutes per side. Salt both sides during the cooking.

4. On the top bun, spread the catsup, mustard, and onion, in that order, and top with the pickle slice.
5. Put the beef patty on the bottom bun and slap the top and bottom together.
6. Microwave the burger on high for 10 to 15 seconds.

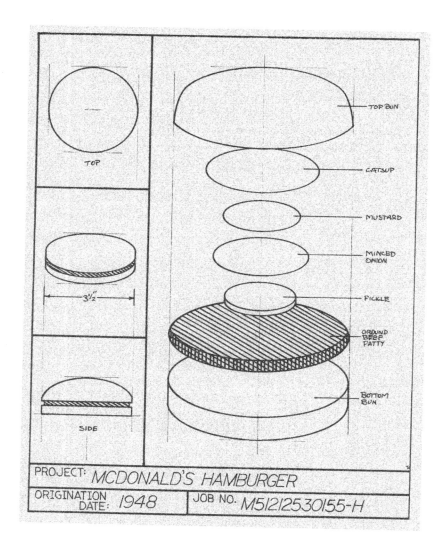

TOP

3½"

SIDE

TOP BUN

CATSUP

MUSTARD

MINCED ONION

PICKLE

GROUND BEEF PATTY

BOTTOM BUN

PROJECT: MCDONALD'S HAMBURGER

ORIGINATION DATE: 1948

JOB NO. M51212530155-H

MCDONALD'S CHEESEBURGER

Follow the recipe above, but add a slice of American cheese (not processed cheese food) on top of the beef patty in the final assembly. Microwave for 15 seconds on high to get that "just out from under the heat lamp" taste.

• • • •

MCDONALD'S
QUARTER POUNDER
(WITH CHEESE)

What is McDonald's sign referring to when it says "Over 100 billion served"? That's not the number of customers served, but actually the number of beef patties sold since McDonald's first opened its doors in the forties. A hamburger counts as one patty. A Big Mac counts as two.

McDonald's sold its 11 billionth hamburger in 1972, the same year that this sandwich, the Quarter Pounder, was added to the growing menu. That was also the year large fries were added and founder Ray Kroc was honored with the Horatio Alger Award (the two events were not related). In 1972, the 2,000th McDonald's opened its doors, and by the end of that year McDonald's had finally become a billion-dollar corporation.

1 sesame-seed bun	1/2 teaspoon prepared mustard
1/4 pound ground beef	1 teaspoon chopped onion
Salt to taste	2 dill pickle slices
1 tablespoon catsup	2 slices American cheese

1. Brown the faces of the bun in a large frying pan over medium heat.
2. Roll the ground beef into a ball and then flatten on wax paper until about 1/4 inch thick.
3 Cook the burger for 3 to 4 minutes per side. Salt each side during the cooking.
4. Spread catsup and then the mustard on the top bun; then add the onion and pickle.

5. Place 1 slice of cheese on the bottom bun, then the beef patty, then the other slice of cheese.
6. Top off the sandwich with the top bun.
7. Microwave on high for 15 seconds.

• MAKES 1 BURGER.

• • • •

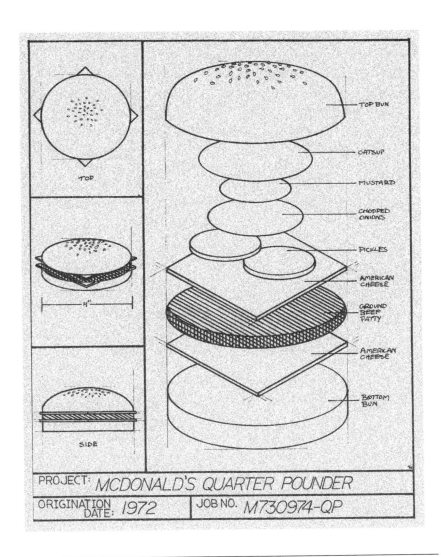

TOP

SIDE

4"

TOP BUN
CATSUP
MUSTARD
CHOPPED ONIONS
PICKLES
AMERICAN CHEESE
GROUND BEEF PATTY
AMERICAN CHEESE
BOTTOM BUN

PROJECT: MCDONALD'S QUARTER POUNDER
ORIGINATION DATE: 1972   JOB NO. M730974-QP

PAL'S
SAUCEBURGER

Here's a simple, great-tasting burger from a small, yet beloved, Tennessee-based hamburger chain famous for its quirky buildings and simple, tasty food. Established in 1956 by Pal Barger, this 17-unit fast-service chain has been making a name for itself by recently winning the Malcolm Baldrige National Quality Award and performing admirably in markets among huge chains such as McDonald's, Burger King, and Wendy's. The signature sandwich from this little drive-thru comes slathered with a simple sauce—a combination of ketchup, mustard, and relish—that makes quick production of scores of these tasty sandwiches a breeze when the line of cars grows long, as it often does.

⅛ pound ground beef
1 small hamburger bun
salt

2 tablespoons ketchup
1 teaspoon sweet pickle relish
½ teaspoon yellow mustard

1. Pat out the ground beef until about the same diameter as the bun. If you like, you can freeze this patty ahead of time to help keep the burger from falling apart when you cook it.
2. Brown or toast the faces of the top and bottom buns. You can do this in a frying pan over medium heat or by toasting them in the oven (or toaster oven).
3. As the buns are browning, grill the hamburger patty, in a hot frying pan over medium heat. Salt the meat generously.

4. Combine the ketchup, relish, and mustard in a small bowl.
5. When the meat is cooked to your liking, place it on the face of the bottom bun.
6. Slather the sauce on the face of the top bun and place it onto the meat.

- MAKES 1 BURGER.

TIDBITS

To multiply this recipe, use this handy multiplier for the sauce:

Sauce for 2 burgers:	*¼ cup ketchup*	*2 teaspoons relish*	*1 teaspoon mustard*
Sauce for 4 burgers:	*½ cup ketchup*	*4 teaspoons relish*	*2 teaspoons mustard*
Sauce for 6 burgers:	*¾ cup ketchup*	*2 tablespoons relish*	*1 tablespoon mustard*

• • • •

PAPA JOHN'S
DIPPING SAUCES

☆   ✌   ✦   ✏   ☯   ✂   ☞

John Schnatter was only 23 years old when he used 1600 dollars of start-up money to buy a pizza oven and have it installed in the broom closet of an Indiana tavern. John started delivering his hot, fresh pizzas, and in 1984, the first year of his business, he sold 300 to 400 pizzas a week. One year later, he opened the first Papa John's restaurant, and his chain has become another American success story. Today the company has expanded to over 2500 locations in 49 states with revenues of 1.7 billion dollars a year. That makes John's place the country's fastest-growing pizza chain.

John has kept the Papa John's menu simple. You won't find salads or subs or chicken wings on his menu. The company just sells pizza, with side orders of breadsticks and cheesesticks made from the same pizza dough recipe. With each order of breadsticks or cheesesticks comes your choice of dipping sauces. I've got clones here for all three of those tasty sauces. You can use these easy clones as dips for a variety of products, or you can simply make your own breadsticks by baking your favorite pizza dough, then slicing it into sticks. If you want cheesesticks, just brush some of the Garlic Sauce on the dough, then sprinkle it with mozzarella cheese and bake. Slice the baked dough into sticks and use the dipping sauce of your choice. It's a cinch.

SPECIAL GARLIC SAUCE

½ cup margarine
¼ teaspoon garlic powder

dash salt

1. Combine ingredients in a small bowl.
2. Microwave on ½ power for 20 seconds. Stir.

• MAKES ½ CUP.

CHEESE SAUCE

½ cup milk
2 teaspoons cornstarch
¼ cup Cheez Whiz

2 teaspoons juice from canned
  jalapeños (nacho slices)

1. Combine cornstarch with milk in a small bowl and stir until cornstarch has dissolved.
2. Add Cheez Whiz and stir to combine. Microwave on high for 1 minute, then stir until smooth.
3. Add juice from jalapeño slices, and stir.

• MAKES ½ CUP.

PIZZA SAUCE

One 10¾-ounce can tomato puree
¼ cup water
1 tablespoon sugar
1 teaspoon olive oil
¼ teaspoon lemon juice

¼ teaspoon salt
¼ teaspoon oregano
⅛ teaspoon basil
⅛ teaspoon thyme
⅛ teaspoon garlic powder

1. Combine ingredients in a small saucepan over medium heat. Bring to a boil.
2. Reduce heat and simmer for 15 to 20 minutes.

• MAKES 1 CUP.

• • • •

SKYLINE
CHILI

Nope, there's no chocolate in it. Or coffee. Or Coca-Cola. The ingredient rumors for Skyline Chili are plentiful on the Internet, but anyone can purchase cans of Skyline chili from the company and find the ingredients listed right on the label: beef, water, tomato paste, dried torula yeast, salt, spices, corn starch, and natural flavors. You can trust that if chocolate were included in the secret recipe, the label would reflect it—that's something that comes in handy for those with a chocolate allergy. So go ahead and eat your chocolate bar then wash it down with Coca-Cola, since all it takes to re-create the unique flavor of Skyline is a special blend of easy-to-find spices plus some beef broth. Let the chili simmer for an hour or so, then serve it up on its own or in one of the traditional Cincinnati-style serving suggestions (the "ways" they call 'em) with the chili poured over cooked spaghetti noodles, topped with grated cheddar cheese and other good stuff:

3-Way: Pour chili over cooked spaghetti noodles and top with grated cheddar cheese.

4-Way: Add a couple teaspoons of grated onion before adding the cheese.

5-Way: Add cooked red beans over the onions before adding the cheese.

1 pound ground beef
2 14.5-ounce cans Swanson beef broth
1/2 cup water
6-ounce can tomato paste
2 tablespoons cornstarch
4 teaspoons chili powder
1 tablespoon white distilled vinegar

1 1/4 teaspoons salt
1 teaspoon cardamom
1 teaspoon nutmeg
1/4 teaspoon allspice
1/4 teaspoon cayenne pepper
1/4 teaspoon coriander
1/4 teaspoon garlic powder
1/8 teaspoon ground black pepper
1/8 teaspoon ground cinnamon

1. Brown ground beef in a large saucepan over medium heat. Do not drain. Use a potato masher to mash the ground beef into very small pieces that are about the size of uncooked rice.
2. Turn off the heat, then add the rest of the ingredients to the pan. Whisk the ingredients so that the tomato paste and cornstarch is mixed in. Crank heat back up to medium and bring mixture to a boil. Reduce heat and simmer for 60 to 75 minutes or until thick.

- MAKES 5 CUPS.

• • • •

STARBUCKS CLASSIC COFFEE CAKE

☆ ✌ 💣 ✏ ☯ ✂ ☞

A good coffee house will have good coffee cake, and Starbucks is no exception. The world's biggest coffee house chain offers cake that is tasty and moist, with a perfect cinnamon streusel crumb topping that goes great with a hot cup of joe. Since Starbucks works with local bakeries, you may find slight variations of the cake at different Starbucks locations. Sometimes there is a ribbon of cinnamon running through the middle of the cake, and sometimes the cake is dusted with a bit of powdered sugar. You'll also find some versions with a few chopped pecans in the topping; and that's the version cloned here. You can certainly leave the pecans out if you like yours a bit less nutty.

TOPPING

1 cup all-purpose flour
1 cup light brown sugar, packed
1/2 cup butter, softened
1 teaspoon cinnamon
1/2 cup chopped pecans

1 cup butter, softened
3/4 cup light brown sugar, packed

1/2 cup granulated sugar
2 eggs
1 1/2 teaspoons vanilla
2 cups all-purpose flour
1 teaspoon baking powder
1/4 teaspoon salt
1/3 cup milk

1. Preheat oven to 325°F.
2. Make topping by combining 1 cup flour with brown sugar, a stick of softened butter, and 1 teaspoon cinnamon in a medium bowl. Mixture should have the consistency of moist sand. Add ½ cup chopped pecans.
3. In a large bowl, cream together 1 cup butter, ¾ cup light brown sugar, and ½ cup granulated sugar with an electric mixer until smooth and fluffy. Add eggs and vanilla and mix well.
4. In a separate bowl, combine flour, baking powder, and salt. Add this dry mixture to the moist ingredients a little bit at a time. Add milk and mix well.
5. Spoon the batter into a 9 x 13–inch baking pan that has been buttered and dusted with a light coating of flour.
6. Sprinkle the crumb topping over the batter. Be sure the topping completely covers the batter.
7. Bake cake for 50 minutes, or until the edges just begin to turn light brown. Cool and slice into 8 pieces.

- SERVES 8.

• • • •

STARBUCKS
CRANBERRY BLISS BAR

☆　　✌　　💣　　✒　　☯　　✂　　☞

Each holiday season Starbucks brings out one of its most beloved dessert recipes: a soft triangle of white chocolate and cranberry cake, covered with delicious creamy lemon frosting and dried cranberries. But, when the holidays leave us, so do the Cranberry Bliss Bars, and that's when the dozens of requests to clone the dessert start rolling in here at TSR. Each of the more than 3,500 Starbucks stores contracts with local bakeries so that the Bliss Bars are fresh for customers each day. The end result may vary slightly from city to city, but the basic recipe is the same, and it rules. Now you can get your Bliss Bar fix anytime of the year, at a fraction of the cost of the real thing, with a little sneaky kitchen cloning.

CAKE
1 cup (2 sticks) butter, softened
1 1/4 cups light brown sugar, packed
3 eggs
1 1/2 teaspoons vanilla
1 teaspoon ginger
1/4 teaspoon salt
1 1/2 cups all-purpose flour
3/4 cup dried cranberries, diced

6 ounces white chocolate, cut into
   chunks

FROSTING
4 ounces cream cheese, softened
3 cups powdered sugar
4 teaspoons lemon juice
1/2 teaspoon vanilla extract

TOPPING
1/4 cup dried cranberries, diced

DRIZZLED ICING
1/2 cup powdered sugar
1 tablespoon milk
2 teaspoons vegetable shortening

1. Preheat oven to 350°F.
2. Make cake by beating butter and brown sugar together with an electric mixer until smooth. Add eggs, vanilla, ginger, and salt and beat well. Mix in flour until smooth. Mix ¾ cup diced dried cranberries and white chocolate into the batter by hand. Pour batter into a greased 9 x 13–inch baking pan. Use a spatula to spread the batter evenly across the pan. Bake for 35 to 40 minutes or until cake is light brown on the edges. Allow the cake to cool.
3. Make frosting by combining softened cream cheese, 3 cups powdered sugar, lemon juice, and vanilla extract in a medium bowl with an electric mixer until smooth. When the cake has cooled, use a spatula to spread frosting over the top of the cake.
4. Sprinkle ¼ cup of diced cranberries over the frosting on the cake.
5. Whisk together ½ cup powdered sugar, 1 tablespoon milk, and shortening until smooth. Drizzle icing over the cranberries in a sweeping motion or use a pastry bag with a fine tip to drizzle frosting across the top of the cake.
6. Allow cake to sit for several hours, then slice the cake lengthwise (the long way) once through the middle. Slice the cake across the width three times, making a total of 8 rectangular slices. Slice each of those 8 slices once diagonally, creating 16 triangular slices.

• MAKES 16 BARS.

• • • •

SUBWAY
SWEET ONION SAUCE

The Sweet Onion Chicken Teriyaki Sandwich is one of Subway's biggest new product rollouts. The sandwich is made with common ingredients: Teriyaki glazed chicken-breast strips, onions, lettuce, tomatoes, green peppers, and olives. But what sets it apart from all other teriyaki chicken sandwiches is Subway's delicious Sweet Onion Sauce. You can ask for as much of the scrumptious sauce as you want on your custom-made sub at the huge sandwich chain, but you won't get any extra to take home, even if you offer to pay. Now, with this recipe, you can add a clone version of the sauce to your home-built sandwich masterpieces whenever you want.

½ cup light corn syrup
1 tablespoon minced white onion
1 tablespoon red wine vinegar
2 teaspoons white distilled vinegar
1 teaspoon balsamic vinegar
1 teaspoon brown sugar

1 teaspoon buttermilk powder
¼ teaspoon lemon juice
⅛ teaspoon poppy seeds
⅛ teaspoon salt
pinch cracked black pepper
pinch garlic powder

1. Combine all ingredients in a small microwave-safe bowl.
2. Heat mixture uncovered in the microwave for 1 to 1½ minutes on high until mixture boils rapidly.
3. Whisk well, cover, and cool.

- MAKES ABOUT ⅔ CUP.

•   •   •   •

TACO BELL
BAJA SAUCE

☆   ✌   💣   ✏   ☯   ✄   ☞

This is the spicy sauce that you can order on your Gordita or Chalupa at Taco Bell, but you won't get much extra sauce—even if you order it on the side—to use later at home. That's too bad since this stuff is good enough to use on all sorts of homemade Mexican masterpieces, from tacos to fajitas to breakfast burritos. Now, with this original TSR clone of the creamy sauce, you'll have enough to hold you over for a while. You need a food processor to puree the vegetables, but don't expect to use all the puree. I've made the measurements for the puree larger than required so that your food processor will have something to grab on to. And, by the way, this is a mayo-based sauce, so if you want to knock down the fat grams, use light mayonnaise in the recipe. You won't even be able to tell the difference.

¼ of a red bell pepper, seeded and
    coarsely chopped
1 large jalapeño, chopped in half
2 tablespoons diced Spanish onion
1 cup mayonnaise

1 tablespoon vinegar
¼ teaspoon cracked black pepper
dash garlic powder
dash cumin

1. Using a food processor, puree peppers and onion.
2. Mix 1 cup mayonnaise and 4 teaspoons of the vegetable puree in a medium bowl. Add remaining ingredients and mix well. Chill for several hours to let flavors develop.

- MAKES 1 CUP.

•   •   •   •

TACO BELL
MILD BORDER SAUCE

☆　　　✌　　　💣　　　✎　　　☯　　　✂　　　☞

If you like the flavor of Taco Bell's sauce, but don't like the burn, this is the sauce for you to clone. It used to be that you could only get this sauce in the little blister packs from Taco Bell restaurants, but now the chain has partnered with Kraft Foods to sell the stuff in 7.5-ounce bottles in most supermarkets. For the record, those bottles of hot sauce will set you back around $1.59 at the store, while the 6-ounce can of tomato paste required for this recipe is only 59 cents—and you end up with more than three times the amount of sauce!

3 cups water
2 teaspoons cornstarch
1 6-ounce can tomato paste
3 tablespoons white distilled vinegar

4 teaspoons chili powder
2 teaspoons salt
1 teaspoon cayenne pepper

1. Dissolve cornstarch in water in a medium saucepan.
2. Add remaining ingredients and stir well. Bring mixture to a boil over medium heat, then reduce heat and simmer for 5 minutes. Turn off heat and cover until cool. Keep in a covered container in the refrigerator to store.

• MAKES 3 CUPS (24 OUNCES).

• • • •

TACO BELL CHICKEN QUESADILLA

Taco Bell takes the fast-food quesadilla into new territory with three different cheeses and a creamy jalapeño sauce, all of which you can now cheerfully re-create in the comfort of your warm kitchen. Gather up the crew, since this recipe will make four of the tasty tortilla treats.

CREAMY JALAPEÑO SAUCE

1/4 cup mayonnaise
2 teaspoons minced jalapeño slices (nacho slices)
2 teaspoons juice from jalapeño slices (nacho slices)
3/4 teaspoon sugar
1/2 teaspoon paprika
1/2 teaspoon cumin
1/8 teaspoon cayenne pepper
1/8 teaspoon garlic powder
dash salt

4 chicken breast tenderloins
vegetable oil
salt
pepper
4 large flour tortillas (10-inch)
1 cup shredded cheddar cheese
1 cup shredded monterey jack cheese

2 slices American cheese

1. Prepare creamy jalapeño sauce by combining all ingredients in a small bowl. Cover and chill so that flavors develop. Stir occasionally.
2. Preheat your barbecue grill to medium heat.
3. Rub chicken tenderloins with vegetable oil. Salt and pepper each side of each tenderloin. Grill for 3 to 5 minutes per side. When chicken is done, slice it very thin.

4. When you are ready to build your quesadillas, preheat a 12-inch skillet over medium-low heat.
5. When the pan is hot, lay one tortilla in the pan. Arrange about ¼ cup of shredded cheddar cheese and ¼ cup of shredded jack cheese on half of the tortilla. Tear up half a slice of American cheese and arrange the pieces on the other cheeses.
6. Arrange about ¼ cup of sliced chicken over the cheese.
7. Spread about 1 tablespoon of jalapeño sauce over the tortilla on the half with no ingredients on it.
8. Fold the sauced-covered half of the tortilla over onto the ingredients on the other half, and press down with a spatula. Cook for about 1 minute, then turn the quesadilla over and cook for a couple more minutes or until the cheese inside is melted. Slice into four pieces and serve hot. Repeat with the remaining ingredients.

• MAKES 4 QUESADILLAS.

•   •   •   •

TACO BELL BURRITO SUPREME

☆　　✌　　💣　　✏　　☯　　✂　　☞

To copy Taco Bell's most famous burrito at home you first must assemble the meaty foundation of many of the chain's top-selling products: the spiced ground beef. Toss it and seven other tasty ingredients into a large flour tortilla and fold using the same technique as taught to new recruits at the chain. If you like a bit of heat, throw on some of the hot sauce from the Taco Bell Fire Border Sauce clone recipe found on page 72.

1 pound lean ground beef	1 16-ounce can refried beans
¼ cup all-purpose flour	8 10-inch flour tortillas
1 tablespoon chili powder	½ cup enchilada sauce
1 teaspoon salt	¾ cup sour cream
½ teaspoon dried minced onion	2 cups shredded lettuce
½ teaspoon paprika	2 cups shredded cheddar cheese
¼ teaspoon onion powder	1 medium tomato, diced
dash garlic powder	½ cup diced yellow onion
½ cup water	

1. In a medium bowl, combine the ground beef with the flour, chili powder, salt, minced onion, paprika, onion powder, and garlic powder. Use your hands to thoroughly mix the ingredients into the ground beef.
2. Add the seasoned beef mixture to the water in a skillet over medium heat. Mix well with a wooden spoon or spatula, and break up the meat as it cooks. Heat for 5 to 6 minutes, or until

browned. The finished product should be very smooth, some-what pasty, with no large chunks of beef remaining.

3. Heat up the refried beans in a covered container in the microwave set on high temperature for 1 1/2 to 2 minutes.

4. Place the flour tortillas in a microwave-safe tortilla steamer, or on a plate and cover with plastic wrap. Heat the tortillas for 30 to 45 seconds in the microwave on high temperature.

5. Build each burrito by first spreading about 1/4 cup of refried beans on the center of a heated flour tortilla. Spread one-eighth of the meat mixture over the beans, then pour about a tablespoon of the enchilada sauce over the meat.

6. Stir the sour cream well, so that it is smoother, then spread about 1 1/2 tablespoons onto the burrito. Arrange some of the lettuce, cheese, tomato, and onion onto the tortilla, and then you're ready to roll.

7. Fold the end of the tortilla closest to you over the filling ingre-dients. Fold either the left or right end over next. Then fold the top edge over the filling. You will be leaving one end of the bur-rito open and unfolded. Repeat with the remaining ingredients and serve immediately.

• MAKES 8 BURRITOS.

• • • •

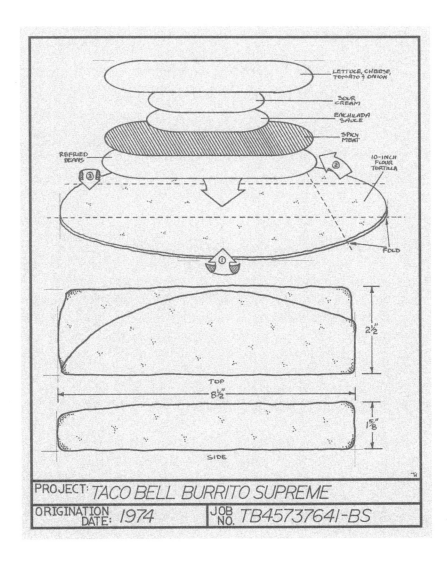

LETTUCE, CHEESE, TOMATO & ONION

SOUR CREAM

ENCHILADA SAUCE

SPICY MEAT

REFRIED BEANS

10-INCH FLOUR TORTILLA

FOLD

TOP

2 1/2"

8 1/2"

SIDE

1 5/8"

PROJECT: *TACO BELL BURRITO SUPREME*

ORIGINATION DATE: *1974*

JOB NO. *TB45737641-BS*

TACO BELL CHICKEN FAJITA! SEASONING MIX

☆ ✌ 💣 ✏ ☯ ✂ ☞

A couple years ago Taco Bell and Kraft Foods got together to produce a line of products—everything from taco kits to salsas and spice mixes—all stamped with the familiar Taco Bell logo and available in supermarkets across the country. The idea was a winner, and now the Taco Bell line of products is among Kraft's top sellers. The clone of this mix, made with a combination of common spices and cornstarch, can be kept indefinitely until your brain's fajita-craving neurons begin firing. When you're set to cook, you'll just need some chicken, a bell pepper, and an onion, and then you simply follow the same instructions that you find on the package of the real thing, which I've handily included for you below in the recipe.

1 tablespoon cornstarch
2 teaspoons chili powder
1 teaspoon salt
1 teaspoon paprika
1 teaspoon sugar

¾ teaspoon crushed chicken bouillon cube
½ teaspoon onion powder
¼ teaspoon garlic powder
¼ teaspoon cayenne pepper
¼ teaspoon cumin

1. Combine all of the ingredients in a small bowl.
2. Prepare fajitas using the following ingredients:

4 skinless chicken breast fillets (1 to 1 ¼ pound), cut into thin strips
2 tablespoons oil

⅓ cup water
1 green bell pepper, cut into strips
1 medium onion, sliced

Prepare the fajitas using the same directions found on the package of the original seasoning mix:

1. Cook and stir chicken in hot oil in a large nonstick skillet 5 minutes on medium-high heat. Add Taco Bell Fajita Seasoning Mix, water, green pepper, and onion; cook and stir on medium heat 5 minutes or until chicken is cooked through and the vegetables are tender.
2. Place tortillas on microwavable plate. Cover with plastic wrap. Microwave on high 1 minute.
3. Spoon chicken mixture onto each tortilla. Top as desired with Taco Bell salsa. Roll up tortillas."

• MAKES 5 SERVINGS.

• • • •

TACO BELL
FIRE BORDER SAUCE

For years Taco Bell customers had only the "mild" and "hot" varieties of free taco sauce blister packs to choose from to add a bit of zing to their fistful of tacos. That is, until the latest addition to the hot sauce selection kicked the heat-o-meter up a few notches. While true hot sauce freaks might find this sauce still on the mild side when compared with the glut of habanero-based sauces on the market today, it's definitely a recipe that improves on the Mexican fast-food chain's original formulas. This one's for those of you who get a rush from a good tastebud tingle.

1 6-ounce can tomato paste
3 cups water
3 tablespoons vinegar
3 tablespoons finely minced canned
    jalapeño slices
1 tablespoon chili powder
1 tablespoon dried minced onion

2 teaspoons salt
2 teaspoons cornstarch
1 teaspoon cayenne pepper
1 teaspoon sugar
1/4 teaspoon onion powder
dash garlic powder

1. Combine the tomato paste with the water in a medium saucepan and whisk until smooth.
2. Add remaining ingredients and stir until combined.
3. Heat mixture over medium high heat until it begins to boil. Continue to cook for about 3 minutes, stirring often. Remove from heat.
4. When sauce has cooled, pour it into a sealed container and refrigerate.

• MAKES 3 CUPS.

TACO BELL MEXICAN PIZZA

Hope you're hungry, 'cause this recipe makes four of the Mexican Pizzas like those served at the Bell. Prepare to blow your diners away with this one if they're at all familiar with the real thing.

½ pound ground beef
2 tablespoons all-purpose flour
1 ½ teaspoons chili powder
    (Spanish blend is best)
¾ teaspoon salt
¼ teaspoon dried minced
    onion
¼ teaspoon paprika
dash garlic powder
dash onion powder
2 tablespoons water

1 cup Crisco shortening
8 small (6 inch diameter) flour
    tortillas
1 16-ounce can refried beans
⅔ cup mild Picante salsa
½ cup shredded cheddar
    cheese
½ cup shredded Monterey Jack
    cheese
⅓ cup diced tomato
¼ cup chopped green onion

1. In a medium bowl, combine the ground beef with the flour, chili powder, salt, dried onion, paprika, garlic powder, and onion powder. Use your hands to thoroughly incorporate everything into the ground beef.
2. Preheat a skillet over medium heat and add the ground beef mixture to the pan along with the water. Brown the beef mixture for 5 to 6 minutes, using a wooden spoon or spatula to break up the meat as it cooks.
3. Heat shortening in a frying pan over medium heat. When shortening is hot, fry each tortilla for about 30 to 45 seconds per side and set aside on paper towels. When frying each

tortilla, be sure to pop any bubbles that form so that tortilla lies flat in the shortening. Tortillas should become golden brown.

4. Heat up refried beans in a small pan over the stove or in the microwave. Preheat oven to 400ºF.

5. When meat and tortillas are done, stack each pizza by first spreading about ⅓ cup refried beans on the face of one tortilla. Next spread ¼ to ⅓ cup of meat, then another tortilla. Coat your pizzas with 2 tablespoons of salsa on each, then combine the cheeses and sprinkle the blend evenly over the top of each pizza. Split up the diced tomato and arrange it evenly over the cheese on each pizza, followed by the green onion.

6. Place pizzas in your hot oven for 8 to 12 minutes or until the cheese on top is melted. Cut each pizza into four slices, and serve.

- MAKES 4 PIZZAS.

• • • •

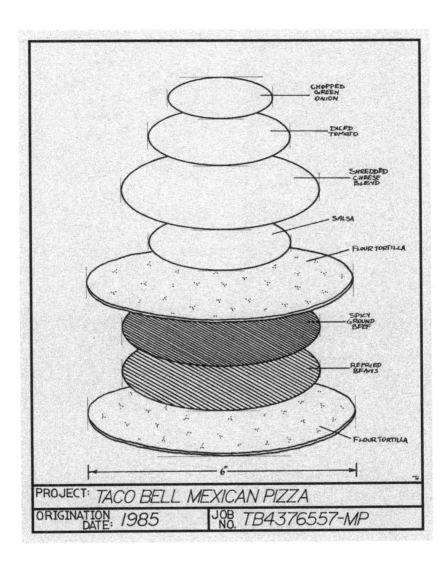

CHOPPED GREEN ONION

DICED TOMATO

SHREDDED CHEESE BLEND

SALSA

FLOUR TORTILLA

SPICY GROUND BEEF

REFRIED BEANS

FLOUR TORTILLA

6"

PROJECT: TACO BELL MEXICAN PIZZA

ORIGINATION DATE: 1985

JOB NO. TB4376557-MP

TACO BELL
SOFT TACO

If you don't think those packets of Taco Bell spices you buy in the grocery stores make spiced ground meat that tastes like the stuff they use at the giant Mexican food chain, you'd be correct. If you want the taco meat to taste like the chain's then you're going to have to whip it up from scratch using this original *TSR* recipe. Once you've prepped your meat, the steps below will help you build your tacos the Taco Bell way, hopefully without any pesky talking Chihuahuas running through the kitchen. If you want crispy tacos, just replace the flour tortillas with crunchy corn shells.

1 pound lean ground beef
¼ cup all-purpose flour
1 tablespoon chili powder
1 teaspoon salt
½ teaspoon dried minced onion
½ teaspoon paprika
¼ teaspoon onion powder

dash garlic powder
½ cup water
12 soft taco flour tortillas (6-inch tortillas)
2 cups shredded lettuce
1 cup shredded cheddar cheese

1. In a medium bowl, combine the ground beef with the flour, chili powder, salt, minced onion, paprika, onion powder, and garlic powder. Use your hands to thoroughly mix the ingredients into the ground beef.
2. Add the seasoned beef mixture to the water in a skillet over medium heat. Mix well with a wooden spoon or spatula, and break up the meat as it cooks. Heat for 5 to 6 minutes, or until browned. The finished product should be very smooth, somewhat pasty, with no large chunks of beef remaining.

3. Heat up the flour tortillas in your microwave for 20 to 30 seconds, or until warm.
4. Build each taco by spooning 2 to 3 tablespoons of the meat into a warm tortilla. Spread some of the shredded lettuce over the meat and then sprinkle some cheese over the top. Repeat with the remaining ingredients and serve immediately.

• MAKES 12 SOFT TACOS.

• • • •

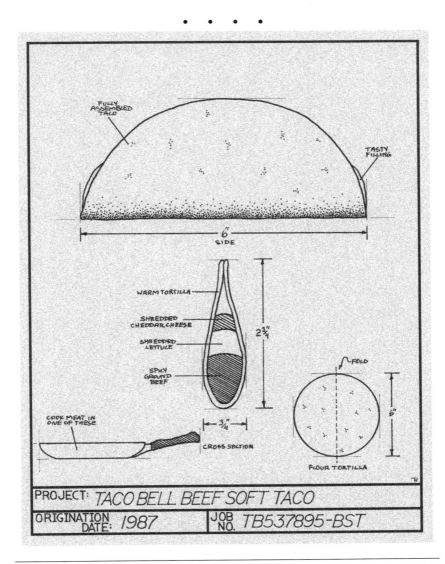

FULLY ASSEMBLED TACO

TASTY FILLING

6"
SIDE

WARM TORTILLA

SHREDDED CHEDDAR CHEESE

SHREDDED LETTUCE

SPICY GROUND BEEF

2¾"

FOLD

6"

COOK MEAT IN ONE OF THESE

¾"
CROSS SECTION

FLOUR TORTILLA

PROJECT: TACO BELL BEEF SOFT TACO

ORIGINATION DATE: 1987   JOB NO. TB537895-BST

TACO BELL
TACO SEASONING MIX

This is a simple recipe to clone the contents of the seasoning packet that bears the Taco Bell logo found in practically all the grocery stores these days. You probably expect the seasoning mix to make meat that tastes exactly like the stuff you get at the big chain. Well, uh, nope. It's more like the popular Lawry's taco seasoning mix, which still makes good spiced ground meat, and works great for a tasty bunch of tacos. But if it's the mushy, spiced meat that's packed into tacos and burritos at America's largest taco joint that you want, you'll have to use the clone recipe for the Taco Bell Soft Taco that precedes this one.

2 tablespoons flour
2 teaspoons chili powder
1 ½ teaspoons dried minced onion
1 ¼ teaspoons salt
1 teaspoon paprika
¾ teaspoon crushed beef bouillon
    cube

¼ teaspoon sugar
¼ teaspoon cayenne pepper
¼ teaspoon garlic powder
dash onion powder

1. Combine all of the ingredients in a small bowl.
2. Prepare taco meat using 1 pound of ground beef and following the same spunky directions as on the original package:

   1. Brown ground beef; drain. Add seasoning mix and ¾ cup of water. Bring to a boil; reduce heat. Simmer uncovered, 10 minutes, stirring occasionally.
   2. Heat taco shells or tortillas as directed on package.

3. Serve bowls of seasoned ground beef, lettuce, tomato, and cheese. Pass the taco shells or tortillas and let everyone pile on the fun!

- Makes 12 tacos.

• • • •

TACO BELL
HOT
TACO SAUCE

You can't buy it in grocery stores, so if you want a substantial portion of Taco Bell's great Taco Sauce to smother your own creations in, you'll have to collect pocketfuls of those little blister packs. But that would be mooching. So here's a way to make plenty of hot sauce just like the stuff people are pouring over the 4 million tacos served at 4,200 Taco Bell restaurants in forty states and around the world every day.

One 6-ounce can tomato paste
2 teaspoons cornstarch
3 cups water
2 teaspoons distilled white vinegar
2 teaspoons cayenne pepper

1 tablespoon minced dried onion
1 1/2 tablespoons chili powder
2 tablespoons canned jalapeño slices ("nacho slices")
2 1/2 teaspoons salt

1. Combine the tomato paste with the water in a saucepan over medium heat. Stir until smooth.
2. Add the cayenne pepper, chili powder, salt, cornstarch, vinegar, and dried onion and stir.
3. Chop the jalapeño slices very fine. You can use a food processor, but don't puree. The best kind of jalapeños to use are those bottled for nachos or pizza. Add them to the mixture.
4. Heat the mixture to boiling. Continue to stir about 3 minutes and remove from the heat.
5. Let the sauce stand until cool, and then put in a tightly sealed container and refrigerate. This will last for 1 to 2 months.

- MAKES 3 1/2 CUPS.

TOMMY'S ORIGINAL WORLD FAMOUS HAMBURGERS

This clone recipe may be for the whole hamburger, but anybody who knows about Tommy's goes there for the chili—and that's the part of this clone recipe they seek. That's also the part that required the most kitchen sleuthing. Turns out it's an old chili con carne recipe created back in 1946 by Tommy's founder, Tommy Koulax, for his first hamburger stand on the corner of Beverly and Rampart Boulevards in Los Angeles. By adding the right combination of water and flour and broth and spices to the meat we can create a thick, tomato-less chili sauce worthy of the gajillions of southern California college students who make late-night Tommy's runs a four-year habit. And if you don't live near one of the two dozen Tommy's outlets, you can still get a gallon of Tommy's famous chili shipped to you. But I hope you really dig the stuff, because you'll shell out around 70 bucks for the dry ice packaging and overnight shipping. And don't expect to see the ingredients on the label, since the chili comes packed in a gallon-size mustard jug.

CHILI

1 pound ground beef
    (not lean)
1/4 cup flour plus 1 1/4 cups flour
1 1/3 cups beef broth
4 cups water
3 tablespoons chili powder
2 tablespoons grated (and then
    chopped) carrot

1 tablespoon white vinegar
2 teaspoons dried minced onion
2 teaspoons salt
1 teaspoon granulated sugar
1 teaspoon paprika
1/4 teaspoon garlic powder

3 pounds ground beef

8 hamburger buns
16 slices Kraft Singles cheddar
    cheese
½ cup diced onion

32 to 40 hamburger pickles (slices)
8 slices large beefsteak tomato
    (½ inch thick)
¼ cup yellow mustard

1. Prepare the chili by first browning the meat in a large saucepan over medium heat. Crumble the meat as it browns. When the meat has been entirely cooked (7 to 10 minutes), pour the meat into a strainer over a large cup or saucepan. Let the fat drip out of the meat for about 5 minutes, then return the meat to the first saucepan. Cover and set aside.

2. With the fat from the meat, we will now make a roux—a French contribution to thicker sauces and gravies usually made with fat and flour. Heat the drippings in a saucepan over medium heat (you should have drained off around ½ cup of the stuff). When the fat is hot, add ¼ cup flour to the pan and stir well. Reduce heat to medium low, and continue to heat the roux, stirring often, until it is a rich caramel color. This should take 10 to 15 minutes. Add the beef broth to the pan and stir. Remove from heat.

3. Meanwhile, back at the other pan, add the water to the beef, then whisk in the remaining 1¼ cups flour. Add the roux/broth mixture and the other chili ingredients and whisk until blended. Make sure your grated carrot is chopped up to the size of rice before you add it.

4. Crank the heat up to medium high. Stir often until you see bubbles forming on the surface of the chili. Turn the heat down to medium low, and continue to simmer for 15 to 20 minutes, or until thick. The chili should be calmly bubbling like lava as it simmers. When it's done cooking, take the chili off the heat, cover it, and let it sit for 30 minutes to an hour before using it on the burgers. It should thicken to a tasty brown paste as it sits.

5. To make your hamburgers, you'll first divide 3 pounds of hamburger into 16 portions of 3 ounces each. Grill the burgers in a hot skillet or on an indoor griddle for 4 to 5 minutes per side or until done. Sprinkle some salt and pepper on each patty.

6. Build the burgers by lightly toasting the faces of the hamburger

buns. Turn them over into a hot skillet or a griddle on medium heat.

7. Place one patty onto the bottom bun.
8. Position two slices of cheese on the meat.
9. Place another beef patty on the cheese.
10. Spoon about ⅓ cup of chili onto the beef patty.
11. Sprinkle about 1 tablespoon of diced onion onto the chili.
12. Arrange 4 to 5 pickle slices on the onion.
13. Place a thick slice of tomato on next.
14. Spread mustard over the face of the top bun and top off your hamburger by turning this bun over onto the tomato.

• MAKES 8 BURGERS, 6 CUPS OF CHILI.

• • • •

WENDY'S CHICKEN CAESAR FRESH STUFFED PITA

☆   ✌   💣   ✏   ☯   ✂   ☞

Early in 1997 Wendy's introduced its selection of cold "Fresh Stuffed" pita sandwiches—perhaps thinking that America was ready for fast food fare that seemed healthier than your standard greasy burger. I love these sandwiches, but apparently most customers didn't agree, since the company discontinued the item in many of the 5000 Wendy's outlets. If you miss the pita sandwiches, and even if you don't, here now is a way to re-create the delicious salads-in-a-flatbread in the comfort of your own home.

DRESSING

½ cup water
⅛ teaspoon dry, unflavored gelatin
⅓ cup white vinegar
½ cup olive oil
½ teaspoon finely minced red bell pepper
½ teaspoon salt
¼ teaspoon garlic powder
¼ teaspoon Worcestershire sauce
⅛ teaspoon coarse ground black pepper
dash parsley
dash oregano
dash thyme
dash basil

1 tablespoon grated Romano cheese
1 tablespoon grated Parmesan cheese
2 tablespoons egg substitute

2 skinless chicken breast fillets
salt
pepper
6 cups romaine lettuce, chopped
¼ cup red cabbage, shredded
¼ cup carrot, shredded
4 pita breads (pocketless, if you can find them)
4 teaspoons shredded, fresh Parmesan cheese

1. Make the dressing by first dissolving the gelatin in the water. Heat the mixture in the microwave on high for 2 minutes or until it begins to boil rapidly. Add the vinegar, then whisk while adding the oil. Add bell pepper, salt, garlic powder, Worcestershire, black pepper, parsley, oregano, thyme, and basil. Let dressing cool for about 15 minutes before adding cheeses and egg substitute. Whisk until slightly thicker, then chill. Overnight refrigeration makes the dressing thicker.
2. Preheat a barbecue or indoor grill to medium heat. Salt and pepper the chicken, then grill it for 5 minutes per side, or until done. Remove chicken from the grill and dice it.
3. While chicken cooks, prepare the salad by combining the romaine lettuce, red cabbage, and shredded carrot in a large bowl and toss.
4. Prepare the sandwiches by first microwaving each pita for 20 seconds.
5. Fold each pita in half like a taco, then add 1 to 1½ cups of the romaine salad into the bread.
6. Add about ⅓ cup of diced chicken on top of the salad in the pita.
7. Pour about a tablespoon of dressing over each sandwich.
8. Sprinkle about a teaspoon of shredded fresh Parmesan on top of each one and serve.

• SERVES 4.

•   •   •   •

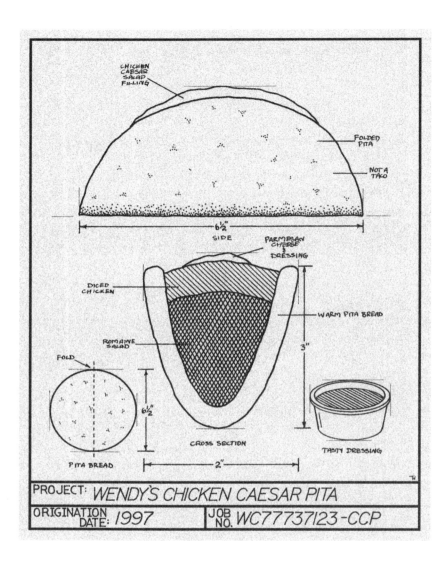

CHICKEN CAESAR SALAD FILLING

FOLDED PITA

NOT A TACO

6½"

SIDE

PARMESAN CHEESE + DRESSING

DICED CHICKEN

WARM PITA BREAD

ROMAINE SALAD

3"

FOLD

6½"

PITA BREAD

CROSS SECTION

2"

TASTY DRESSING

PROJECT: *WENDY'S CHICKEN CAESAR PITA*

ORIGINATION DATE: *1997*

JOB NO. *WC77737123-CCP*

WENDY'S CLASSIC GREEK FRESH STUFFED PITA

☆   ✌   💣   ✏   ☯   ✂   ☞

The Classic Greek Pita uses the same salad base and dressing as the previous clone for the Chicken Caesar Pita, but replaces the chicken and Parmesan with a Greek topping that's a breeze to make. Even though Wendy's uses a special custom pocketless pita that can be tough to find in stores, you can use the more common pocketed pita, just without opening the pocket. Instead, you heat up the pita, then fill up the center and fold it like a soft taco.

DRESSING
1/2 cup water
1/8 teaspoon dry, unflavored gelatin
1/3 cup white vinegar
1/2 cup olive oil
1/2 teaspoon finely minced red bell pepper
1/2 teaspoon salt
1/4 teaspoon garlic powder
1/4 teaspoon Worcestershire sauce
1/8 teaspoon coarse ground black pepper
dash parsley
dash oregano
dash thyme
dash basil

1 tablespoon grated Romano cheese
1 tablespoon grated Parmesan cheese
2 tablespoons egg substitute

1 cup (4-ounce package) crumbled feta cheese
1/2 cup tomato, seeded and diced
1/4 cup cucumber, thinly sliced and chopped
1/4 cup red onion, diced
6 cups romaine lettuce, chopped
1/4 cup red cabbage, shredded
1/4 cup carrot, shredded
4 pita breads (pocketless, if you can find them)

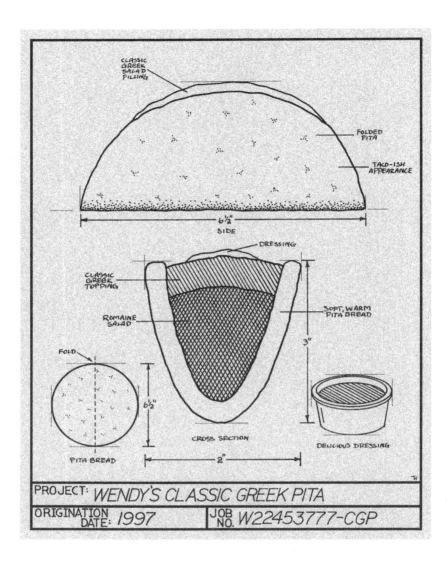

CLASSIC GREEK SALAD FILLING

FOLDED PITA

TACO-ISH APPEARANCE

6½"
SIDE

DRESSING

CLASSIC GREEK TOPPING

ROMAINE SALAD

SOFT, WARM PITA BREAD

3"

FOLD

6½"

PITA BREAD

CROSS SECTION

2"

DELICIOUS DRESSING

PROJECT: WENDY'S CLASSIC GREEK PITA

ORIGINATION DATE: 1997

JOB NO. W22453777-CGP

1. Make the dressing by first dissolving the gelatin in the water. Heat the mixture in the microwave on high for 2 minutes or until it begins to boil rapidly. Add the vinegar, then whisk while adding the oil. Add bell pepper, salt, garlic powder, Worcestershire, black pepper, parsley, oregano, thyme, and basil. Let dressing cool for about 15 minutes before adding cheeses and egg substitute. Whisk until slightly thicker, then chill. Overnight refrigeration makes the dressing thicker.
2. Make the Greek topping for the sandwiches by combining the crumbled feta cheese, tomato, cucumber, and red onion in a small bowl.
3. Prepare the salad by combining the romaine lettuce, red cabbage, and shredded carrot in a large bowl and toss.
4. Prepare the sandwiches by first microwaving each pita for 20 seconds.
5. Fold each pita in half like a taco, then add 1 to 1½ cups of the romaine salad into the bread.
6. Add ½ to ⅓ cup of the Greek topping to each sandwich.
7. Pour about a tablespoon of dressing over each sandwich and serve.

- SERVES 4.

• • • •

WENDY'S
SPICY CHICKEN FILLET
SANDWICH

☆　　✌　　💣　　✐　　☯　　✂　　☞

There once was a time when Wendy's offered this sandwich for a "limited time only." Apparently the tasty zing from this breaded chicken sandwich won it many loyal customers and a permanent place on the fast food chain's menu. Now you can re-create the spicy kick of the original with a secret blend of spices in the chicken's crispy coating. Follow the same stacking order as the original, and you've just made four sandwich clones at a fraction of the cost of the real thing.

6 to 8 cups vegetable oil
1/3 cup Frank's Original Red Hot Pepper Sauce
2/3 cup water
1 cup all-purpose flour
2 1/2 teaspoons salt
4 teaspoons cayenne pepper
1 teaspoon coarse ground black pepper

1 teaspoon onion powder
1/2 teaspoon paprika
1/8 teaspoon garlic powder
4 skinless chicken breast fillets
4 plain hamburger buns
8 teaspoons mayonnaise
4 lettuce leaves
4 tomato slices

1. Preheat 6 to 8 cups of oil in a deep fryer to 350°F.
2. Combine the pepper sauce and water in a small bowl.
3. Combine the flour, salt, cayenne pepper, black pepper, onion powder, paprika, and garlic powder in another shallow bowl.
4. Pound each of the chicken pieces with a mallet until about

⅜-inch thick. Trim each breast fillet if necessary to help it fit on the bun.

5. Working with one fillet at a time, coat each piece with the flour, then dredge it in the diluted pepper sauce. Coat the chicken once again in the flour mixture and set it aside until the rest of the chicken is coated.

6. Fry the chicken fillets for 8 to 12 minutes or until they are light brown and crispy. Remove the chicken to a rack or to paper towels to drain.

7. As chicken is frying, prepare each sandwich by grilling the face of the hamburger buns on a hot skillet over medium heat. Spread about 2 teaspoons of mayonnaise on the face of each of the inverted top buns.

8. Place a tomato slice onto the mayonnaise, then stack a leaf of lettuce on top of the tomato.

9. On each of the bottom buns, stack one piece of chicken.

10. Flip the top half of each sandwich onto the bottom half and serve hot.

- MAKES 4 SANDWICHES.

• • • •

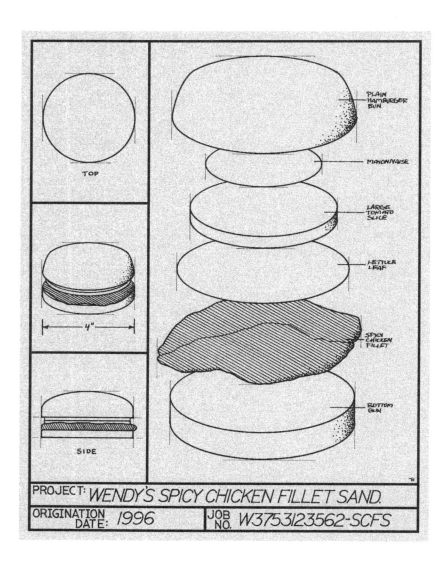

TOP

SIDE

4"

PLAIN HAMBURGER BUN

MAYONNAISE

LARGE TOMATO SLICE

LETTUCE LEAF

SPICY CHICKEN FILLET

BOTTOM BUN

PROJECT: *WENDY'S SPICY CHICKEN FILLET SAND.*

ORIGINATION DATE: *1996*

JOB NO. *W3753123562-SCFS*

WENDY'S GARDEN SENSATIONS MANDARIN CHICKEN SALAD

☆   ✌   💣   ✏   ☯   ✂   ☞

Of the four salads on Wendy's new "Garden Sensations" menu, this is the one that draws all the cloning requests. It's the sesame dressing that everyone's nuts about. The clone below gives you a nice 1 ½ cups of the tasty stuff, so it'll fit perfectly into a standard dressing cruet. Once you've got your dressing made, building the rest of the salad is a breeze.

SESAME DRESSING

½ cup corn syrup
3 tablespoons white distilled vinegar
2 tablespoons pineapple juice
4 teaspoons granulated sugar
1 tablespoon light brown sugar
1 tablespoon rice wine vinegar
1 tablespoon soy sauce
1 teaspoon sesame oil
¼ teaspoon ground mustard
¼ teaspoon ground ginger
⅛ teaspoon salt
⅛ teaspoon paprika

dash garlic powder
dash ground black pepper

½ cup vegetable oil
½ teaspoon sesame seeds

4 chicken breast fillets
1 large head iceberg lettuce, chopped
4 cups red leaf lettuce, chopped
1 ⅓ cups canned mandarin orange wedges
1 cup rice noodles
1 cup roasted sliced almonds

1. Prepare dressing by combining all dressing ingredients except vegetable oil and sesame seeds in a blender on high speed. Slowly add oil to mixture (to create an emulsion). Add sesame seeds and blend for just a couple seconds. Pour dressing into a covered container (such as a dressing cruet) and chill until needed.
2. Rub each chicken breast fillet with oil, then lightly salt and pepper each piece. Grill on medium-high heat until done. Chill chicken breasts in refrigerator until cold.
3. When chicken is cold, build each salad by first arranging about 4 cups of iceberg lettuce in the bottom of a large salad bowl or on a plate.
4. Arrange a cup of red leaf lettuce on the iceberg lettuce.
5. Dice each chicken breast into bite-size pieces and sprinkle the pieces from each one over each salad.
6. Arrange about $1/3$ cup of mandarin orange wedges on each salad.
7. Next, sprinkle about $1/4$ cup of rice noodles and $1/4$ cup of roasted sliced almonds on top of each salad.
8. Add desired amount of sesame dressing and serve.

• MAKES 4 LARGE SALADS.

•   •   •   •

WENDY'S GRILLED CHICKEN FILLET SANDWICH

In 1990, Wendy's not only added this new sandwich to its growing menu, but also added more international restaurants to the chain, including stores in Indonesia, Greece, Turkey, and Guatemala. Wendy's now claims more than 4,000 outlets around the world, with more than $3 billion in sales.

This is an excellent sandwich if you like grilled chicken, and it contains only nine grams of fat, if you're counting.

1 plain hamburger bun
1/2 skinned, boneless chicken breast
salt to taste

1 tablespoon Wishbone Honey Dijon
  salad dressing
1 lettuce leaf
1 large tomato slice

1. Heat the grill or broiler to medium heat.
2. Brown the faces of the bun in a frying pan over medium heat.
3. Cook the chicken breast for 6 to 10 minutes per side, or until done. Salt each side during the cooking.
4. Spread the salad dressing on the top bun.
5. Place the cooked chicken on the bottom bun. Top with the lettuce leaf, tomato slice, and top bun, in that order.
6. Microwave on high for 15 seconds.

- MAKES 1 SANDWICH.

• • • •

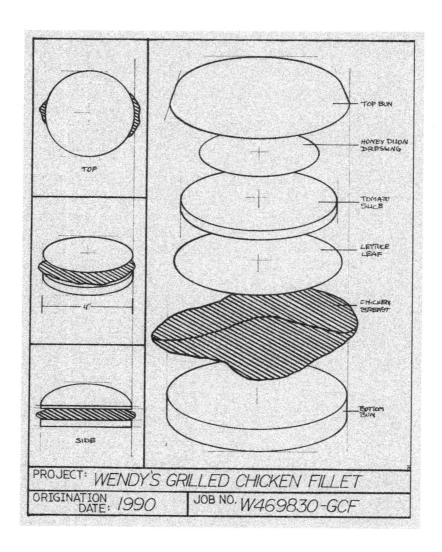

TOP

4'

SIDE

TOP BUN

HONEY DIJON DRESSING

TOMATO SLICE

LETTUCE LEAF

CHICKEN BREAST

BOTTOM BUN

PROJECT: *WENDY'S GRILLED CHICKEN FILLET*	
ORIGINATION DATE: *1990*	JOB NO. *W469830-GCF*

WENDY'S
JUNIOR BACON
CHEESEBURGER

☆   ✌   💣   ✏   ☯   ✂   ☞

Surely when Dave Thomas opened his first Wendy's Old Fashioned Hamburgers restaurant in 1969 and named it after his daughter, he never imagined the tremendous success and growth his hamburger chain would realize. He also could not have known that in 1989 he would begin starring in a series of television ads that would give Wendy's the biggest customer awareness level since its famous "Where's the beef?" campaign.

In that same year, Wendy's introduced the Super Value Menu, a selection of items all priced under a buck. The Junior Bacon Cheeseburger was added to the selection of inexpensive items and quickly became a hit.

1 plain hamburger bun	1 slice American cheese
$1/3$ pound ground beef	2 strips cooked bacon
salt to taste	1 lettuce leaf
1 tablespoon mayonnaise	1 tomato slice

1. Brown the faces of the bun in a frying pan over medium heat. Keep the pan hot.
2. Form the ground beef into a square patty approximately 4 × 4 inches.
3. Cook the patty in the pan for 3 to 4 minutes per side, or until done. Salt each side during the cooking.

4. Spread the mayonnaise on the top bun.
5. Place the patty on the bottom bun. On top, stack the cheese, bacon (side by side), lettuce leaf and tomato slice, in that order. Top off with the top bun.

•   MAKES 1 BURGER.

•   •   •   •

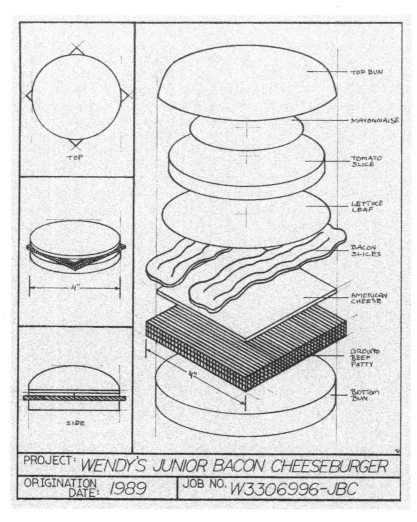

WENDY'S
SINGLE

In 1984, the diminutive Clara Peller blurted out in a series of four television ads the memorable phrase that would pop up on T-shirts and in presidential campaigns: "Where's the beef?" The ad was devised by Wendy's advertising agency to attack the misconception that its Single hamburger was smaller than its competitors' "big name" hamburgers. The campaign was so original that it stole the show at the 1984 Clio Awards, winning the advertising industry's highest honors and registering the highest consumer awareness level in the industry's history.

1 plain hamburger bun
1/4 pound ground beef
salt to taste
1 teaspoon catsup
1 tablespoon mayonnaise

1/2 teaspoon prepared mustard
1 lettuce leaf
3 raw onion rings
1 large tomato slice
3 to 4 dill pickle slices

1. Brown the faces of the bun in a large frying pan over medium heat. Keep the pan hot.
2. On wax paper, shape the ground beef into an approximately 4×4-inch square. It's best to freeze this patty ahead of time for easier cooking. Don't defrost before cooking.
3. Cook the burger in the pan for 3 minutes per side, or until done. Salt both sides during the cooking.
4. Spread the catsup and then the mayonnaise on the top bun.
5. Put the cooked patty on the bottom bun. On top of the meat,

spread the mustard, then place the lettuce, onion, tomato, and pickles, in that order.

6. Top off with the top bun and microwave for 15 seconds.

- MAKES 1 BURGER.

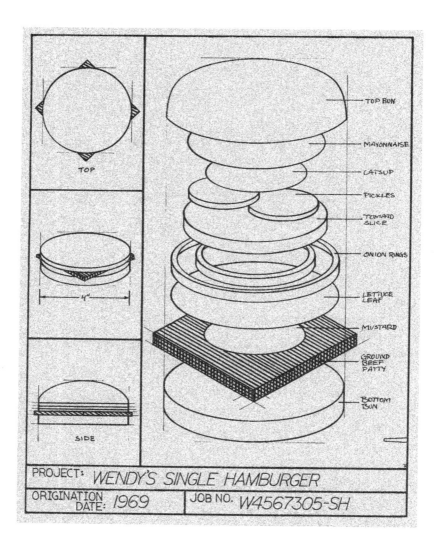

Single with Cheese

For a Single with cheese, place 1 slice of American cheese (not processed cheese food) on the beef patty when assembling the burger.

Double and Double with Cheese

Make this burger the same way as the Single, but stack another patty on the first one so that you have a total of $1/2$ pound ground beef.

If you want a Double with cheese, put one slice of cheese between the two beef patties.

• • • •

WIENERSCHNITZEL CHILI SAUCE

The real version of this chili sauce comes to each Wienerschnitzel unit in big 'ol 6-pound, 12-ounce cans of concentrated brown goo with bits of ground pork already in it. But after adding 64 ounces of water and 15 chopped hamburger patties to the sauce the magic begins to happen; the stuff transforms into the familiar thick and spicy chili sauce that gets dolloped over hot dogs and french fries for the drooling customers at America's largest hot dog chain. The proper proportion of spices, tomato paste, and meat is crucial, but the real challenge in cloning this recipe is figuring out a common grocery store equivalent for the "modified food starch" that's used in large quantities in the real chili sauce as a thickener. After a couple days sealed up in the underground lab with Starbucks lattes on intravenous drip, I finally came out squinting at the bright sunshine—victorious—with a killer solution to the chili conundrum! This secret combination of cornstarch and Wondra flour (and plenty of salt and chili powder) gives you a chili sauce that says nothing but "Wienerschnitzel" all over it (even without the MSG!). So get out the hot dogs, baby! The top requested secret clone recipe from this 40-year-old chain has finally been cracked.

¾ pound ground beef
¼ pound ground pork
6 cups water
¼ cup cornstarch

½ cup Wondra flour (see Tidbits)
6-ounce can tomato paste
¼ cup chili powder (McCormick)
3 tablespoons white vinegar

1 tablespoon salt
1 tablespoon dried minced onion
1 1/2 teaspoons granulated sugar

1/4 teaspoon garlic powder
1/4 teaspoon ground black pepper

1. Brown ground beef and ground pork in a large saucepan over medium heat. Crumble and chop the meat with a spoon or spatula as it cooks. When the meat is completely browned cover saucepan and turn heat to low. This way the ground meat will slowly simmer in its own juices.
2. After 10 minutes, remove the ground meat from the heat and drain off most of the fat. Keep some of it in the pan.
3. While the meat is still off the heat add the water and the cornstarch to the pan. Whisk the cornstarch thoroughly as it's added until it's dissolved into the water. Do the same for the Wondra flour.
4. You can now set the pan back over medium heat and add the remaining ingredients. Bring mixture to a boil, stirring often.
5. When chili begins to boil, reduce heat and simmer for 30 minutes. When chili is done it will be much thicker and darker, like the real thing. And, like the original, you can use this chili sauce on hot dogs, hamburgers, and french fries, or take it solo.

• MAKES 6 CUPS.

TIDBITS

Wondra flour is a finely ground, quick-mixing flour used in sauces and gravies. It is made by Gold Medal and can usually be found in the baking aisle next to all the other flours.

• • • •

BISQUICK
BAKING MIX

☆   ✌   💣   ✐   ☯   ✂   ☞

So you've got a hankerin' for pancakes, but you're all out of Bisquick. Not to worry, home cloners. Now you can easily whip up your own version of the popular baking mix with just four simple ingredients. Since the real thing includes shortening, salt, flour, and leavening, that's exactly what we'll use here to duplicate it. This recipe makes about 6 cups of the stuff, which, just like the original, you can keep sealed up in a container in your pantry until it's flapjack time. Then you simply add milk and eggs for pancakes or waffles, or just milk if it's biscuits you want. You'll find the specifics on those recipes in the Tidbits section.

4 cups all-purpose flour
2 tablespoons baking powder

1 ½ teaspoons salt
1 cup shortening

1. Combine all dry ingredients in a large bowl.
2. Add shortening and mix with an electric mixer on medium speed until all shortening is blended with the flour.
3. Use the mix as you would the real thing. Check out the Tidbits below.

• MAKES 6 CUPS.

Follow these recipes to use the baking mix you just cloned like a champ:

Pancakes: Stir 2 cups baking mix with 1 cup milk and 2 eggs in a bowl until blended. Pour ¼ cup portions onto a hot griddle. Cook until edges are dry. Turn; cook until golden. Makes 14 pancakes.

Waffles: Stir 2 cups baking mix with 1⅓ cups milk, 1 egg, and 2 tablespoons vegetable oil in a bowl until blended. Pour onto a hot waffle iron. Bake until the steaming stops. Makes 12 4-inch waffles.

Biscuits: Preheat oven to 450°F. Stir 2¼ cups baking mix with ⅔ cup milk. When the dough forms, turn it out onto a surface sprinkle with extra mix. Knead 10 times. Roll dough ½-inch thick. Cut with 2½–inch cutter. Place on an ungreased cookie sheet. Bake for 8 to 10 minutes or until golden brown.

• MAKES 9 BISCUITS.

•   •   •   •

BORDEN CRACKER JACK

In 1871 a German immigrant named F. W. Reuckheim came to Chicago with $200 in his pocket. He used all of his money to open a small popcorn shop in the city and started selling a sweet caramel-and molasses–coated popcorn confection. Rueckheim's big break came in 1893, when the treat was served at Chicago's first world's fair. From then on the popcorn's popularity grew enormously. In 1896 a salesman tasting the treat for the first time said, "That's a cracker jack," and the name stuck. Shortly after Cracker Jack's debut another customer commented, "The more you eat, the more you want," and that's still the slogan today.

In 1912 the Cracker Jack Company started adding toy surprises, ranging from small books to miniature metal toy trains. To date they have given away more than 17 billion toy surprises. In 1964 Borden, Inc. bought the Cracker Jack Company, and today the Cracker Jack division is the largest user of popcorn in the world, popping more than twenty tons of corn a day.

4 quarts popped popcorn (or
    1 1/3 bags microwave popcorn)
1 cup Spanish peanuts
4 tablespoons (1/2 stick) butter

1 cup brown sugar
1/2 cup light corn syrup
2 tablespoons molasses
1/4 teaspoon salt

1. Preheat the oven to 250ºF.
2. Combine the popcorn and peanuts in a metal bowl or on a cookie sheet and place in the preheated oven.
3. Combine all of the remaining ingredients in a saucepan.
4. Stirring over medium heat, bring the mixture to a boil.

5. Using a cooking thermometer, bring the mixture to the hard-crack stage (290°F, or the point at which the syrup, when dripped into cold water, forms a hard but pliable ball). This will take about 20 to 25 minutes (or until you notice the mixture turning a slightly darker brown).
6. Remove the popcorn and peanuts from the oven and, working quickly, pour the caramel mixture in a fine stream over them. Then place them back in the oven for 10 minutes.
7. Mix well every five minutes, so that all of the popcorn is coated.
8. Cool and store in a covered container to preserve freshness.

• MAKES 4 QUARTS.

•   •   •   •

BULL'S-EYE ORIGINAL BBQ SAUCE

Some say it's the best off-the-shelf barbecue sauce in the business. That secret combination of molasses, liquid smoke, and spices makes this stuff irresistible on chicken, ribs, or juicy hamburger. If it's grilling time and you're all out of sauce, why not whip up a clone batch of your own when it's this friggin' easy?

1 cup water
¾ cup light corn syrup
½ cup tomato paste
⅔ cup vinegar
⅓ cup dark brown sugar
3 tablespoons molasses
1 ¼ teaspoons liquid smoke
   (see Tidbits)

1 teaspoon salt
¼ teaspoon onion powder
¼ teaspoon ground black pepper
¼ teaspoon ground mustard
⅛ teaspoon paprika
⅛ teaspoon garlic powder
dash cayenne pepper

1. Combine all ingredients in a medium saucepan over high heat and whisk until smooth.
2. Bring mixture to a boil, then reduce heat and simmer uncovered for 45 minutes or until thick.
3. Cool, then store in a covered container in the refrigerator overnight.

• MAKES 1 ½ CUPS.

TIDBITS

Liquid smoke is a flavoring found near the barbecue sauces and marinades. Use hickory-flavored liquid smoke if you have a choice.

CADBURY'S CREME EGG

Here's a way to get your Easter candy fix, even when it's not Easter-time. It's a clone version of the first soft fondant-filled egg candy to hit the market many Easters ago. Each spring Cadbury candy machines whip out 66,000 of these cool candies every hour. And now, because of the success of these chocolates with the orange, yolk-colored center, other candy companies have come out with their own milk chocolate eggs. Some are filled with Snickers or Milky Way centers, while others contain peanut butter, coconut, caramel, or the same type of fondant center as the original . . . right down to the colors. Still, nothing compares with the original eggs that are sold only once a year, for the Easter holiday. Enjoy your own version at home anytime you like. With this recipe that won't require you to make anything close to 66,000 of 'em.

½ cup light corn syrup
¼ cup butter, softened
1 teaspoon vanilla
¼ teaspoon salt
3 cups powdered sugar

4 drops yellow food coloring
2 drops red food coloring
1 12-ounce bag milk chocolate chips
2 tablespoons vegetable shortening

1. Combine the corn syrup, butter, vanilla, and salt in a large bowl. Beat well with an electric mixer until smooth.
2. Add powdered sugar, one cup at a time, mixing by hand after each addition. Mix well until creamy.
3. Remove about ⅓ of the mixture and place it into a small bowl. Add the yellow and red food coloring and stir well to combine.

4. Cover both mixtures and refrigerate for at least 2 hours, or until firm.
5. When mixtures are firm, roll a small, marble-size ball from the orange filling, and wrap a portion of the white filling around it that is roughly twice the size. Form this filling into the shape of an egg and place it onto a cookie sheet that has been brushed with a light coating of shortening. Repeat for the remaining filling ingredients, then refrigerate these centers for 3 to 4 hours or until firm.
6. Combine the milk chocolate chips with the shortening in a glass or ceramic bowl. Microwave chocolate on high speed for 1 minute, then stir gently and microwave again for 1 more minute, and stir gently. Be very careful not to overcook the chocolate or it could seize up on you and become unusable.
7. Use a fork to dip each center into the chocolate, tap the fork on the side of the bowl, then place each candy onto wax paper. Chill.
8. After 1 to 2 hours of chilling, dip each candy once more and chill for several hours, or until completely firm.

• MAKES 2 DOZEN CANDY EGGS.

•   •   •   •

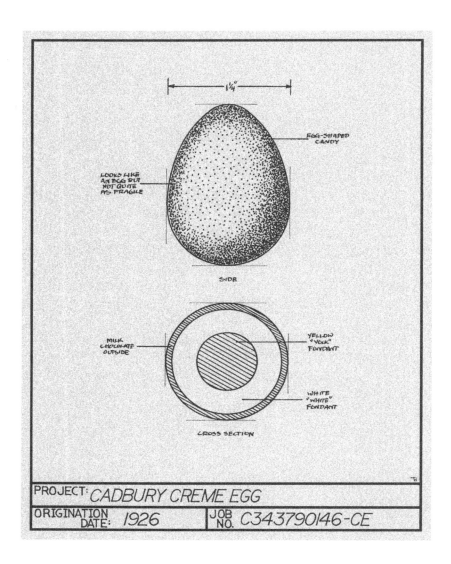

1¼"

EGG-SHAPED
CANDY

LOOKS LIKE
AN EGG BUT
NOT QUITE
AS FRAGILE

SIDE

MILK
CHOCOLATE
OUTSIDE

YELLOW
"YOLK"
FONDANT

WHITE
"WHITE"
FONDANT

CROSS SECTION

PROJECT: CADBURY CREME EGG

ORIGINATION DATE: 1926

JOB NO. C343790146-CE

CHEF PAUL PRUDHOMME'S POULTRY MAGIC

Louisiana chef Paul Prudhomme, America's number one Dom DeLuise lookalike, hit it big in supermarkets with his magical brand of Cajun spice blends. Chef Paul developed his seasonings after years of making little batches and passing them out to customers in the restaurants where he worked. Now his Magic Seasoning Blends come in several varieties and are produced in a whopping 30,000-square-foot plant by 38 employees. Fortunately, it'll take only one of you in a small kitchen to make a clone of one of the most popular versions of the blend. Use it when you barbecue, roast, grill, or sauté your favorite chicken, turkey, duck, or Cornish game hens.

1 ½ teaspoons salt
½ teaspoon paprika
¼ teaspoon cayenne
¼ teaspoon onion powder
¼ teaspoon garlic powder

¼ teaspoon ground black pepper
¼ teaspoon dried thyme
¼ teaspoon dried oregano
¼ teaspoon rubbed sage
dash cumin

Combine all ingredients in a small bowl. Store in a covered container. Sprinkle on any poultry to taste.

• MAKES 4 TEASPOONS.

DOLLY MADISON ZINGERS (DEVIL'S FOOD)

Former U.S. president James Madison's wife did not create this baking company, despite the fact that her name is on every carrot cake, crumb cake, and Zinger that comes off the production line. It was instead company founder Roy Nafziger's brainstorm to use the former first lady's name, since she was notorious for throwing huge shindigs featuring a fine selection of desserts and baked goods. Nafziger said his company would create cakes "fine enough to serve at the White House." While I don't expect you'll be treated to a tray of Zingers on your next stay in the Lincoln Bedroom, I will agree that these little snack cakes are a tasty way to appease a sweet tooth.

The cake batter is easy, since you just use any instant devil's food cake mix. I like Duncan Hines. As for the frosting, it may not come out as dark brown as the original since the recipe here doesn't include brown food coloring (caramel coloring). But the taste will be right on. And I think former president Clinton would agree that as long as the sweet little treats taste good, appearance is secondary.

CAKE
Duncan Hines devil's food cake mix
1 1/3 cups water
1/2 cup oil
3 large eggs

FILLING
2 teaspoons hot water
1/4 teaspoon salt
2 cups marshmallow creme
(one 7-ounce jar)
1/2 cup shortening
1/3 cup powdered sugar
1/2 teaspoon vanilla

FROSTING
1 cup powdered sugar
1/4 cup Hershey's chocolate syrup

2 tablespoons shortening
1/2 teaspoon vanilla
dash salt

1. Prepare the cake batter following the directions on the box. If you use Duncan Hines brand, you will need 1 1/3 cups of water, 1/2 cup of oil, and 3 eggs. Preheat oven to 350°F.

2. To prepare the cake pans that will make cakes the size of Zingers, tear off 20 pieces of aluminum foil that are each about 8 inches wide. Fold the foil in half and then in half once more so that you have a rectangular piece of foil. Wrap this piece of foil around a small prescription medicine bottle. Tuck in the ends and take the bottle out, leaving the foil open at the top. This will form a little pan. Flatten the bottom so that the mini pan stands up straight. Place this into a baking pan and repeat with the remaining pieces of foil. When you have arranged all of the foil pans in a baking pan, spray the inside of all the pans with non-stick cooking spray. Fill each little pan about halfway with cake batter. Bake cakes for 15 to 17 minutes or until a toothpick stuck in the center comes out clean. Remove the cakes from the oven and allow them to cool completely.

3. To make the filling, combine the hot water with the salt in a small bowl and stir until the salt is dissolved. Let this mixture cool.

4. Combine the marshmallow creme, shortening, powdered sugar, and vanilla in a medium bowl and mix well with an electric mixer on high speed until fluffy. Add the salt mixture to the bowl and mix.

5. To make the chocolate frosting, combine all the frosting ingredients in a medium bowl and mix well with an electric mixer until smooth.

6. To assemble your snack cakes first poke three holes with a toothpick or skewer in the top of a cake and swirl around inside the holes, making little caverns for your filling.

7. Use a pastry bag with a small tip to squeeze some filling into each hole. Careful not to overfill, or your cake will burst open. Sure, it looks cool when they explode, but this mess won't make for a very good clone.

8. Once the cake is filled, use a butter knife to spread frosting on top of the cake over the holes, concealing your secret injection work. Drag a fork lengthwise over the frosting, making grooves just like the real thing.

• MAKES 20 SNACK CAKES.

•   •   •   •

MOLD MADE FROM FOIL   FILL TO HERE

THE FOIL MOLD

PILL BOTTLE

INJECT FILLING HERE

BAKED CAKE

INJECT FILLING

FILLING

DEVIL'S FOOD CAKE

3"

1⅜"

CHOCOLATE FROSTING

1"

CROSS SECTION

PROJECT: DOLLY MADISON ZINGERS (DEVIL'S FOOD)

ORIGINATION DATE: CIRCA 1968   JOB NO. DM59037463-ZDF

DRAKE'S DEVIL DOGS

Here's a clone recipe for a favorite east coast treat that could even fool Rosie O'Donnell. The snack food–loving talk show hostess professes her love for these tasty Drake's goodies all the time on her daytime show. And who could blame her? It's hard not to relish the smooth, fluffy filling sandwiched between two tender devil's food cake fingers. I'll take a Devil Dog over a Twinkie any day of the week. For this clone recipe, we'll make the cakes from scratch. This will help us to create a flavor and texture closest to the original. But if you're feeling especially lazy, you can certainly use a devil's food cake mix in place of the scratch recipe here. Just make the filling with the recipe below and assemble your cakes the same way.

CAKE
1 egg
½ cup shortening
1¼ cups granulated sugar
1 cup milk
1 teaspoon vanilla
2⅓ cups all-purpose flour
½ cup cocoa
½ teaspoon salt
½ teaspoon baking powder

FILLING
2 cups marshmallow creme
    (1 7-ounce jar)
1 cup shortening
½ cup powdered sugar
½ teaspoon vanilla
⅛ teaspoon salt
2 teaspoons very hot water

1. Preheat oven to 400ºF.
2. In a medium bowl, blend together the egg, shortening, and sugar with an electric mixer. Continue beating while adding the milk and vanilla.

3. In another bowl sift together remaining cake ingredients—flour, cocoa, salt, and baking powder.
4. Combine the dry ingredients with the wet ingredients and beat until smooth.
5. Spoon about a tablespoon of the batter in strips about 4 inches long and 1 inch wide on a lightly greased cookie sheet. Bake for 5 to 6 minutes or until the cakes are done. Cool.
6. In another bowl combine the marshmallow creme, shortening, powdered sugar, and vanilla. Dissolve the ⅛ teaspoon of salt in the 2 teaspoons of very hot water in a small bowl. Add this salt solution to the filling mixture and beat on high speed with an electric mixer until the filling is smooth and fluffy.
7. When the cakes have cooled, spread about a tablespoon of filling on the face of one cake and top it off with another cake. Repeat with the remaining ingredients.

• MAKES 20 TO 24 SNACK CAKES.

•   •   •   •

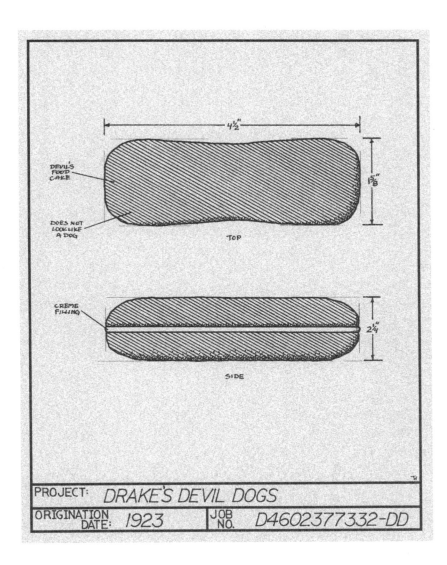

DEVIL'S
FOOD
CAKE

DOES NOT
LOOK LIKE
A DOG

4½"

1⅝"

TOP

CREME
FILLING

2¼"

SIDE

PROJECT: DRAKE'S DEVIL DOGS

ORIGINATION
DATE: 1923

JOB
NO. D4602377332-DD

119

FRITOS
HOT BEAN DIP

Re-create the popular bean dip at home in just minutes with a food processor—simply pour all the ingredients in and fire it up. The best part about this recipe is that we can duplicate the taste of the popular dip without any added fat. If you check out the label of the real thing, you'll see that there's hydrogenated oil in there. We can avoid this saturated fat without sacrificing flavor in our home clone, which is a perfectly satisfying and healthy choice for dipping. Now bring on the greasy chips!

1 15-ounce can pinto beans, drained
4 bottled jalapeño slices (nacho slices)
1 tablespoon juice from bottled jalapeño slices

½ teaspoon salt
½ teaspoon sugar
¼ teaspoon onion powder
¼ teaspoon paprika
⅛ teaspoon garlic powder
⅛ teaspoon cayenne pepper

1. Combine drained pinto beans with the other ingredients in a food processor. Puree ingredients on high speed until smooth. Cover and chill for at least an hour before serving.

• MAKES 1 ¼ CUPS.

• • • •

GIRL SCOUT COOKIES
SHORTBREAD

Since they only sell these once a year, right around springtime, you're bound to crave them again sometime in the fall. If you're still holding on to a box, by that time they may have begun to taste a bit like used air-hockey pucks. Now you can toss out those relics and fill the box with a fresh batch, made from this clone recipe for the first variety of cookies sold by the Girl Scouts back in 1917.

½ cup butter-flavored shortening
1 cup powdered sugar
½ teaspoon vanilla
¼ teaspoon salt
2 tablespoons beaten egg

½ teaspoon baking soda
2 tablespoons buttermilk
1 ½ cups all-purpose flour (plus an
    extra ¼ cup reserved for rolling)
⅛ teaspoon baking powder

1. In a large mixing bowl, cream together the shortening, sugar, vanilla, and salt with an electric mixer.
2. Add the egg and beat mixture until it's fluffy. Add the baking soda and mix for about 20 seconds, then add the buttermilk and mix for an additional 30 seconds.
3. In another bowl, combine the flour and baking powder.
4. Pour dry ingredients into wet ingredients and mix well with an electric mixer until flour is incorporated.
5. Roll the dough into a ball, cover it with plastic wrap, and chill it for 1 hour.
6. Preheat oven to 325⁰F.
7. Roll dough out on a well-floured surface to ⅛ inch thick and punch out cookies with a 1 ½ to 2-inch cutter (a medium-size

spice bottle lid works well). Arrange cookies on an ungreased cookie sheet.

8. Bake for 12 to 15 minutes or until golden brown.

- MAKES 60 COOKIES.

• • • •

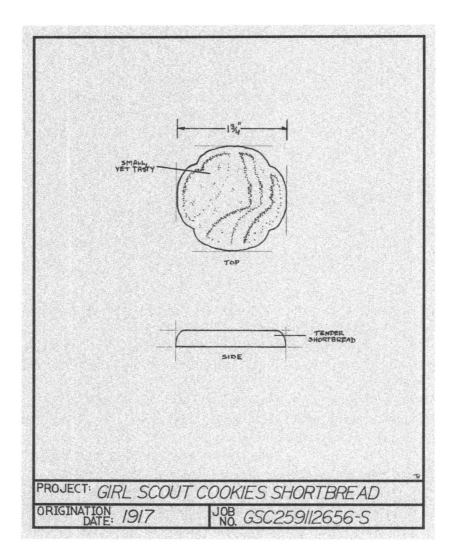

PROJECT: *GIRL SCOUT COOKIES SHORTBREAD*

ORIGINATION DATE: *1917*   JOB NO. *GSC259112656-S*

GIRL SCOUT COOKIES
THIN MINTS

☆   ✌   💣   ✏   ☯   ✂   ☞

If those cute little cookie peddlers aren't posted outside the market, it may be tough to get your hands on these—the most popular cookies sold by the Girl Scouts each year. One out of every four boxes of cookies sold by the girls is Thin Mints. This recipe uses an improved version of the chocolate wafers created for the Oreo cookie clone in the second *TSR* book, *More Top Secret Recipes*. That recipe creates 108 cookie wafers, so when you're done dipping, you'll have the equivalent of three boxes of the Girl Scout Cookies favorite. (See? That's why you bought those extra cookie sheets.) You could, of course, reduce the recipe by baking only 1/3 of the cookie dough for the wafers and then reducing the coating ingredients by 1/3, giving you a total of 36 cookies.

CHOCOLATE COOKIE WAFERS
1 18.25-ounce package Betty
   Crocker chocolate fudge cake
   mix
3 tablespoons shortening, melted
1/2 cup cake flour, measured then
   sifted
1 egg

3 tablespoons water
non-stick cooking spray

COATING
3 12-ounce bags semi-sweet
   chocolate chips
3/4 teaspoon peppermint extract
6 tablespoons shortening

1. Combine the cookie ingredients in a large bowl, adding the water a little bit at a time until the dough forms. Cover and chill for 2 hours.
2. Preheat oven to 350ºF.

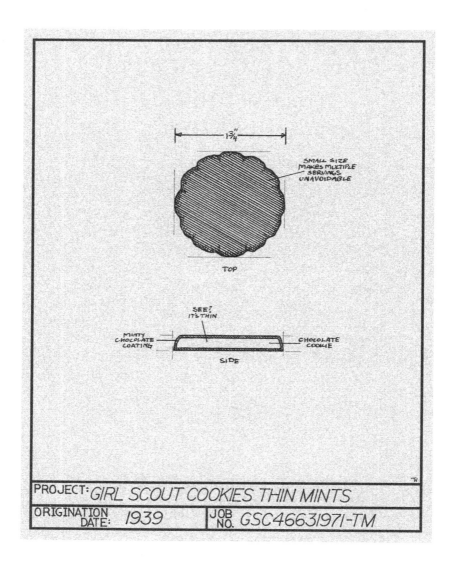

1¾"

SMALL SIZE
MAKES MULTIPLE
SERVINGS
UNAVOIDABLE

TOP

SEE?
IT'S THIN

MINTY
CHOCOLATE
COATING

CHOCOLATE
COOKIE

SIDE

PROJECT: *GIRL SCOUT COOKIES THIN MINTS*

ORIGINATION DATE: *1939*   JOB NO. *GSC46631971-TM*

3. On a lightly floured surface roll out a portion of the dough to just under $\frac{1}{16}$ of an inch thick. To cut, use a lid from a spice container with a $1\frac{1}{2}$-inch diameter (Schilling brand is good). Arrange the cut dough rounds on a cookie sheet that is sprayed with a light coating of non-stick spray. Bake for 10 minutes. Remove wafers from the oven and cool completely.

4. Combine chocolate chips with peppermint extract and shortening in a large microwave-safe glass or ceramic bowl. Heat on 50 percent power for 2 minutes, stir gently, then heat for an additional minute. Stir once again, and if chocolate is not a smooth consistency, continue to zap in microwave in 30-second intervals until smooth.

5. Use a fork to dip each wafer in the chocolate, tap the fork on the edge of the bowl so that the excess chocolate runs off, and then place the cookies side-by-side on a wax paper–lined baking sheet. Refrigerate until firm.

- MAKES 108 COOKIES.

•　•　•　•

GRANDMA'S COOKIES OATMEAL RAISIN BIG COOKIES

☆ ✌ 💣 ✏ ☯ ✂ ☞

GrandMa's Cookie Company was founded back in 1914 by Foster Wheeler, but it wasn't until 1977 that the company introduced the popular Big Cookie. This large, soft cookie comes two to a pack and is offered in several varieties, including oatmeal raisin. Now you can bake up a couple batches all your own with this spiffy kitchen clone. Just be sure not to overdo it in the oven. You want these cookies soft and chewy when cool—just like a happy grandma would make 'em. So be sure to take the cookies out when they are just beginning to turn light brown around the edges.

½ cup raisins	2 cups all-purpose flour
⅓ cup water	1¼ cups oats (not instant)
½ cup vegetable shortening	2 teaspoons baking soda
1 egg	¾ teaspoon cinnamon
1½ cups dark brown sugar	1 teaspoon salt
1½ teaspoons vanilla	½ cup raisins

1. Preheat oven to 275ºF.
2. Combine ½ cup raisins with water in a food processor and blend on high speed for about 1 minute or until very smooth.
3. Combine this raisin puree with the vegetable shortening, egg, brown sugar, and vanilla in a large bowl. Mix well with electric mixer until smooth.
4. In a separate bowl, combine the flour with the oats, baking soda, cinnamon, and salt. Pour this dry mixture into the wet

mixture and mix well until ingredients are incorporated. Mix in ½ cup raisins.

5. Roll 3-tablespoon-size portions of the dough into a ball in your hands and press to ½ inch flat on an ungreased baking sheet. Bake for 18 to 20 minutes. Be careful not to overcook, or the cookies will not be chewy. Store in a sealed container.

• MAKES 16 TO 18 COOKIES.

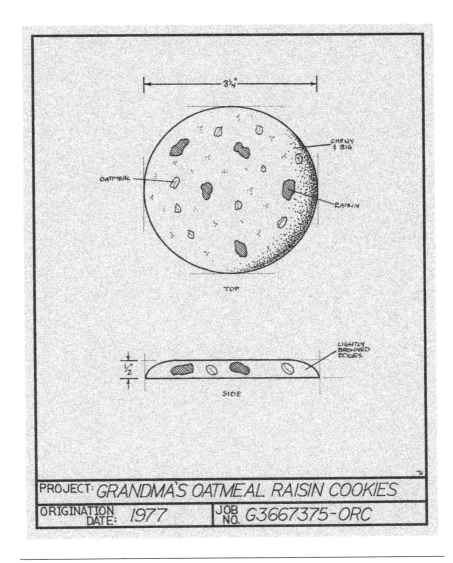

HEINZ
57 SAUCE

In the late 1800s Henry John Heinz established the slogan "57 Varieties," which you can still find printed on Heinz products even though the company now boasts over 5700 varieties in 200 countries. Today Heinz is the world's largest tomato-product producer, but interestingly the first product for the company that was launched in 1869 had nothing to do with tomatoes; it was grated horseradish. It wasn't until 1876 that ketchup was added to the growing company's product line. Tomato is also an important ingredient in this tangy steak sauce. But you'll find some interesting ingredients in there as well, such as raisin puree, malt vinegar, apple juice concentrate, and mustard. And don't worry if your version doesn't come out as brown as the original. Heinz uses a little caramel coloring in its product to give it that distinctive tint. It's just for looks, though, so I've left that ingredient out of this clone recipe. Besides, I've found that the turmeric and yellow mustard will still help get this version pretty close to the color of the real deal.

RAISIN PUREE
½ cup raisins
½ cup water

1⅓ cups white vinegar
1 cup tomato paste
⅔ cup malt vinegar
⅔ cup sugar
½ cup water

1 tablespoon yellow prepared
    mustard
2 teaspoons apple juice concentrate
1½ teaspoons salt
1 teaspoon vegetable oil
1 teaspoon lemon juice
½ teaspoon onion powder
¼ teaspoon garlic powder
⅛ teaspoon turmeric

1. Make the raisin puree by combining the raisins with the water in a food processor or blender. Blend on high speed for 1 minute or until the puree is smooth. Measure ¼ cup of this puree into a medium saucepan.
2. Add the remaining ingredients and whisk until smooth.
3. Turn heat up to medium high and bring mixture to a thorough boil. Reduce heat to low and simmer, uncovered, for ½ hour or until thick. Let sauce cool and then refrigerate it in a covered container for at least 24 hours.

• MAKES 3 CUPS.

•   •   •   •

HEINZ KETCHUP

By the age of 12 Henry John Heinz was peddling produce from his family's garden in post–Civil War Pittsburgh. By age 25, he and a friend had launched Heinz & Noble to sell bottled horseradish in clear glass bottles to reveal its purity. Henry's pickling empire grew as he added jams, jellies, and condiments to the line, including ketchup, which hit the markets in 1876. You'll still see the famous Heinz pickle logo on every product, and if you want a quick tip on how to get the thick stuff out of the bottle easily, don't pound on the backside like a maniac. Instead Heinz recommends a good smack to the embossed "57" found on the neck of every bottle. Today Heinz is the world's largest tomato processor, with the famous ketchup bottles in over half of U.S. households. But if you find your house is all out, just create a simple clone with a few common ingredients. You'll get a whole 12-ounce bottle's worth of thick, tasty ketchup with this one-of-a-kind secret recipe.

one 6-ounce can tomato
   paste
½ cup light corn syrup
½ cup white vinegar
¼ cup water

1 tablespoon sugar
1 teaspoon salt
¼ teaspoon onion
   powder
⅛ teaspoon garlic powder

1. Combine all ingredients in a medium saucepan over medium heat. Whisk until smooth.
2. When mixture comes to a boil, reduce heat and simmer for 20 minutes, stirring often.

3. Remove pan from heat and cover until cool. Chill in a covered container.

• MAKES 1 ½ CUPS.

•   •   •   •

HOSTESS TWINKIE

The Twinkie was invented in 1930 by the late James A. Dewar, then the Chicago-area regional manager of Continental Baking Company, the parent corporation behind the Hostess trademark. At the time, Continental made "Little Short Cake Fingers" only during the six-week strawberry season, and Dewar realized that the aluminum pans in which the cakes were baked sat idle the rest of the year. He came up with the idea of injecting the little cakes with a creamy filling to make them a year-round product and decided to charge a nickel for a package of two.

But Dewar couldn't come up with a catchy name for the treat—that is, until he set out on a business trip to St. Louis. Along the road he saw a sign for TWINKLE TOE SHOES, and the name TWINKIES evolved. Sales took off, and Dewar reportedly ate two Twinkies every day for much of his life. He died in 1985.

The spongy treat has evolved into an American phenomenon, from which nearly everyone has slurped the creamy center. Today the Twinkie is Continental's top Hostess-line seller, with the injection machines filling as many as 52,000 every hour.

You will need a spice bottle (approximately the size of a twinkie), ten 12 × 14-inch pieces of aluminum foil, a cake decorator or pastry bag, and a toothpick.

CAKE

nonstick spray
4 egg whites
one 16-ounce box golden pound
*   cake mix*
⅔ cup water

FILLING

2 teaspoons very hot water
rounded ¼ teaspoon salt
2 cups marshmallow creme (one
   7-ounce jar)

½ cup shortening
⅓ cup powdered sugar
½ teaspoon vanilla

1. Preheat the oven to 325ºF.
2. Fold each piece of aluminum foil in half twice. Wrap the folded foil around the spice bottle to create a mold. Leave the top of the mold open for pouring in the batter. Make ten of these molds and arrange them on a cookie sheet or in a shallow pan. Grease the inside of each mold with a light coating of nonstick spray.
3. Disregard the directions on the box of cake mix. Instead, beat the egg whites until stiff. In a separate bowl combine cake mix with water, and beat until thoroughly blended (about 2 minutes). Fold egg whites into cake batter, and slowly combine until completely mixed.
4. Pour the batter into the molds, filling each one about ¾ inch. Bake in the preheated oven for 30 minutes, or until the cake is golden brown and a toothpick stuck in the center comes out clean.
5. For the filling, combine the salt with the hot water in a small bowl and stir until salt is dissolved. Let this mixture cool.
6. Combine the marshmallow creme, shortening, powdered sugar, and vanilla in a medium bowl and mix well with an electric mixer on high speed until fluffy.
7. Add the salt solution to the filling mixture and combine.
8. When the cakes are done and cooled, use a toothpick or skewer to make three small holes in the bottom of each one. Move the toothpick around the inside of each cake to create space for the filling.
9. Using a cake decorator or pastry bag, inject each cake with filling through all three holes.

- MAKES 10.

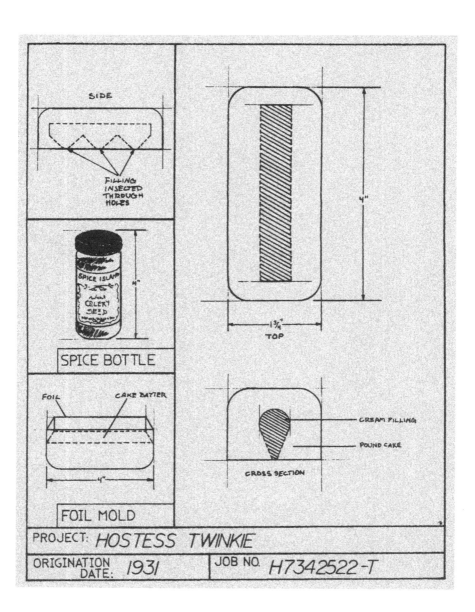

SIDE

FILLING INJECTED THROUGH HOLES

SPICE ISLAND CELERY SEED

4"

SPICE BOTTLE

FOIL   CAKE BATTER

4"

FOIL MOLD

4"

1¾"

TOP

CREAM FILLING

POUND CAKE

CROSS SECTION

PROJECT: HOSTESS TWINKIE

ORIGINATION DATE: 1931

JOB NO. H7342522-T

JIMMY DEAN
BREAKFAST SAUSAGE

☆   ✌   💣   ✏   ☯   ✂   ☞

Before he became America's sausage king, Jimmy Dean was known for crooning the country hit "Big Bad John." That song came out in 1962 and sold over 8 million copies. His singing success launched a television career on ABC with *The Jimmy Dean Show,* on which Roy Clark, Patsy Cline, and Roger Miller got their big breaks. The TV exposure led to acting roles for Jimmy as a regular on *Daniel Boone* and in feature films, including his debut in the James Bond flick *Diamonds Are Forever.* Knowing that a show business career is an unpredictable one, Jimmy socked his money away in hog-farming investments. In 1968, the Jimmy Dean Meat Company developed a special recipe to transform those piggies into the sausage that has now become a household name. Today, the company is part of the Sara Lee Corporation, but Jimmy is still chairman of the board of his division, and he still appears on TV in commercials for the brand, even at the age of 71.

This clone recipe re-creates three varieties of the famous roll sausage that you form into patties and cook in a skillet. Use ground pork found at the supermarket (make it lean pork, if you like), or grind some up yourself if you have a meat grinder lying around, for some good old-fashioned fun.

SAGE

16 ounces ground pork
1 teaspoon salt
1/2 teaspoon dried parsley
1/4 teaspoon rubbed sage
1/4 teaspoon ground black pepper

1/4 teaspoon dried thyme
1/4 teaspoon crushed red
   pepper
1/4 teaspoon coriander
1/4 teaspoon MSG (such as Accent)

HOT

16 ounces ground pork
1 teaspoon salt
1/2 teaspoon cayenne pepper
1/4 teaspoon rubbed sage
1/4 teaspoon ground black pepper
1/4 teaspoon crushed red pepper
1/4 teaspoon coriander
1/4 teaspoon MSG
   (such as Accent)

MAPLE

16 ounces ground pork
3 tablespoons maple-flavored syrup
1 teaspoon salt
1/2 teaspoon MSG
   (such as Accent)
1/4 teaspoon coriander

1. Combine all ingredients for the flavor of your choice in a medium bowl. Form the sausage into patties and cook in a skillet over medium heat until brown.

- MAKES 1 POUND OF SAUSAGE.

•　•　•　•

K.C. MASTERPIECE
ORIGINAL BBQ SAUCE

Even though it's now owned and produced by the Clorox Company, the taste of Original K.C. Masterpiece barbecue sauce is the same as when it was first created in good ol' Kansas City, USA. This is the sauce that steals awards from all the other popular meat slathers on the market. Now it's sold in a variety of flavors. But this is the clone for the original, and you'll find it very easy to make. Just throw all of the ingredients in a saucepan, crank it up to a boil, and simmer for about an hour. Done deal. And just like the original Masterpiece, this stuff will make a work of art out of any of your grilled meats, or burgers and sandwiches, and as a dipping sauce or marinade.

2 cups water
¾ cup light corn syrup
½ cup tomato paste
½ cup vinegar
3 tablespoons molasses
3 tablespoons brown sugar

1 teaspoon liquid smoke (see Tidbit)
½ teaspoon salt
¼ teaspoon onion powder
¼ teaspoon pepper
⅛ teaspoon paprika
⅛ teaspoon garlic powder

1. Combine all ingredients in a medium saucepan over high heat and whisk until smooth.
2. Bring mixture to a boil, then reduce heat and simmer for 45 to 60 minutes or until mixture is thick.
3. Cool, then store in a covered container in the refrigerator overnight so that flavors can develop.

- Makes 1½ cups.

TIDBITS

Liquid smoke is a flavoring found near the barbecue sauces and marinades. Use hickory-flavored liquid smoke if you have a choice.

•   •   •   •

M&M/MARS
ALMOND BAR

☆　　✌　　💣　　✏　　☯　　✂　　☞

What started in Tacoma, Washington, in 1911 as a small home-based candy shop has now grown to be one of the largest privately held companies in the world. Mars products are found in more than 100 countries, and the Mars family pulls in revenues in the range of a sweet $11 billion each year.

The Mars Almond Bar was first produced in 1936, when it was known as the Mars Toasted Almond Bar. It was reformulated in 1980 and the name was changed to Mars Bar; in 1990 it was renamed once again, becoming Mars Almond Bar.

You'll need a heavy-duty mixer to handle the nougat in this recipe.

2 cups granulated sugar
1/2 cup light corn syrup
1/2 cup plus 2 tablespoons water
pinch salt
2 egg whites

35 unwrapped Kraft caramels
2/3 cup whole roasted almonds
two 12-ounce bags milk chocolate
chips

1. In a large saucepan over medium heat, combine the sugar, corn syrup, 1/2 cup of the water, and the salt. Heat to boiling, then cook using a candy thermometer to monitor the temperature.
2. Beat the egg whites until they are stiff and form peaks. Don't use a plastic bowl for this.
3. When the sugar mixture reaches 270°F, or the *soft-crack stage*, remove from the heat and pour the mixture in thin streams

into the egg whites, blending completely with an electric mixer set on low.

4. Continue to mix about 20 minutes, or until the nougat begins to harden and thickens to the consistency of dough. Mix in the almonds.

5. Press the nougat into a greased 9 × 9-inch pan and chill until firm, about 30 minutes.

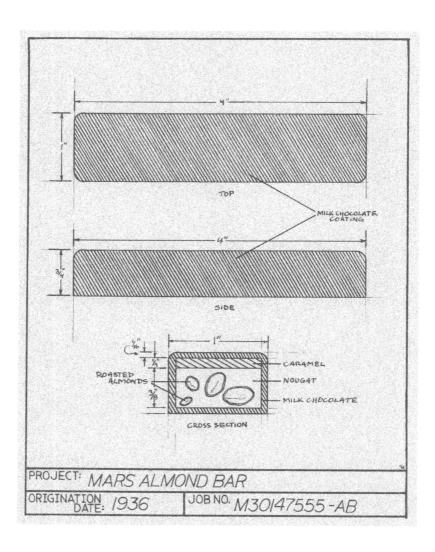

TOP

MILK CHOCOLATE COATING

SIDE

ROASTED ALMONDS

CARAMEL

NOUGAT

MILK CHOCOLATE

CROSS SECTION

PROJECT: MARS ALMOND BAR

ORIGINATION DATE: 1936   JOB NO. M30147555-AB

6. Melt the caramels with the remaining 2 tablespoons water in a small saucepan over medium heat.
7. Pour the caramel over the nougat and return the pan to the refrigerator.
8. When the caramel and nougat are firm (about 30 minutes), slice down the middle of the pan with a sharp knife, and then slice across into 7 segments to make a total of 14 bars.
9. Melt the milk chocolate chips in a microwave for 2 minutes on half power, stirring halfway through the cooking time. Melt completely, but be careful not to overheat.
10. Resting the bar on a fork (and using your fingers if needed), dip each bar into the chocolate to coat completely and tap the fork against the side of the bowl to knock off the excess chocolate. Place on waxed paper and let cool at room temperature until the chocolate is firm, 1 to 2 hours.

• MAKES 14 CANDY BARS.

• • • •

M&M/MARS
MILKY WAY

I find that some people are confused by the brand name M&M/Mars. The company is actually a snack division within the parent company Mars, Incorporated, which produces food products around the world as diverse as Uncle Ben's rice and Kal Kan dog food. When the founder's son, Forrest E. Mars, Sr., returned from England (where he had established the first canned pet food business in that country), he formed a company in Newark, New Jersey, to make small chocolate candies that could be sold throughout the year, not melting in the hot summer months. Those were the first M&M's. The company, called M&M Limited, consolidated with other Mars confectionery businesses in the United States in 1967 to form M&M/Mars as it exists today.

The Mars Milky Way bar was the first chocolate-covered candy bar to find widespread popularity in the United States. It was developed in 1923 by the Mars family, and became so successful so quickly that the company had to build a new manufacturing plant in Chicago just to keep up with demand.

You'll need a heavy-duty mixer for this recipe.

2 cups granulated sugar
1/2 cup light corn syrup
1/2 cup plus 2 tablespoons water
pinch salt
2 egg whites

35 unwrapped Kraft caramels
1/4 cup semisweet chocolate chips
two 12-ounce bags milk chocolate
  chips

1. In a large saucepan over medium heat, combine the sugar, corn syrup, 1/2 cup of the water, and the salt. Stir often until the mixture begins to boil, then continue to cook, using a candy thermometer to monitor the temperature.
2. While the candy boils, beat the egg whites until they are stiff and form peaks. Don't use a plastic bowl for this.

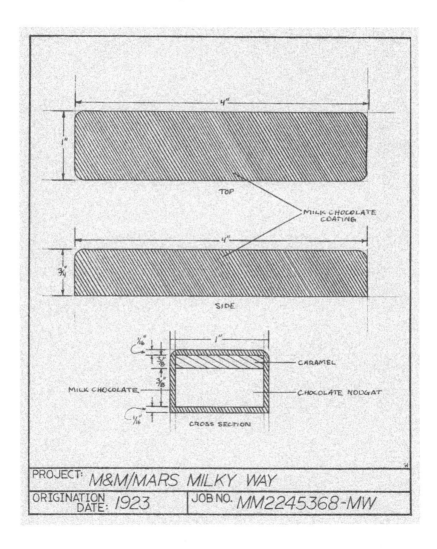

TOP

MILK CHOCOLATE COATING

4"

1"

SIDE

4"

3/4"

CROSS SECTION

1"

CARAMEL

MILK CHOCOLATE

CHOCOLATE NOUGAT

3/8"

3/8"

3/16"

1/16"

PROJECT: M&M/MARS MILKY WAY

ORIGINATION DATE: 1923

JOB NO. MM2245368-MW

3. When the sugar mixture reaches 270ºF, or the *soft-crack stage*, remove from the heat and pour the mixture in thin streams into the egg whites, blending with a mixer set on low speed.

4. Continue to mix for 15 minutes or so. The mixture will thicken as you mix, until it reaches the consistency of cookie dough. At this point, add the semisweet chocolate chips. Be warned; the mixture will not get any thicker after the chocolate is added, so be sure the candy is very thick and fluffy before adding the chips.

5. When the chocolate chips are completely blended into the candy, press the mixture into a greased 9 × 9-inch pan and refrigerate until cool, about 30 minutes.

6. Heat the caramels with the remaining 2 tablespoons water in a small saucepan until thoroughly melted. Pour the caramel over the refrigerated candy.

7. While the candy cools, melt the milk chocolate chips in the microwave for 2 minutes on medium power. Stir halfway through the heating time. Melt completely, but be careful not to overheat.

8. When the caramel is set, use a sharp knife to cut down the center of the pan. Then cut the candy across into 7 segments, making a total of 14 bars.

9. Resting a bar on a fork (and using your fingers if needed), dip each bar into the chocolate to coat completely, then tap the fork against the side of the bowl to knock off the excess chocolate.

10. Place each bar on waxed paper and cool until firm at room temperature, 1 to 2 hours.

• MAKES 14 CANDY BARS.

•   •   •   •

M&M/MARS
3 MUSKETEERS

☆   ✄   💣   🖉   ●   ✂   ☞

Nougat is an important ingredient in the 3 Musketeers Bar, as well as in many other candy bars created by M&M/Mars. Nougat is made by mixing a hot sugar syrup with whipped egg whites until the solution cools and stiffens, creating a *frappe*. Other ingredients may be added to the nougat during this process to give it different flavors. In this recipe, you'll add chocolate chips to create a dark, chocolaty nougat.

But the 3 Musketeers Bar wasn't always filled with just a chocolate nougat. In fact, when the candy bar was created back in 1932, it was actually three pieces with three flavors: vanilla, strawberry, and chocolate. After World War II, the product was changed to a single chocolate bar because that was the favorite flavor, and customers wanted more of it. Thankfully they didn't decide to change the name to 1 Musketeer!

You'll need a heavy-duty electric mixer for this recipe.

3 cups granulated sugar
3/4 cup light corn syrup
3/4 cup water
1/8 teaspoon salt

3 egg whites
1/3 cup semisweet chocolate chips
two 12-ounce bags milk chocolate
   chips

1. In a large saucepan over medium heat, combine the sugar, corn syrup, water, and salt. Heat, stirring, to boiling, then continue to cook, using a candy thermometer to monitor the temperature.
2. Beat the egg whites until they are stiff and form peaks. Don't use a plastic bowl for this.

3. When the sugar solution comes to 270°F, or the *soft-crack stage,* remove from the heat and pour the mixture in thin streams into the egg whites, blending completely with a mixer set on low speed.
4. Continue to mix until the candy begins to harden to the consistency of dough. This may take as long as 20 minutes. At this point, add the semisweet chocolate chips. Remember that the

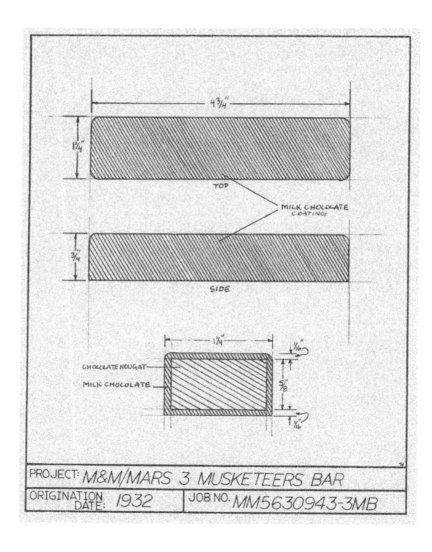

PROJECT: M&M/MARS 3 MUSKETEERS BAR

ORIGINATION DATE: 1932   JOB NO. MM5630943-3MB

candy *must* already be at the consistency of dough when you add the chocolate; the nougat will thicken no more after the chocolate is added.

5. When the chocolate is thoroughly blended and the nougat has thickened, press it into a greased 9 × 9-inch pan. Refrigerate until firm, about 30 minutes.

6. With a sharp knife, cut the candy in half down the middle of the pan. Then cut across into 7 segments to create a total of 14 bars.

7. Melt the milk chocolate chips in the microwave for 2 minutes on half power, stirring halfway through the heating time. Melt completely, but be careful not to overheat.

8. Resting a bar on a fork (and using your fingers if needed), dip each bar into the chocolate to coat completely and place on wax paper. Cool till firm at room temperature, 1 to 2 hours.

•   MAKES 14 CANDY BARS.

•   •   •   •

M&M/MARS
SNICKERS BAR

In 1992 *Fortune* magazine estimated the Mars family's personal worth at somewhere around $12.5 billion—quite a fistful of peanuts. This solid foundation of wealth, built on the country's undying passion for chocolate and other sweets, has made this clan the richest family in America—and the most reclusive. A family rule prohibits photographs to be taken of the Mars family and corporate executives. According to *Fortune*, a photographer who once tried to get a shot of Forrest Mars, Sr., found himself enveloped in a cloth that was thrown as he was about to snap the picture.

The empire started in 1902, when nineteen-year-old Franklin C. Mars began selling homemade candy. In 1910 he started a wholesale candy business in Tacoma, Washington. Ten years later Frank moved to Minneapolis, where he used the family kitchen to make buttercreams, which were personally delivered to retailers in the city by his wife, Ethel. Business grew steadily, and in 1940 Frank's son Forrest established M&M Limited in Newark, New Jersey.

By 1967 the family's confectionery business in the United States had been consolidated into M&M/Mars. The fortune grew steadily larger as the corporation routinely kept four brands in the top-ten-selling chocolates in the country: Milky Way, M&M's Plain and Peanut, and, in the number-one spot, Snickers.

1 tablespoon plus 2 tablespoons water
¼ cup light corn syrup
2 tablespoons butter
1 teaspoon vanilla extract
2 tablespoons peanut butter
dash salt

3 cups powdered sugar
35 unwrapped Kraft caramels
1 cup (or two 3.5-ounce packages)
    dry-roasted unsalted peanuts
two 12-ounce bags milk-chocolate
    chips

1. With the mixer on high speed, combine 1 tablespoon water, corn syrup, butter, vanilla, peanut butter, and salt until creamy. Slowly add the powdered sugar.
2. When the mixture has the consistency of dough, remove it from the bowl with your hands and press it into a lightly greased 9 × 9-inch pan. Set in the refrigerator.
3. Melt the caramels in a small pan with 2 tablespoons water over low heat.
4. When the caramel is soft, mix in the peanuts. Pour the mixture over the refrigerated nougat in the pan. Let this cool in the refrigerator.
5. When the refrigerated mixture is firm, melt the chocolate over low heat in a double boiler or in a microwave oven set on high for 2 minutes. Stir halfway through cooking time.
6. When the mixture in the pan has hardened, cut it into 4 × 1-inch sections.
7. Set each chunk onto a fork and dip into the melted chocolate. Tap the fork against the side of the bowl or pan to knock off any excess chocolate. Then place the chunks on waxed paper to cool at room temperature (less than 70ºF). This could take several hours, but the bars will set best this way. You can speed up the process by placing the bars in the refrigerator for 30 minutes.

• MAKES ABOUT 2 DOZEN BARS.

• • • •

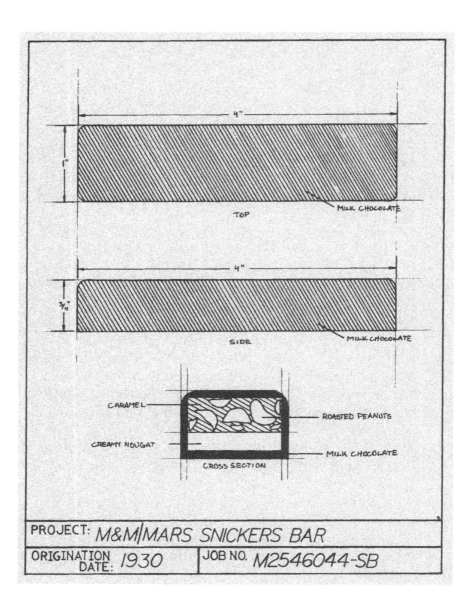

4"

1"

MILK CHOCOLATE

TOP

4"

3/4"

MILK CHOCOLATE

SIDE

CARAMEL

ROASTED PEANUTS

CREAMY NOUGAT

MILK CHOCOLATE

CROSS SECTION

PROJECT:	M&M/MARS SNICKERS BAR	
ORIGINATION DATE:	1930	JOB NO. M2546044-SB

MRS. DASH
SALT-FREE SEASONING
BLEND

So here's the challenge with this clone recipe: Not only do we have to get the right ratios for nearly 20 different spices, but we also have to come up with a way to get the same lemony tang that makes the real Mrs. Dash the tasty salt-free seasoning blend we've come to know and love over the years. Sure, we could use powdered citric acid that is sometimes found in health food stores, but not everyone is going to have that ingredient readily available. Then we still need to figure out the "lemon juice solids" part. Ah, but wait, there's citric acid *and* lemon juice solids in Kool-Aid unsweetened lemonade drink mix. It's perfect! Add a little of that drink powder to the spice blend and we have a clone that in a blindfold taste test could fool even Mr. Dash.

¼ cup crushed dried minced onion
   flakes (see Tidbits)
4 teaspoons crushed dried vegetable
   flakes (Schilling) (see Tidbits)
1 tablespoon garlic powder
1 tablespoon dried orange peel
2 teaspoons coarse ground black
   pepper
1 teaspoon dried parsley
½ teaspoon dried basil
½ teaspoon dried marjoram

½ teaspoon dried oregano
½ teaspoon dried savory
½ teaspoon dried thyme
½ teaspoon cayenne pepper
½ teaspoon cumin
½ teaspoon coriander
½ teaspoon dried mustard
¼ teaspoon celery seed
¼ teaspoon Kool-Aid unsweetened
   lemonade drink mix
dash crushed dried rosemary

1. Combine all of the ingredients in a small bowl and stir well. As you stir, crush the leafy spices for a finer blend.
2. Store the spice blend in a covered container or a sealed shaker bottle.

- MAKES ABOUT ⅔ CUP.

TIDBITS

It's best to use a mortar and pestle to crush these sometimes tough little onion and vegetable flakes to about the size of rice, before adding them to the mix. But if you don't have one of those handy kitchen tools, you may also use the back of a spoon and a small bowl—plus a little grease. You know, the elbow kind.

• • • •

NABISCO CHIPS AHOY!

As you bake these cookies, imagine producing a quarter of a million cookies and crackers every minute. That's what Nabisco does—which is why the conglomerate is the largest manufacturer of cookies and crackers in the world. Chips Ahoy! Chocolate Chip Cookies were developed in 1964, along with Chicken In A Biscuit Crackers and Mister Salty Pretzels. But Chips Ahoy! became the big winner for the company. Today it's the world's top-selling chocolate-chip cookie, with more than 6 billion sold every year.

1 1/2 cups vegetable shortening
1 cup packed light brown sugar
1 cup granulated sugar
2 teaspoons salt
1 1/2 teaspoons vanilla extract

1 teaspoon baking soda
4 cups all-purpose flour
1/4 cup water
one 12-ounce bag mini semi-sweet
  chocolate chips

1. Preheat the oven to 325ºF.
2. In a large mixing bowl, combine the shortening and sugars and blend with an electric mixer until smooth.
3. Add the salt, vanilla, and baking soda.
4. While beating at low speed, slowly add the flour. Then add the water. Mix thoroughly. Stir in the chocolate chips. Add extra water to dough if needed to make it stick together.
5. Form the cookies by breaking off bits of dough and patting them out with your fingers into 2-inch rounds about 1/8 inch thick.
6. Place the cookies on ungreased cookie sheets and bake for 12

to 18 minutes, or until golden brown on the top and around the edges.

- MAKES ABOUT 3 DOZEN COOKIES.

• • • •

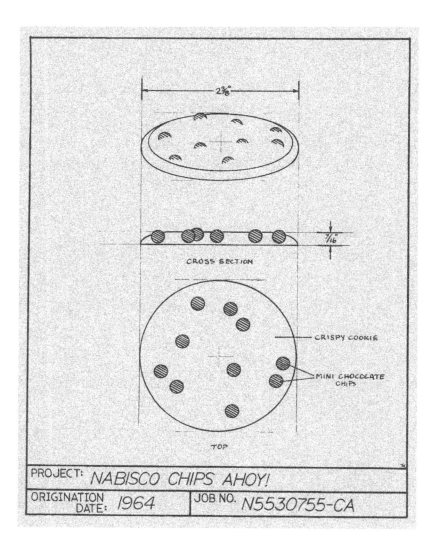

CROSS SECTION

CRISPY COOKIE

MINI CHOCOLATE CHIPS

TOP

PROJECT: NABISCO CHIPS AHOY!

ORIGINATION DATE: 1964

JOB NO. N5530755-CA

NESTLÉ CRUNCH

☆　　✌　　💣　　✏　　☯　　✂　　☞

In 1867, infant mortality rates in Vevey, Switzerland, had been climbing and Henri Nestlé was working hard on a concoction of concentrated milk, sugar, and cereal for babies who were refusing their mother's milk. Eventually he discovered a formula that helped infants to stay strong and healthy. He called his new product Farine Lactée and merged with two American brothers, Charles and George Page, who had come to Switzerland to capitalize on Swiss canned milk technology. Their new company was called Nestlé & Anglo-Swiss Condensed Milk Company, and quickly expanded into fifteen other countries. Seven years later, Nestlé sold the company to three local businessmen for one million francs.

The new company kept the Nestlé name and started selling chocolate in 1904. In 1929, the company acquired Cailler, the first company to mass-produce chocolate bars, and Swiss General, the company credited with inventing milk chocolate. This company was the core of the chocolate business as we know it today. The Nestlé Crunch bar was introduced in 1928 and is now the company's top-selling candy bar.

two 12-ounce bags milk chocolate
chips (Nestlé is best)

1 1/2 cups Rice Krispies

1. Melt the chocolate chips in a microwave-safe bowl in a microwave set on medium for 2 minutes. Stir halfway through the heating time. Melt thoroughly, but be careful not to overheat.
2. Gently mix the Rice Krispies into the chocolate and pour into a greased 9 × 12-inch pan.

3. Slam the pan on the counter or floor to level the chocolate.
4. Refrigerate until firm, about 30 minutes.
5. Cut the candy in half widthwise and then cut it twice length-wise, making 6 bars.

- MAKES 6 KING-SIZE BARS.

• • • •

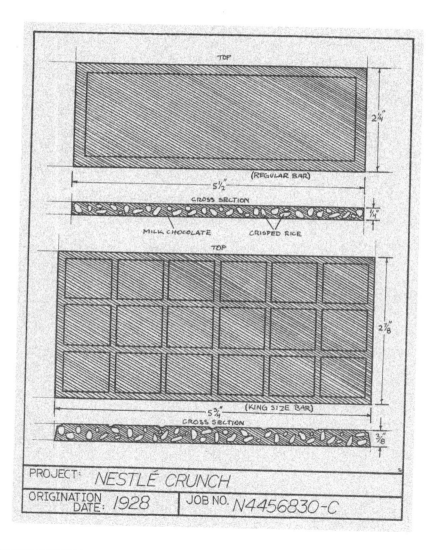

OLD BAY SEASONING

With spice grinder in hand, Gustav Brunn traveled to America from Germany, and settled down in Baltimore on the Chesapeake Bay. There on the bay, steamed crabs are a staple. So Gustav started grinding. In 1939, Gustav found just the right mix for his top-secret blend of spices that for generations would be the most used seasoning on steamed crabs, shrimp, lobster, and other tasty seafood dishes. But the celery salt–based blend is not just for seafood, according to McCormick & Co., which purchased Old Bay in 1990. You can also use the blend on chicken, french fries, popcorn, baked potatoes, deviled eggs, hamburgers, and even pizza. If you've got a recipe that requires Old Bay, but don't have any in the cupboard, head to the spice cabinet and throw these ingredients together to make the perfect clone.

1 tablespoon celery salt
1/4 teaspoon paprika
1/8 teaspoon black pepper
1/8 teaspoon cayenne pepper
pinch ground dry mustard
pinch mace

pinch cinnamon
pinch cardamom
pinch allspice
pinch ground clove
pinch ginger

1. Combine all ingredients in a small bowl. Store in a sealed container.

- MAKES 4 TEASPOONS.

•   •   •   •

NESTLÉ
BABY RUTH
CANDY BAR

☆   ✌   💣   ✏   ☯   ✂   ☞

Beneath the chocolate of Nestlé's popular candy bar is a chewy, peanut-covered center that resembles Hershey's PayDay.

CENTERS

¼ cup whole milk	1¼ cups powdered sugar
5 unwrapped caramels	
1 tablespoon light corn syrup	20 unwrapped caramels
1 teaspoon butter	1½ teaspoons water
¼ teaspoon vanilla	2 cups dry roasted peanuts
⅛ teaspoon salt	1 12-ounce bag milk chocolate chips

1. Combine all ingredients for the centers, except the powdered sugar, in a small saucepan over low heat. Stir often as the caramel slowly melts. When the mixture is smooth, add ¾ cup of powdered sugar. Stir. Save the remaining ½ cup of powdered sugar for later.
2. Use a candy thermometer to bring the mixture to exactly 230ºF, stirring often, then turn off the heat.
3. When the temperature of the candy begins to drop, add the remaining ½ cup powdered sugar to the pan, then use a hand mixer on high speed to combine. Keep mixing until the candy cools and thickens and can no longer be mixed. That should take a minute or two.

4. Let the candy cool in the pan for 10 to 15 minutes, or until it can be touched. Don't let it sit too long—you want the candy to still be warm and pliable when you shape it. Take a tablespoon-size portion and roll it between your palms or on a countertop until it forms a roll the width of your index finger, and measuring about 4½ inches long. Repeat with the remaining center candy mixture and place the rolls on wax paper. You should have 8 rolls. Let the center rolls sit out for an hour or two to firm up.

5. Combine the 20 caramels with the 1½ teaspoons of water in a small saucepan over low heat. Stir often until the caramels melt completely, then turn off the heat. If you work fast this caramel will stay warm while you make the candy bars.

6. Pour the peanuts onto a baking sheet or other flat surface. Using a basting brush and working quickly, "paint" a coating of caramel onto one side of a center roll. Quickly turn the center over, caramel side down, onto the peanuts and press gently so that the peanuts stick to the surface of the candy. Paint more caramel onto the other side of the roll and press it down onto the peanuts. The candy should have a solid layer of peanuts covering all sides. If needed, brush additional caramel onto the roll, then turn it onto the peanuts to coat the roll completely. Place the candy bar onto wax paper, and repeat with the remaining ingredients. Place these bars into your refrigerator for an hour or two so that they firm up.

7. Pour the milk chocolate chips into a glass or ceramic bowl and zap it in the microwave for 2 minutes on 50 percent power. Gently stir the chips, then heat for an additional 30 seconds at 50 percent power. Repeat if necessary, stirring gently after each 30 seconds. Don't overcook the chips or the chocolate will burn and seize up on you.

8. Drop a candy bar center into the melted milk chocolate. Cover the candy bar with chocolate using two forks, one in each hand. When the candy is covered with chocolate, balance the bar on both of the forks, one at each end of the candy bar, and tap the forks on the top edge of the bowl so that much of the chocolate drops off. Carefully place the candy bar onto wax

paper and remove the two forks. Repeat with the remaining ingredients, and then chill the candy bars until firm.

• MAKES 8 CANDY BARS.

• • • •

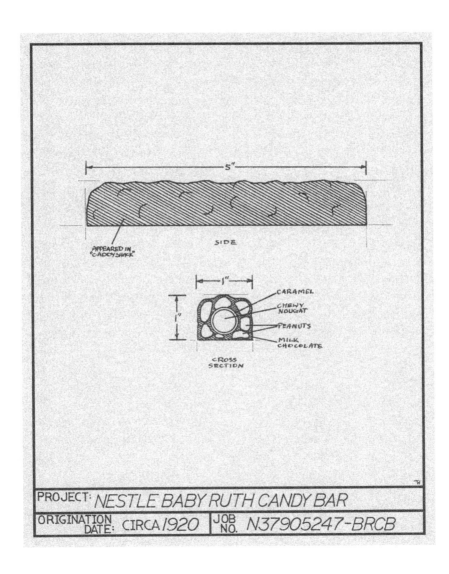

5"

SIDE

APPEARED IN "CADDY SHACK"

1"

1"

CARAMEL

CHEWY NOUGAT

PEANUTS

MILK CHOCOLATE

CROSS SECTION

PROJECT: NESTLE BABY RUTH CANDY BAR

ORIGINATION DATE: CIRCA 1920   JOB NO. N37905247-BRCB

PACE
PICANTE SAUCE

☆ ✌ 💣 ✏ ☯ ✂ ☞

Texan David Pace had been selling 58 different varieties of jam, jellies, and sauces from the back of his liquor store in the 1940s when he came up with a recipe for a thick and spicy tomato-based sauce he dubbed "Picante." When sales of David's new sauce took off, he concentrated all his efforts on marketing his all-natural, preservative-free product, and designed the sauce's famous hourglass-shaped jar (to keep it from tipping over). Now America's number-one Mexican hot sauce brand, Pace Foods makes it known that it still uses only fresh jalapeño peppers in the sauces, rather than the brined, less flavorful jalapeños—like those canned nacho slices. Each year all the fresh jalapeños used by the company weigh in at around 30 million pounds, and the nation gobbles up around 120 million pounds of the zingy sauces. Here's a simple recipe to make a kitchen copy of the medium heat–level Pace Picante Sauce, which was the first variety David created. The mild and hot versions were added in 1981, and you'll find clones for those at the bottom of the recipe in Tidbits.

one 10 ¾-ounce can tomato puree
1 can full of water (1 ⅓ cups)
⅓ cup chopped Spanish onion
¼ cup chopped fresh jalapeño
    peppers, with seeds (3 to
    4 peppers)

2 tablespoons white vinegar
rounded ¼ teaspoon salt
¼ teaspoon dried minced onion
¼ teaspoon dried minced garlic

1. Combine all ingredients in a saucepan over medium high heat.
2. Bring to a boil, reduce heat, and simmer for 30 minutes or until thick.
3. When cool, bottle in 16-ounce jar and refrigerate overnight.

• MAKES 2 CUPS (16 OUNCES).

TIDBITS

For the mild version of the salsa, reduce the amount of fresh jalapeños to 2 rounded tablespoons (2 to 3 peppers).

For the hot variety, increase the amount of jalapeños to ⅓ cup (4 to 5 peppers).

•　•　•　•

PEPPERIDGE FARM
GINGER MAN COOKIES

When cloning cookies for the holidays, why not clone the best? Pepperidge Farm's Ginger Man cookies bring a sweet gingery crunch to the seasonal or non-seasonal festivities. And so will your version no matter what shape they end up.

1 cup packed dark brown sugar
3/4 cup granulated sugar
1/2 cup shortening
1/4 cup molasses
2 eggs
1/2 teaspoon vanilla
2 cups all-purpose flour
1 teaspoon baking soda

1 teaspoon baking powder
1 teaspoon ground ginger
1 teaspoon salt
1 teaspoon ground cinnamon
1/4 teaspoon ground cloves
red sugar crystals (for cake
    decorating)

1. Preheat oven to 300ºF.
2. Cream together the sugars, shortening, molasses, eggs, and vanilla in a large bowl. Beat with an electric mixer until smooth.
3. In another large bowl, combine flour, baking soda, baking powder, ginger, salt, cinnamon, and cloves.
4. Add the dry mixture to the wet mixture, stirring while you add it.
5. Roll a portion of the dough out on a heavily floured surface. Roll to under 1/4 inch thick. Cut the cookies using a man-shaped cookie cutter, or any other cookie cutter shape you've got in the bottom drawer.

6. Place cookies on an oiled cookie sheet and bake for 15 to 18 minutes. Bake only one cookie sheet of cookies at a time.

• MAKES AROUND 3 DOZEN COOKIES.

•   •   •   •

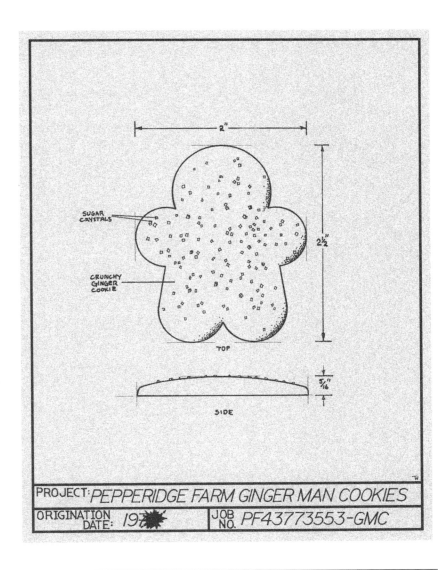

SUGAR CRYSTALS

CRUNCHY GINGER COOKIE

2"

2½"

TOP

5/16"

SIDE

PROJECT: *PEPPERIDGE FARM GINGER MAN COOKIES*

ORIGINATION DATE: *197*   JOB NO. *PF43773553-GMC*

PROGRESSO ITALIAN-STYLE BREAD CRUMBS

Here's a real easy one that clones the most popular brand of seasoned bread crumbs. Just throw all of the ingredients into a small bowl, mix it up, and you're done. Use the finished product for an Italian-style breading—when frying or baking chicken, fish, pork chops, eggplant, etc.—just as you would the store-bought stuff.

1 cup plain bread crumbs
1/2 teaspoon salt
1/2 teaspoon parsley flakes
1/4 teaspoon garlic powder

1/4 teaspoon onion powder
1/4 teaspoon sugar
dash oregano

Combine all ingredients in a small bowl.

• MAKES 1 CUP.

• • • •

SABRETT
ONIONS IN SAUCE

Here's a cool clone for the tangy orange/red onion sauce slathered over hot dogs ordered from Sabrett's push carts. For a buck or two you can grab a hot dog with the works on the fly from these popular umbrella-covered food carts in many major cities. You find hundreds of 'em in New York City, especially around Central Park. In fact, that's where the sample for this re-creation was obtained. While most of the Sabrett toppings are standard hot dog fare—ketchup, mustard, sauerkraut—the onion sauce is a real Top Secret Recipe. And it's one that we can now slam into the "solved" file.

1 ½ teaspoons olive oil
1 medium onion, sliced thin and
    chopped
2 cups water
1 tablespoon corn syrup
2 tablespoons tomato paste

1 teaspoon cornstarch
½ teaspoon salt
¼ teaspoon crushed red pepper
    flakes
¼ cup vinegar

1. Heat the oil in a large saucepan over medium heat.
2. Sauté sliced onion in the oil for 5 minutes, until onions are soft but not brown.
3. Add water, corn syrup, tomato paste, cornstarch, salt, and red pepper flakes, and stir.

4. Bring mixture to a boil, then reduce heat and simmer for 20 minutes. Add vinegar. Continue to simmer for an additional 10 minutes or until most of the liquid has reduced and the sauce is thick.

• MAKES ABOUT 1 1/2 CUPS.

• • • •

SCHILLING
SALAD SUPREME

This orange-colored spice blend has been perking up salads, pasta, potatoes, hamburgers, and vegetables for years now, but I've never seen a homegrown clone for the stuff. Time to change that. While it's obvious that sesame seeds are a major part of this blend, you may not know that the main ingredient is Romano cheese (in the bottle, it's been dyed orange by the paprika). Be sure to store this one in the refrigerator. You might even want to keep the seasoning in an empty shaker-top spice bottle. And if you're in the mood for some tasty pasta salad, just check out the Tidbit below that comes right off the bottle of the original product.

2 tablespoons Romano cheese
1 1/2 teaspoons sesame seeds
1 teaspoon paprika
3/4 teaspoon salt
1/2 teaspoon poppy seeds
1/2 teaspoon celery seeds

1/4 teaspoon garlic powder
1/4 teaspoon coarse ground black
   pepper
dash cayenne pepper

1. Combine all ingredients in a small bowl and mix well.
2. Pour blend into a sealed container (such as an empty spice bottle) and store chilled.

• MAKES 1/4 CUP.

The label of the original product includes an easy recipe for Supreme Pasta Salad.

"Combine 1 pound cooked pasta, 8 ounces Italian dressing and 4 tablespoons Salad Supreme [or the amount made in the above clone recipe]. Toss with an assortment of chopped fresh vegetables. Chill."

•   •   •   •

SNICKERS MUNCH BAR

☆   ✌   💣   ✏   ☯   ✂   ☞

It was only recently that the bigwigs at M&M/Mars, Inc. chose to capitalize on the company's bestselling candy bar, Snickers, by slapping the brand name on the peanut riddled, butter toffee Munch Bar. Despite the new moniker, the candy bar is the same simple, peanut-brittle recipe the company has used for decades, which makes it easy for us to clone with only four common ingredients, plus a candy thermometer. With this *Top Secret Recipe* you can produce the equivalent of 12 of these addictive candy bars in your own kitchen. Just be sure the dry-roasted peanuts you use are the salted kind, and watch that thermometer closely once the candy gets simmering.

2 cups salted dry-roasted peanuts
½ cup butter (1 stick)

½ cup granulated sugar
¼ cup light corn syrup

1. Spread peanuts out on a baking sheet and heat them up in your oven set on 300°F. This will warm up the peanuts so that they don't cool the candy too quickly when added later. There's no need to preheat the oven.
2. Melt the butter in a medium saucepan over medium/low heat.
3. Add sugar and corn syrup and simmer, stirring occasionally. Put a candy thermometer in the mixture and watch it closely.

4. When the mixture reaches 300°F, add the warm peanuts and stir well until all of the peanuts are coated with candy. Pour the candy onto the warm baking sheet and spread it flat. When the candy cools, break it into chunks and store it in a covered container.

- MAKES THE EQUIVALENT OF 12 1.5-OUNCE CANDY BARS.

• • • •

STARK
MARY JANE

☆ ✌ 💣 ✏ ☯ ✂ ☞

In 1914, Charles H. Miller came up with this molasses and peanut butter candy and named it after his favorite aunt. His candy company flourished, selling many confections, but none as popular as the Mary Jane. Eventually all the other candies were eliminated and Mary Janes came to be the only candy produced by the Miller company. Miller tried playing with the formula to improve the candy, but none could compare to the original. In 1985, Stark Candy Company bought the Miller company and added the Stark name to the wrapper. The candy is much the same today as it was eighty years ago.

1 cup granulated sugar	1 egg white
1 cup light corn syrup	1/2 cup peanut butter
1/2 cup water	1/4 cup powdered sugar
3 tablespoons molasses	cornstarch for dusting

1. Combine the sugar, corn syrup, and water in a saucepan over medium heat.
2. Heat, stirring, until the sugar begins to boil, then continue to cook, using a candy thermometer to monitor the temperature.
3. When the sugar reaches 240ºF, or the *soft-ball stage*, beat the egg white in a microwave-safe bowl until it is stiff and forms peaks. Divide the beaten egg white, and throw out half. (We only need 1/2 egg white for this recipe, and it is easier to divide when beaten.)
4. When the sugar reaches 265°F, or the *hard-ball stage*, stir in the

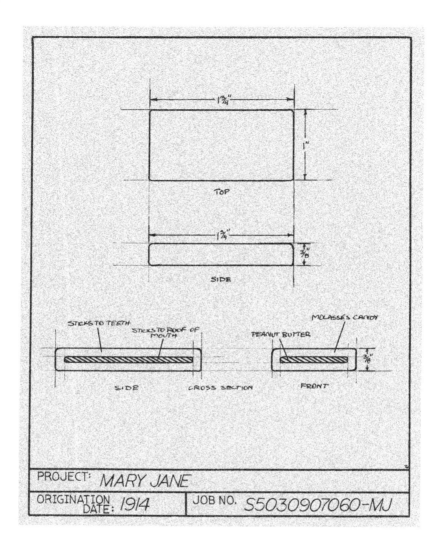

TOP

$1\frac{3}{4}''$

$1''$

SIDE

$1\frac{3}{4}''$

$\frac{3}{8}''$

STICKS TO TEETH

STICKS TO ROOF OF MOUTH

MOLASSES CANDY

PEANUT BUTTER

$\frac{3}{8}''$

SIDE   CROSS SECTION   FRONT

PROJECT: MARY JANE

ORIGINATION DATE: 1914

JOB NO. S5030907060-MJ

molasses, then pour the mixture in thin streams into the egg white while beating with an electric mixer on low speed.

5. Beat for 3 to 4 minutes and then pour half the mixture into a 9 × 9-inch greased pan and let it firm up in the refrigerator for 5 to 10 minutes.

6. Combine the peanut butter and powdered sugar.

7. When the candy is firm, spread a thin layer of the peanut butter mixture on top.

8. Microwave the remaining candy mixture for 1 minute on high, or until it becomes soft again.

9. Pour the softened candy over the peanut butter layer.

10. When the candy is cool but still pliable, (about 20 minutes later) turn it out onto a surface dusted lightly with cornstarch. Use a cornstarch-dusted rolling pin to roll the candy about 1/4 inch thick.

11. Use kitchen scissors or a sharp knife to cut the candy into 1 1/2 × 1/2-inch rectangles.

• MAKES 30 CANDIES.

• • • •

SUNSHINE LEMON COOLERS

Brothers Jacob and Joseph Loose had a dream of creating products in a bakery filled with sunshine. In 1912 they got their wish by opening the famous "Thousand Window Bakery" in Long Island City, New York. It was the largest bakery in the world until 1955. Today Sunshine Biscuits has moved to another location in Sayerville, New Jersey, where ovens the size of football fields bake like crazy. Sunshine is now owned by Keebler and continues to produce many baked treats you're likely familiar with, such as Hydrox Cookies, Saltine Crackers, Vienna Fingers, Cheez-it Crackers, and these sweet Lemon Coolers. You know the ones—those little round cookies dusted with lemon-flavored powdered sugar. To make that coating, we'll just use a little unsweetened Kool-Aid lemonade drink mix combined with powdered sugar. Shake the cookies in a bag with this mixture (I call it bake 'n shake) and you've got yourself another tasty knock-off.

½ cup powdered sugar
⅓ cup sugar
⅓ cup shortening
1 egg
½ teaspoon vanilla

⅛ teaspoon salt
1 ½ cups cake flour
1 ½ teaspoons baking powder
1 tablespoon water

LEMON POWDERED SUGAR

1 cup powdered sugar

rounded ½ teaspoon Kool-Aid unsweetened lemonade drink mix

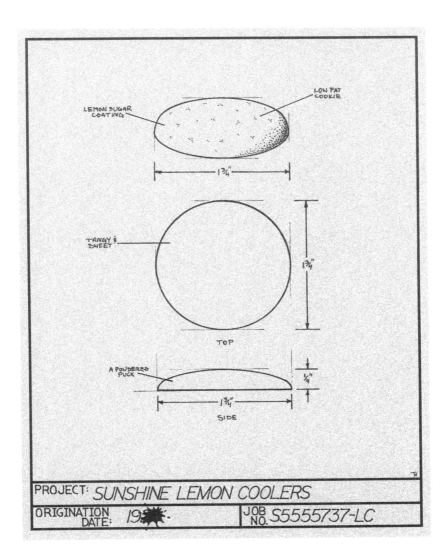

LOW FAT COOKIE

LEMON SUGAR COATING

1¾"

TANGY & SWEET

1¾"

TOP

A POWDERED PUCK

¼"

1¾"

SIDE

PROJECT: *SUNSHINE LEMON COOLERS*

ORIGINATION DATE: 19██.

JOB NO. *S5555737-LC*

1. Preheat oven to 325°F.
2. Cream together sugars, shortening, egg, vanilla, and salt in a large bowl.
3. Add the flour and baking powder. Add 1 tablespoon of water and continue mixing until dough forms a ball.
4. Roll dough into ¾-inch balls and flatten slightly onto a lightly greased cookie sheet. Bake for 15 to 18 minutes or until cookies are light brown.
5. As cookies bake, combine 1 cup powdered sugar with the lemonade drink mix in a large plastic bag and shake thoroughly to mix.
6. When the cookies are removed from the oven and while they are hot, add 4 or 5 at a time to the bag and shake it until the cookies are well coated. Repeat with the remaining cookies.

- Makes 50 to 56 cookies.

• • • •

SUPER PRETZELS

Gerry Shreiber, a college dropout, wasn't happy with the metal-working business he had been operating for about seven years with a friend, so the two decided to sell out. Shreiber's take was about $60,000, but he needed a new job. By chance one day, he wandered into a Philadelphia waterbed store and struck up a conversation with an investor in a troubled soft pretzel company. After touring the rundown plant, Shreiber thought he could turn the company around, so he put his money to work and bought J&J Soft Pretzels for $72,100. That was in 1971. At the time, J&J had at least ten competitors in the soft pretzel business, but over the years Shreiber devised a strategy that would eliminate this competition and help his company grow—he simply bought most of them out.

Today J&J Super Pretzels are uncontested in the frozen soft pretzel market, and they currently constitute about 70 percent of the soft pretzels that are sold in the country's malls, convenience stores, amusement parks, stadiums, and movie theaters.

one 1/4-ounce package active dry
    yeast
1 cup warm water (105 to 110°F)
3 3/4 cups all-purpose flour
3 tablespoons light corn syrup
2 tablespoons (1/4 stick) butter,
    softened

1 teaspoon salt
4 cups cold water
1/3 cup baking soda
coarse pretzel salt (such as kosher
    salt)

1. Dissolve the yeast in the warm water in a large bowl.
2. Add 2 cups of the flour and beat until smooth.
3. Add the corn syrup, butter, and salt, and mix well about 2 minutes.
4. Add the remaining flour and knead with your hands until all the flour is worked into the dough.

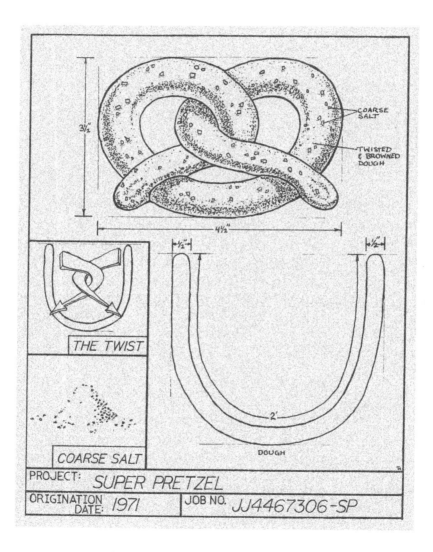

COARSE SALT

TWISTED & BROWNED DOUGH

3½"

4½"

THE TWIST

COARSE SALT

DOUGH

2'

PROJECT: SUPER PRETZEL

ORIGINATION DATE: 1971   JOB NO. JJ4467306-SP

5. Cover the bowl and set the dough in a warm, cozy place where it can ponder the meaning of "Rise, you gooey glob!" Allow the dough to double in size, from 1 to 1 1/2 hours.

6. Remove the dough from the bowl and divide into 10 equal pieces.

7. With your hands, roll each piece of dough out on a flat surface until it's about 2 feet long.

8. Holding the dough at both ends, give each strip of dough a twist. Lay the twists well spaced on greased cookie sheets (refer to the illustration for design specifics). Let these rise for another 30 to 45 minutes.

9. When the dough has nearly doubled again, combine the cold water and baking soda in a large saucepan and bring to a boil. This will be your browning solution (a.k.a. *caustic bath*).

10. Preheat the oven to 350ºF.

11. Drop each pretzel, one at a time, into the boiling solution. Soak each pretzel for 1 minute, carefully turning after 30 seconds. Return to the cookie sheets.

12. Bake the pretzels for 12 to 15 minutes, or until they are golden brown.

13. Eat the pretzels hot or allow them to cool and freeze them. If you want salt, lightly moisten the surface of the pretzel with a pastry brush and apply a generous sprinkling of coarse salt.

14. Frozen pretzels can be reheated in a microwave set on high for about 30 seconds.

- MAKES 10 PRETZELS.

• • • •

TASTYKAKE CHOCOLATE CUPCAKES

In 1914, the founders of the Tasty Baking Company set out to create "the cake that made Mother stop baking." The idea of small, prewrapped cakes made fresh at the bakery and delivered to local grocery stores was especially appealing back then. Tastykake products remain popular; every day the company ships and sells millions of Tastykake products. Perhaps the success of the product over the years lies in the secret recipes that have gone remarkably unchanged since they were first created. These chocolate cupcakes in several varieties are the company's top-selling item, with more than 7 million baked weekly.

You'll need a pastry bag to make the filled variety.

CUPCAKES

one 18.25-ounce box Duncan
    Hines Moist Deluxe Devil's Food
    cake mix

3 eggs
$^1/_2$ cup vegetable oil
1$^1/_3$ cups water

CHOCOLATE ICING

5$^1/_3$ tablespoons ($^2/_3$ stick) butter,
    softened
$^1/_2$ cup semisweet chocolate chips

1$^1/_2$ teaspoons vanilla extract
1 tablespoon milk
2$^1/_4$ cups powdered sugar

BUTTERCREAM ICING

5 1/3 tablespoons (2/3 stick) butter, softened
1 1/2 teaspoons vanilla extract

2 1/2 tablespoons milk
1/8 teaspoon salt
3 cups powdered sugar

FILLING

1/2 cup shortening
1/2 teaspoon vanilla extract

pinch salt
1 cup powdered sugar

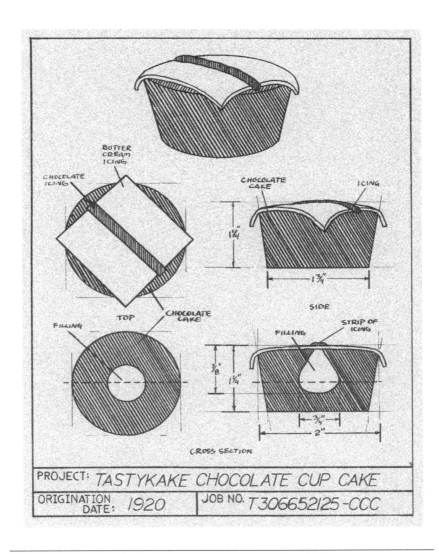

PROJECT: TASTYKAKE CHOCOLATE CUP CAKE

ORIGINATION DATE: 1920   JOB NO. T306652125-CCC

1. Preheat the oven to 350°F.
2. Make the cupcakes according to the directions on the box of cake mix. (Combine the ingredients, mix for 2 minutes, pour into lightly greased muffin cups, and bake for 19 to 22 minutes.)
3. While the cupcakes bake, make the chocolate and/or butter-cream icings.

    Chocolate icing: In a mixing bowl, combine the butter with the chocolate chips melted in a microwave set on high for 30 to 45 seconds. Blend in the vanilla, milk, and powdered sugar and beat with an electric mixer until smooth and creamy.

    Buttercream icing: Combine all the ingredients in a mixing bowl and beat until smooth.
4. If you're making the filled cupcakes, combine the ingredients for the filling in another mixing bowl and beat until fluffy.
5. When the cupcakes are cool, complete each by following the directions below for your preference.

- MAKES 24 CUPCAKES.

CHOCOLATE-ICED CUPCAKES

First spread a layer of chocolate frosting on each cupcake. Then, using a pastry bag with a small, round tip, draw a single straight line of buttercream icing down the middle of the chocolate icing.

BUTTERCREAM-ICED CUPCAKES

First spread a layer of buttercream icing evenly over the top of each cupcake. Then, using a pastry bag with a small, round tip, draw a straight line of chocolate icing down the middle of the buttercream icing.

CREME-FILLED CUPCAKES

If it's filled cupcakes you want, you need to fill them before you spread on the frosting. How do you do this? It's really very easy.

Use a toothpick or wooden skewer to make a hole in the top of the unfrosted cupcake. Stick the toothpick into the middle of the cupcake and then swirl it around to carve out a cavity in the middle of the cake. This is where the filling will go.

Use a pastry bag to inject a small amount (about 1 teaspoon) of filling into each cupcake, to fill the hole. When you ice your cupcakes, the icing will neatly hide the hole you made.

•　•　•　•

TASTYKAKE
BUTTERSCOTCH
KRIMPETS

☆   ✌   💣   ✏   ☯   ✂   ☞

In 1914 Pittsburgh baker Philip J. Baur and Boston egg salesman Herbert T. Morris decided that there was a need for prewrapped, fresh cakes that were conveniently available at local grocers. The two men coined the name *Tastykake* for their new treats and were determined to use only the finest ingredients, delivered fresh daily to their bakery.

The founders' standards of freshness are still maintained. Tastykakes baked tonight are on the shelves tomorrow. That philosophy has contributed to substantial growth for the Tasty Baking Company. On its first day, the firm's sales receipts totaled $28.32; today the company boasts yearly sales of more than $200 million.

Among the top-selling Tastykake treats are the Butterscotch Krimpets, first created in 1927. Today, approximately 6 million Butterscotch Krimpets are baked each and every week.

CAKE

4 egg whites
one 16-ounce box golden pound
   cake mix

⅔ cup water

FROSTING

⅛ cup Nestlé Butterscotch Morsels
   (about 40 chips)

½ (1 stick) cup butter, softened
1½ cups powdered sugar

1. Preheat the oven to 325°F.
2. Beat the egg whites until thick.
3. Blend the egg whites with the cake mix and water.
4. Pour the batter into a greased 9 × 12-inch baking pan. Bake for 30 minutes, or until the top is golden brown and a toothpick inserted in the center comes out clean. Cool.
5. For the frosting, melt the butterscotch morsels in a microwave oven on high for 45 seconds. If you don't have a microwave oven, use a double boiler over hot, not boiling, water.
6. Mix the butter with the melted butterscotch. Add the powdered sugar. Blend with a mixer until the frosting has a smooth consistency.
7. Spread the frosting on top of the cooled pound cake.
8. Cut the cake into nine rows. Then make two cuts lengthwise. This should divide cake into twenty-seven equal pieces.

- MAKES 27 CAKES.

• • • •

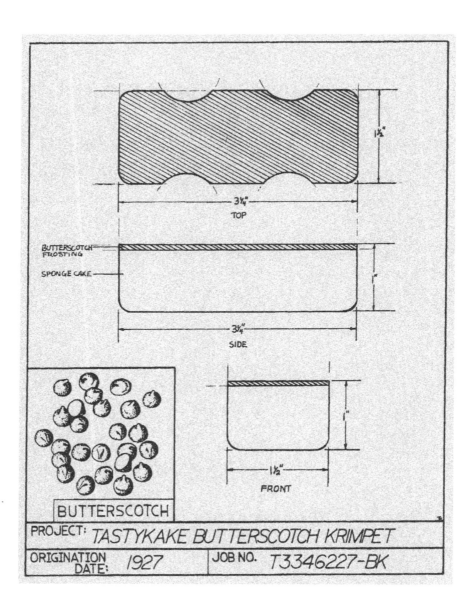

1½"

3¼"

TOP

BUTTERSCOTCH FROSTING

SPONGE CAKE

1"

3¼"

SIDE

1"

1½"

FRONT

BUTTERSCOTCH

PROJECT: TASTYKAKE BUTTERSCOTCH KRIMPET

ORIGINATION DATE: 1927

JOB NO. T3346227-BK

188

TASTYKAKE PEANUT BUTTER KANDY KAKES

Since it was founded in 1914, the Tasty Baking Company has continued to uphold its policy of controlled distribution to ensure freshness of its products. The company delivers only what it will sell promptly and removes cakes from the stores after just a few days in an effort to keep them from becoming stale.

As the years went by and delivery efficiency improved, transportation routes expanded from Philadelphia to New England, the Midwest, and the South. Mixing, baking, wrapping, and packaging of the products have changed from hand operations to sophisticated automated ones, cutting the production cycle from twelve hours to forty-five minutes, and loading time from five hours to forty-five minutes.

Peanut Butter Kandy Kakes made their debut in the early 1930s as *Tandy Takes*. The name was eventually changed, and the company claims you could make almost 8 million peanut butter sandwiches with the quantity of peanut butter used in Kandy Kakes each year.

4 egg whites
one 16-ounce box golden pound
    cake mix
⅔ cup water

1 cup peanut butter
½ cup powdered sugar
one 11.5-ounce bag Hershey milk-
    chocolate chips

1. Preheat the oven to 325ºF.
2. Beat the egg whites until fluffy.
3. Blend the egg whites with the cake mix and water.
4. Pour tablespoon-size dollops of batter into each cup of a well-greased muffin tin. Bake for 10 minutes, or until a toothpick stuck in center of cake comes out clean. Make five batches. Clean muffin tin for later use. Do not grease.
5. Combine the peanut butter and sugar.
6. While the pound-cake rounds cool, heat the chocolate chips in a double boiler over low heat, stirring often. You can also melt them in a microwave oven set on high for 2 minutes, stirring once halfway through the heating time.
7. When the chocolate is soft, line the bottom half of each muffin-tin cup with shortening; then use a spoon to spread a thin layer of chocolate in each cup.
8. With your fingers, spread a thin layer of peanut butter over the chocolate.
9. Place a cake round on the peanut-butter layer.
10. Spread a layer of chocolate over the top of each cake, spreading to the sides to cover the entire surface.
11. Cool in the refrigerator for 10 minutes and turn out of the tin.

• MAKES 30 CAKES.

•   •   •   •

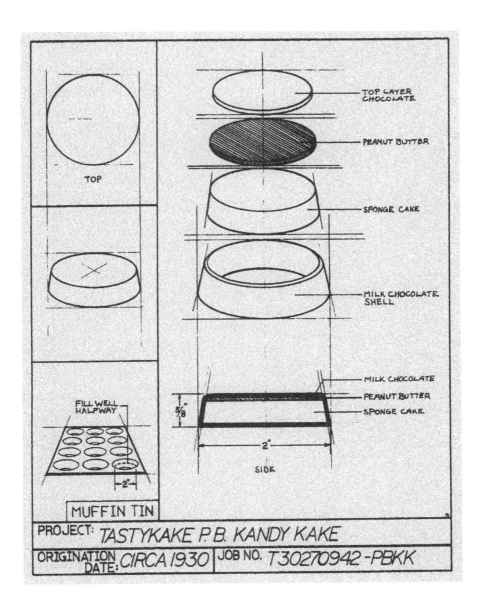

TOP

TOP LAYER
CHOCOLATE

PEANUT BUTTER

SPONGE CAKE

MILK CHOCOLATE
SHELL

MILK CHOCOLATE
PEANUT BUTTER
SPONGE CAKE

5/8"

2"

SIDE

FILL WELL
HALFWAY

2"

MUFFIN TIN

PROJECT: TASTYKAKE P.B. KANDY KAKE

ORIGINATION
DATE: CIRCA 1930

JOB NO. T30270942-PBKK

BENIHANA HIBACHI CHICKEN AND HIBACHI STEAK

☆　　　✌　　　💣　　　✒　　　☯　　　✂　　　☞

When 20-year-old Rocky Aoki came to New York City from Japan with his wrestling team in 1959 he was convinced it was the land of opportunity. Just five years later he used $10,000 he had saved plus another $20,000 that he borrowed to open a Benihana steakhouse on the West Side of Manhattan. His concept of bringing the chefs out from the back kitchen to prepare the food in front of customers on a specially designed hibachi grill was groundbreaking. The restaurant was such a smashing success that it paid for itself within six months.

The most popular items at the restaurant are the Hibachi Chicken and Hibachi Steak, which are prepared at your table on an open hibachi grill. But, since most home kitchens are not fitted with a hibachi grill, you'll have to improvise. You will likely have to use two pans; one for the meat and mushrooms, and the other for the remaining vegetables. And since many of today's cooking surfaces are coated with scratchable, nonstick coatings, we won't be slicing the meat and vegetables while they are sizzling on the hot cooking surface as the Benihana chefs do. Nor will you be required to flip a mushroom into your hat.

4 boneless, skinless chicken breast
    halves
1 large onion
2 medium zucchini
2 cups sliced mushrooms
2 tablespoons vegetable oil
6 tablespoons soy sauce

4 tablespoons butter
salt
pepper
2 teaspoons lemon juice
3 teaspoons sesame seeds
6 cups bean sprouts

ON THE SIDE
Mustard Sauce (page 41)
Ginger Sauce (page 42)

1. Before you begin cooking be sure that the chicken, onion, zucchini, and mushrooms have been sliced into bite-size pieces. For the onion, slice it as if you were making onion rings, then quarter those slices. For the zucchini, first slice them into long, thin strips, then cut across those strips four or five times to make bite-size pieces that are 1 to 1 ½ inches long.

2. Spread 1 tablespoon of oil in a large frying pan over medium/high heat. Spread another tablespoon of oil in another pan over medium/high heat.

3. Begin by sautéing the sliced chicken in one of the pans. Add 1 tablespoon of soy sauce, 1 tablespoon of butter, and a dash of salt and pepper to the chicken.

4. Add the onion and zucchini to the other pan. Add 2 tablespoons soy sauce, 1 tablespoon butter, and a dash of salt and pepper. Sauté the vegetables as long as the chicken is cooking, being sure to stir both pans often.

5. When the chicken has sautéed for about 2 minutes or when it appears white on all sides, slide the meat to one side of the pan, pour lemon juice on it, then add the mushrooms to the other side of the pan. Pour 1 tablespoon of the soy sauce over the mushrooms, then add 1 tablespoon of butter plus a dash of salt and pepper. Continue to stir both pans.

6. After 6 to 8 minutes, or when the chicken is done, sprinkle 1 teaspoon of sesame seeds over the chicken, then mix the

chicken with the mushrooms. Spoon the chicken mixture in four even portions on four plates next to four even portions of the vegetables from the other pan.

7. Pour the bean sprouts into the same pan in which you cooked the vegetables, and cook over high heat. Add 2 tablespoons soy sauce, 1 tablespoon butter, and a dash of salt and pepper.

8. Cook the sprouts for only a minute or two, or until they have tenderized. Just before you serve the sprouts, sprinkle 2 teaspoons of sesame seeds on them. Serve the sprouts next to the chicken and vegetables with mustard sauce and ginger sauce on the side.

• SERVES 3 TO 4 AS AN ENTREE.

HIBACHI STEAK

You can also make a Hibachi Steak like you would find at the restaurant. Just follow the chicken recipe, substituting a 16-ounce sirloin steak for the chicken. Also eliminate the lemon juice and sesame seeds from the recipe.

Keep in mind that your sliced beef will likely cook in half the time of the chicken, depending on how rare you like it.

•   •   •   •

BENIHANA
DIPPING SAUCES

The origin of the name of this chain of Japanese steakhouses dates back to 1935. That's when founder Rocky Aoki's father, Yunosuke Aoki, opened a small coffee shop in Japan and named it "Benihana" after a wild red flower that grew near the front door of his shop. Next time you're at Benihana, look carefully and you'll notice that bright red flower has been incorporated into the restaurant's logo.

With most of the cooking performed before your eyes on an open hibachi grill, Benihana maintains a much smaller kitchen than most restaurants, allowing practically the entire restaurant to become productive, money-generating dining space. The limited space behind the scenes is for storage, office and dressing rooms, and a small preparation area for noncooked items like these sauces. Use them to dip food in—like the Hibachi Steak or Chicken (pages 195 and 193). These sauces will go well with a variety of Asian dishes and can be frozen in sealed containers for weeks at a time.

MUSTARD SAUCE (FOR CHICKEN AND BEEF)
 1/4 cup soy sauce
 1/4 cup water

2 teaspoons Oriental mustard*
2 teaspoons heavy cream
1/2 teaspoon garlic powder

Combine all of the ingredients in a small bowl and mix until well combined. Chill before serving.

*Can be found in the international or Asian food section of your supermarket.

GINGER SAUCE (FOR VEGETABLES AND SEAFOOD)

$1/4$ cup chopped onion
$1/4$ cup soy sauce
1 clove garlic, minced
$1/2$ ounce gingerroot (a nickel-size
    slice), peeled and chopped

juice of $1/2$ lemon
    (2 tablespoons)
$1/2$ teaspoon sugar
$1/4$ teaspoon white vinegar

Combine all of the ingredients in a blender and blend on low speed for 30 seconds or until the gingerroot and garlic have been puréed. Chill before serving.

• MAKES $2/3$ CUP OF EACH SAUCE.

•   •   •   •

BENIHANA
JAPANESE FRIED RICE

☆　　✌　　💣　　✏　　☯　　✂　　☞

The talented chefs at Benihana cook food on hibachi grills with flair and charisma, treating the preparation like a tiny stage show. They juggle salt and pepper shakers, trim food with lightning speed, and flip shrimp and mushrooms perfectly onto serving plates or into their tall chef's hat.

One of the side dishes that everyone seems to love is the fried rice. At Benihana this dish is prepared by chefs with precooked rice on open hibachi grills, and is ordered à la carte to complement any Benihana entree, including Hibachi Steak and Chicken. I like when the rice is thrown onto the hot hibachi grill and seems to come alive as it sizzles and dances around like a bunch of little jumping beans. Okay, so I'm easily amused.

This version of that popular side dish will go well with just about any Japanese entree and can be partially prepared ahead of time, and kept in the refrigerator until the rest of the meal is close to done (check out the "Tidbits").

1 cup uncooked long grain converted
　　or parboiled rice (**not** instant or
　　quick white rice)
2 eggs, beaten
1 cup frozen peas, thawed
2 tablespoons finely grated carrot

1/2 cup diced onion
　　(1/2 small onion)
1 1/2 tablespoons butter
2 tablespoons soy sauce
salt
pepper

1. Cook the rice following the instructions on the package. This should take about 20 minutes. Pour the rice into a large bowl to let it cool.

2. Scramble the eggs in a small pan over medium heat. Chop scrambled chunks of egg into small pea-size bits with your spatula while cooking.
3. When the rice has cooled, add the peas, carrot, eggs, and onion to the bowl. Carefully toss all of the ingredients together.
4. Melt the butter in a large frying pan over medium/high heat.
5. When the butter has completely melted, dump the rice mixture into the pan and add the soy sauce plus a dash of salt and pepper. Cook the rice mixture for 6 to 8 minutes, stirring often.

• SERVES 4 AS A SIDE DISH.

TIDBITS

This fried rice can be prepared ahead of time by cooking the rice, then adding the peas, carrot, and scrambled egg plus half of the soy sauce. Keep this refrigerated until you are ready to fry it in the butter. That's when you add the salt, pepper, and remaining soy sauce.

• • • •

THE CHEESECAKE FACTORY BRUSCHETTA

MENU DESCRIPTION: *"Grilled Bread Topped with Fresh Chopped Tomato, Red Onion, Garlic, Basil and Olive Oil."*

In 1972, Oscar and Evelyn Overton moved from Detroit to Los Angeles to build a wholesale bakery that would sell cheesecakes and other high-quality desserts to local restaurants. Business was a booming success, but some restaurants balked at the high prices the bakery was charging for its desserts. So in 1978 the couple's son David decided to open a restaurant of his own—the first Cheesecake Factory restaurant—in posh Beverly Hills. The restaurant was an immediate success and soon David started a moderate expansion of the concept. Sure, the current total of 20 restaurants doesn't seem like a lot, but this handful of stores earns the chain more than $100 million in business each year. That's more than some chains with four times the number of outlets rake in.

Bruschetta is one of the top-selling appetizers at the restaurant chain. Bruschetta is toasted bread flavored with garlic and olive oil, broiled until crispy, and then arranged around a pile of tomato-basil salad in vinaigrette. This salad is scooped onto the bruschetta, like a dip, and then you open wide. This version makes five slices just like the dish served at the restaurant, but the recipe can be easily doubled.

1 1/2 cups chopped Roma
    plum tomatoes
    (6 to 8 tomatoes)
2 tablespoons diced red onion
1 large clove garlic, minced
2 tablespoons chopped fresh basil (4
    to 6 small leaves)
2 tablespoons olive oil

1/2 teaspoon red wine vinegar
1/4 teaspoon salt
dash ground black pepper
1/2 loaf French baguette or crusty
    Italian bread
    (5 to 7 slices)
1/4 teaspoon garlic salt
2 to 3 sprigs Italian parsley

1. Combine the tomatoes, red onion, garlic, and basil in a medium bowl.
2. Add ½ tablespoon of oil, vinegar, salt, and pepper and mix well. Cover the bowl and let it sit in the refrigerator for at least 1 hour.
3. When you are ready to serve the dish, preheat your broiler

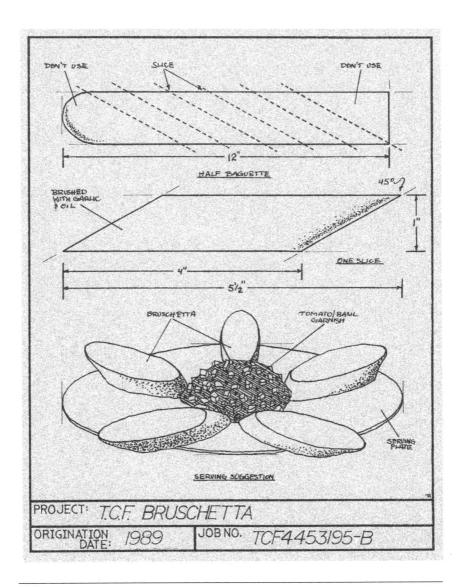

DON'T USE   SLICE   DON'T USE

12"

HALF BAGUETTE

BRUSHED WITH GARLIC & OIL

45°

1"

ONE SLICE

4"

5½"

BRUSCHETTA   TOMATO/BASIL GARNISH

SERVING PLATE

SERVING SUGGESTION

PROJECT: *T.C.F. BRUSCHETTA*

ORIGINATION DATE: *1989*   JOB NO. *TCF4453195-B*

and slice the baguette in 1-inch slices on a 45-degree angle to make 5 slices of bread.

4. Combine the remaining 1½ tablespoons of oil with the garlic salt.

5. Brush the entire surface of each slice of bread (both sides) with the olive oil mixture. Broil the slices of bread in the oven for 1½ to 2 minutes per side or until the surface of the bread starts to turn brown.

6. Arrange the bread like a star or spokes of a wheel on a serving plate. Pour the chilled tomato mixture in a neat pile onto the bread slices where they meet at the center of the plate. Garnish with Italian parsley.

• SERVES 2 AS AN APPETIZER.

TIDBITS

There is a variation on this recipe if your bread has a hard crust. The more traditional method of rubbing the bread with the garlic clove is done as follows:

After you slice the bread, slice a clove of garlic in half and rub it around the edge of the crust on both sides of the bread. Rub the olive oil on the bread and lightly salt each slice, if you like. Grill the bread the same way as above in step 5.

•   •   •   •

THE
CHEESECAKE FACTORY
AVOCADO EGGROLLS

☆   ✌   💣   ✏   ☯   ✂   ☞

MENU DESCRIPTION: *"Chunks of Fresh Avocado, Sun-Dried Tomato, Red Onion and Cilantro Deep Fried in a Crisp Chinese Wrapper."*

In 1995, Forbes Magazine named the Cheesecake Factory in its list of the 200 best small companies in America. At 20 stores now, the Cheesecake Factory plans to grow at a modest rate of about 5 new restaurants per year, and still does not franchise.

Here's something different that I think you'll really like. The Avocado Eggrolls are one of the most popular appetizers on the menu at the Cheesecake Factory, and it's not hard to see why. The combination of hot avocado, sun-dried tomatoes, and the cilantro-tamarind sauce is one of the most unique and tasty flavors I've enjoyed at any of the restaurant chains. The trickiest part might be finding the tamarind pulp at your market. It's a brown, sticky pulp that looks sort of like puréed prunes, and can be found in the spice section or near the ethnic foods—or try a Middle Eastern market. The pulp often contains the large seeds of the fruit, so be sure to remove them before measuring. If you can't find the tamarind, you can get by substituting smashed raisins or prunes.

EGGROLLS

1 large avocado
2 tablespoons chopped sun-dried tomatoes (bottled in oil)
1 tablespoon minced red onion

1/2 teaspoon chopped fresh cilantro
pinch salt
3 eggroll wrappers
1 egg, beaten
vegetable oil for frying

DIPPING SAUCE

1/4 cup chopped cashews
2/3 cup chopped fresh cilantro
2 cloves garlic, quartered
2 green onions, chopped
1 tablespoon sugar
1 teaspoon ground black pepper

1 teaspoon cumin
4 teaspoons white vinegar
1 teaspoon balsamic vinegar
1/2 teaspoon tamarind pulp
1/2 cup honey
pinch ground saffron
1/4 cup olive oil

1. After you peel the avocado and remove the pit, dice it into bite-size pieces.

2. In a small bowl, gently combine the avocado with the tomatoes, red onion, 1/2 teaspoon cilantro, and a pinch of salt. Be careful not to smash the avocado.

3. Prepare the eggrolls by spooning 1/3 of the filling into an eggroll wrapper. With the wrapper positioned so that one corner is pointing toward you, place the filling about 1 inch from the bottom corner and 1 inch from each side. Roll the bottom corner up over the filling, then roll the filling up to about the middle of the wrapper. Brush the remaining corners and edges of the wrapper with the beaten egg. Fold the left and right corners over the filling and "glue" the corners to the wrapper. Finish by rolling the wrapper and filling up over the top corner. Press on the wrapper to ensure it is sealed. Repeat these steps with the remaining two eggrolls and keep them covered in the refrigerator while you make the dipping sauce.

4. Prepare the sauce by combining the cashews, cilantro, garlic, green onions, sugar, black pepper, and cumin in a foo processor or blender. Blend with short bursts until the mixture is well blended, and the cashews and garlic have been chopped into pieces about half the size of a grain of rice.

5. Combine the vinegars, honey, tamarind, and saffron in a small bowl. Heat the mixture for about 1 minute in a microwave, then stir until the tamarind pulp dissolves completely.

6. Pour the tamarind mixture into the blender or food processor with the cashew mixture and mix with short bursts until well combined (about 20 seconds).

7. Pour the blended sauce into a small bowl. Add the oil and stir by hand. Cover and refrigerate the sauce for at least 30 minutes before serving.

8. Heat oil in a deep fryer or a deep pan over medium heat. You want the oil to be deep enough to cover the eggrolls.

9. When the oil is hot, fry the eggrolls for 3 to 4 minutes or until golden brown. Drain on paper towels.

10. When the eggrolls can be safely touched, slice once diagonally across the middle of each one and serve them arranged around a sauce dish filled with the dipping sauce.

• SERVES 1 OR 2 AS AN APPETIZER.

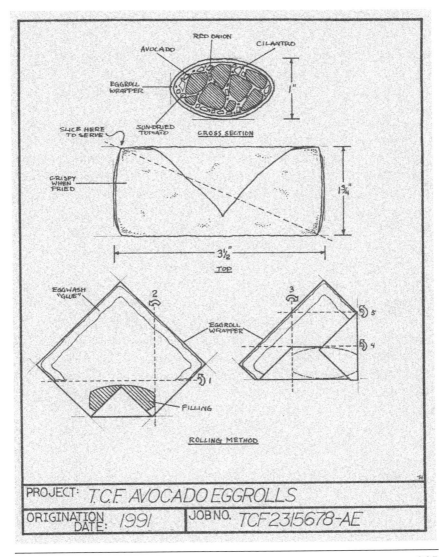

THE
CHEESECAKE FACTORY
CAJUN JAMBALAYA PASTA

MENU DESCRIPTION: *"Our most popular dish! Shrimp and Chicken Sautéed with Onions, Peppers and Tomatoes in a Very Spicy Cajun Sauce. All on top of Fresh Fettuccine."*

The Cheesecake Factory's founder, David Overton, says it was his unfamiliarity with the restaurant business that contributed to the company's success. In an interview with **Nation's Restaurant News** David says, "We did not know anything about running restaurants. We just knew that people valued fresh foods. In some ways our naiveté helped us because we didn't know what you are not supposed to do."

I think we all know it helps to serve good food and that's an area in which the Cheesecake Factory excels. The pastas and salads top the list of big sellers, but it's the Cajun Jambalaya Pasta that holds the pole position, according to the menu description of this dish. Jambalaya is a spicy Creole dish that usually combines a variety of ingredients including tomatoes, onions, peppers, and some type of meat with rice. Rather than the traditional rice, the Cheesecake Factory has designed its version to include two types of fettuccine—an attractive mix of standard white noodles and green spinach-flavored noodles.

This recipe makes 2 huge portions, like those served in the restaurant. It's actually enough food for a family of four.

½ teaspoon white pepper
½ teaspoon cayenne pepper
1½ teaspoons salt
½ teaspoon paprika
¼ teaspoon garlic powder
¼ teaspoon onion powder
2 skinless, boneless chicken breast halves
½ pound large shrimp, peeled and deveined
5 quarts water
6 ounces plain fettuccine
6 ounces spinach fettuccine

2 tablespoons olive oil
2 medium tomatoes, chopped
1 small green bell pepper, sliced
1 small red bell pepper, sliced
1 small yellow bell pepper, sliced
1 small white onion, sliced
1½ cups chicken stock
1 tablespoon arrowroot or cornstarch
2 tablespoons white wine
2 teaspoons chopped fresh parsley

1. Make a Cajun seasoning blend by combining the white pepper, cayenne pepper, salt, paprika, garlic powder, and onion powder in a small bowl.
2. Cut the chicken breasts into bite-size pieces. Use about one-third of the seasoning blend to coat the chicken pieces.
3. In another bowl, sprinkle another one-third of the spice blend over the shrimp.
4. Start your pasta cooking by bringing 5 quarts of water to a boil over high heat. Add both fettuccines to the hot water, reduce the heat to medium, and simmer for 12 to 14 minutes or until the pasta is tender.
5. While the fettuccine cooks, heat 1 tablespoon of the olive oil in a large frying pan or skillet over high heat. When the oil is hot, sauté the chicken in the pan for about 2 minutes per side or until the surface of the chicken starts to turn brown.
6. Add the shrimp to the pan with the chicken and cook for another 2 minutes, stirring occasionally to keep the shrimp from sticking. When the chicken and shrimp have been seared, pour the contents of the pan onto a plate or into a bowl. Do not rinse the pan!
7. Put the pan back over the high heat and add the remaining tablespoon of oil to the pan. Add the tomatoes, peppers, and onion to the oil. Sprinkle the veggies with the remaining spice

blend and sauté for about 10 minutes or until the vegetables begin to turn dark brown or black.

8. Add the chicken and shrimp to the vegetables and pour ¾ cup of the chicken stock in the pan. Cook over high heat until the stock has been reduced to just about nothing. Add the remaining ¾ cup of the stock to the pan. The liquid should become dark as it deglazes the pan of the dark film left by the spices and cooking food. Stir constantly, scraping the blackened stuff on the bottom of the pan. Reduce the broth a bit more, then turn the heat down to low.

9. Combine the arrowroot with the wine in a small bowl. Stir until it is dissolved. Add this to the pan and simmer over low heat until the sauce thickens slightly.

10. When the fettuccine is done, drain it and spoon half onto a plate. Spoon half of the jambalaya over the fettuccine. Sprinkle half of the parsley over the top. Repeat for the second serving.

• SERVES 2 AS A LARGE ENTREE.

TIDBITS

You may also be able to find fettuccine that comes in a 12-ounce box with a combination of plain and spinach noodles. One brand is Ronzoni. This variety is perfect for this recipe, and you won't have any leftover noodles in opened boxes.

• • • •

CHILI'S GRILLED CARIBBEAN SALAD

MENU DESCRIPTION: *"Grilled, marinated chicken breast, mixed greens, pico de gallo, pineapple chunks, tortilla strips & honey-lime dressing."*

Larry Levine started building his chain of Chili's restaurants in Dallas in 1975. At that time Chili's was basically a hamburger joint with a gourmet touch, dining room service and booze. Even though the menu then offered only eleven items, the restaurant was so popular that throngs of hungry customers waited patiently in lines extending into the parking lots. This caught the eye of the persuasive restaurateur Norman Brinker, who, in 1983, convinced Larry to sell his chain of Chili's restaurants, which by then had grown to a total of thirty.

Before Norman had stepped into the picture, more than 80 percent of Chili's business was in hamburgers. Today a much larger menu reflects the current trends in food, and salads are some of the best-selling items. These days the Grilled Caribbean Salad with the tasty honey-lime dressing is the salad of choice.

HONEY-LIME DRESSING

¹/₄ cup Grey Poupon Dijon mustard
¹/₄ cup honey
1 ¹/₂ tablespoons sugar

1 tablespoon sesame oil
1 ¹/₂ tablespoons apple cider vinegar
1 ¹/₂ teaspoons lime juice

Blend all the ingredients in a small bowl with an electric mixer. Cover and chill.

PICO DE GALLO

2   edium tomatoes, diced
¹/₂ cup diced Spanish onion
2 teaspoons chopped fresh jalapeño
    pepper, seeded and de-ribbed

2 teaspoons finely minced fresh
    cilantro*
pinch of salt

Combine all the ingredients in a small bowl. Cover and chill.

SALAD

4 boneless, skinless chicken breast
    halves
1/2 cup teriyaki marinade, store
    bought or your own (page 305)
4 cups chopped iceberg lettuce

4 cups chopped green leaf
    lettuce
1 cup chopped red cabbage
1 5.5-ounce can pineapple chunks in
    juice, drained
10 tortilla chips

1. Marinate the chicken in the teriyaki for at least 2 hours. You can use a resealable plastic bag for this. Put the chicken into the bag and pour in the marinade, then toss it into the fridge.
2. Prepare the barbecue or preheat a stovetop grill. Grill the chicken for 4 to 5 minutes per side or until done.
3. Toss the lettuce and cabbage together, then divide the greens into two large individual-serving salad bowls.
4. Divide the pico de gallo and pour it in two even portions over the greens.
5. Divide the pineapple and sprinkle it on the salads.
6. Break the tortilla chips into large chunks and sprinkle half on each salad.
7. Slice the grilled chicken breasts into thin strips, and spread half the strips onto each salad.
8. Pour the dressing into two small bowls and serve with the salads.

- SERVES 2 AS AN ENTREE.

* Found in the produce section; also known as fresh coriander and Chinese parsley.

CHILI'S PEANUT BUTTERCUP CHEESECAKE

☆ ✌ 💣 ✏ ☯ ✂ ☞

MENU DESCRIPTION: *"Chocolate & vanilla marbled cheesecake on a chocolate cookie crust, topped w/fudge & Reese's Peanut Butter Cup pieces."*

If I had to pick one person in the restaurant business with the most respected and distinguished career, it would have to be Norman Brinker. The 65-year-old CEO of Brinker International is still building on a success story that spans four decades, and recently detailed his life in an autobiography, **On the Brink.** Back in the fifties, Norman took a job with Robert Peterson, who had just a few years earlier opened the first Jack-in-the-Box in San Diego, California. By the age of 34, Norman owned 20 percent of Jack-in-the-Box, giving him enough capital to set out on his own venture. In 1964 he opened a fifties-style coffee shop in downtown Dallas called Brinks. He sold that eatery a year later for $6,000 and sank that cash into a new chain that would become one of his most successful ventures. Norman opened the first Steak and Ale in 1966, took the chain public in 1971, then 10 years later sold the whole kit-and-caboodle for $100 million to the Pillsbury Company (that's some serious dough, boy). Pillsbury kept him on to run the operation, but Norman needed new action. In 1983, he purchased Chili's from founder Larry Levine and within 12 years built the chain into a billion-dollar company. Today Norman continues to watch Brinker International grow as new concepts like Cozymel's and Romano's Macaroni Grill are added to his long list of restaurant chain successes.

Speaking of rich, here's a tasty dessert for anyone who digs cheesecake and peanut butter cups. Use an 8-inch springform pan for this recipe if you have one. If not, you can also use two 9-inch pie pans and make two smaller cheesecakes. For the Oreo cookie crumbs, you can crumble three Oreo cookies, after removing the filling, or you can find packaged Oreo crumbs in the baking section of your supermarket near the graham cracker crumbs.

1 cup graham cracker crumbs
1/4 cup Oreo chocolate cookie crumbs
    (3 cookies with filling removed)
1/3 cup butter, melted
1/4 cup smooth peanut butter (not
    chunky)
3 8-ounce packages cream cheese,
    softened

3 eggs
1 cup sour cream
1 cup sugar
1 1/2 teaspoons vanilla
1/4 cup chocolate syrup
1 cup fudge topping
4 chilled regular-size Reese's peanut
    butter cups
    (not bite-size)

1. Preheat the oven to 375°F.
2. In a medium bowl combine the graham cracker crumbs, chocolate cookie crumbs, and melted butter.
3. Press the crumbs firmly over just the bottom of an 8-inch springform pan. Bake for 6 to 8 minutes.
4. When the crust is cool, spread the peanut butter in a circle in the center of the crust. (You may soften the peanut butter for 30 seconds in the microwave to make it easier to spread.) You don't need to spread the peanut butter to the edge—leave about an inch margin all around.
5. You'll need two separate bowls for the two fillings, one larger than the other. In the larger bowl, with an electric mixer, beat together the cream cheese, eggs, sour cream, sugar, and vanilla until smooth.
6. Remove 1 cup of the cream cheese mixture and pour it into the smaller bowl. Add the chocolate syrup to this mixture and combine.
7. Pour the large bowl of filling into the pan and spread it evenly over the crust.
8. Pour the chocolate filling onto the other filling and spread it out. Using the tip of a knife, swirl the chocolate into the white filling beneath it. A couple of passes should be enough.
9. Lower the oven temperature to 350°F. Bake the cheesecake for 70 to 80 minutes or until it becomes firm in the center. Remove from the oven and allow it to cool.

10. When the cheesecake is completely cool, soften the fudge topping in a double boiler or the microwave for about 45 seconds, then spread it out evenly over the cheesecake. Be sure to cover the entire surface of the filling.
11. Unwrap the peanut butter cups and chop them into small chunks.
12. Sprinkle the peanut butter cup pieces and any crumbs over the top of the cheesecake. Chill.
13. Slice the cake 5 times through the middle to make 10 slices.

• SERVES 10.

• • • •

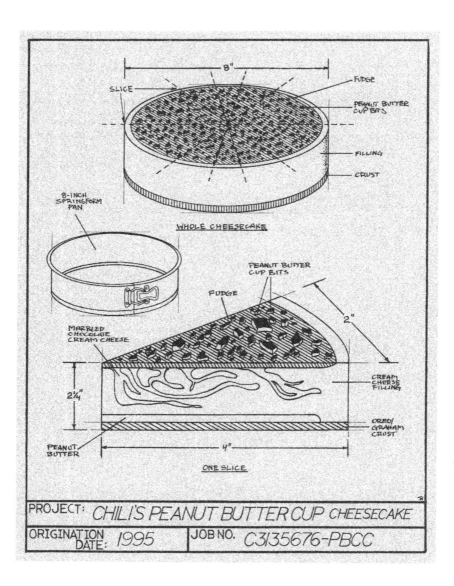

8"

SLICE

FUDGE

PEANUT BUTTER CUP BITS

FILLING

CRUST

8-INCH SPRINGFORM PAN

WHOLE CHEESECAKE

PEANUT BUTTER CUP BITS

FUDGE

MARBLED CHOCOLATE CREAM CHEESE

2"

2¼"

CREAM CHEESE FILLING

OREO/ GRAHAM CRUST

PEANUT BUTTER

4"

ONE SLICE

PROJECT: *CHILI'S PEANUT BUTTER CUP CHEESECAKE*

ORIGINATION DATE: *1995*

JOB NO. *C3135676-PBCC*

DENNY'S
SCRAM SLAM

☆　　❧　　💣　　✐　　☯　　✂　　☞

MENU DESCRIPTION: *"Three eggs scrambled with Cheddar cheese, mushrooms, green peppers and onions, then topped with diced tomatoes. Served with hashed browns, sausage, bacon and choice of toast, Homestyle buttermilk biscuit or English muffin."*

In 1953, Harold Butler realized his dream of opening a donut shop. The little shop in Lakewood, California was called Danny's Donuts, and Harold's philosophy was simple: "We're going to serve the best cup of coffee; make the best donuts; give the best service; keep everything spotless; offer the best value; and stay open 24 hours a day."

That little donut store made $120,000 in its first year—a good bit of change for any restaurant in 1953. When customers requested more than fried dough with a hole in the middle, Harold began offering sandwiches, breakfasts, and other meals, and in 1954 changed the name to Danny's Coffee Shops. The name of the chain would eventually change again, this time to Denny's—now the nation's largest full-service restaurant chain.

In 1977, Denny's introduced the Grand Slam Breakfast—a value-priced breakfast that included eggs, sausage, bacon, and pancakes. Later, the successful Grand Slam Breakfast specials expanded to included other variations including the French Slam, Southern Slam, and the Scram Slam, the last a popular vegetable-and-scrambled-egg creation you can now make for yourself.

1 slice white onion, diced (1/4 cup)	1 1/2 tablespoons butter
1/4 green bell pepper, diced (1/4 cup)	6 eggs, beaten
	1 cup shredded Cheddar cheese
4 mushrooms, sliced (1 cup)	salt
	1/2 tomato, chopped

1. In a small skillet, sauté the onion, green pepper, and mushrooms in 1 tablespoon of the butter over medium heat for about 5 minutes or until the mushrooms are tender.
2. In another larger skillet over medium heat, melt the remaining ½ tablespoon butter. Add the beaten eggs. Stir the eggs as they cook to scramble them.
3. When the eggs have cooked for 5 to 7 minutes and are no longer runny, add the cheese and stir. Add the sautéed onions, green pepper, and mushrooms along with a dash of salt and cook the eggs until done.
4. Divide the eggs onto two plates and sprinkle chopped tomatoes over each helping. Serve with bacon, sausage, and hash browns on the side.

• SERVES 2.

• • • •

DENNY'S
MOONS OVER MY HAMMY

☆   ✌   💣   ✏   ☯   ✂   ☞

MENU DESCRIPTION: *"The supreme ham and egg sandwich, made with Swiss and American cheese on grilled sourdough. Served with choice of hashed browns or French fries."*

With its goofy-yet-memorable name, Moons Over My Hammy is a delicious and versatile scrambled egg sandwich that can be eaten for breakfast with hash browns on the side, or for lunch with a side of French fries. When you get the sourdough bread for this recipe, try to find a good-quality loaf with large slices.

butter, softened
2 eggs, beaten
salt
2 ounces deli-sliced ham
2 slices sourdough bread

1 to 2 slices processed Swiss cheese
   (Kraft Singles)
1 to 2 slices American cheese (Kraft
   Singles)

ON THE SIDE
hash browns

French fries

1. Put two medium-size skillets over medium heat. In one skillet, add a little butter and scramble the two eggs. Salt the eggs to taste. In the other skillet, brown the stack of sliced ham without separating the slices.
2. When the stack of ham slices has browned a bit on both sides, re-move it from the pan. Butter one side of each slice of sourdough bread and put one slice into the pan, buttered side down, to grill.
3. Immediately put the slice(s) of Swiss cheese onto the face-up, unbuttered side of the bread that is grilling.
4. Stack the heated ham slices on the Swiss cheese.
5. Scoop the scrambled eggs out of the other pan with a large spatula and place them on the ham.
6. Place the slice(s) of American cheese on the eggs.

7. Top off the sandwich with the remaining slice of sourdough bread. Make sure the unbuttered side faces the cheese.
8. By this time the bread touching the pan should be grilled to a golden brown. Carefully flip the sandwich over and grill the other side for about 2 minutes or until brown.
9. Slice the sandwich diagonally through the middle and serve with hash browns or French fries on the side.

• SERVES 1 (CAN BE DOUBLED).

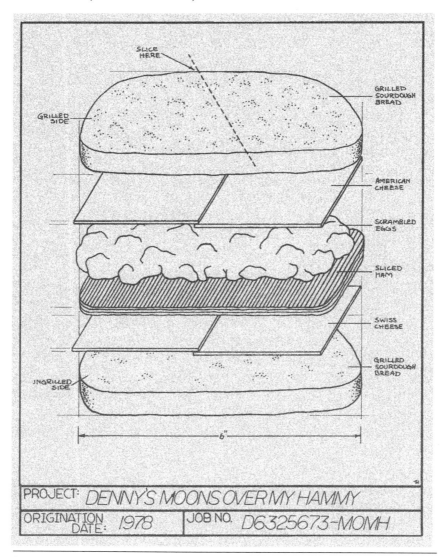

SLICE HERE

GRILLED SOURDOUGH BREAD

GRILLED SIDE

AMERICAN CHEESE

SCRAMBLED EGGS

SLICED HAM

SWISS CHEESE

GRILLED SOURDOUGH BREAD

UNGRILLED SIDE

6"

PROJECT: DENNY'S MOONS OVER MY HAMMY

ORIGINATION DATE: 1978   JOB NO. D6325673-MOMH

DENNY'S
THE SUPER BIRD

☆   ✌   💣   ✏   ☯   ✂   ☞

MENU DESCRIPTION: *"A Denny's original. Sliced turkey breast with Swiss cheese, bacon and tomato on grilled sourdough. Served with French fries and pickle chips."*

Now you can munch down your own clone of this popular palate pleaser, The Super Bird, a cross between a grilled cheese and a club, and Denny's top-selling sandwich. When shopping for sourdough bread, try to find a high-quality loaf with large slices. The thin-sliced turkey breast is best purchased at your market's deli service counter where they cut it while you wait. If you don't have a service counter like this near you, you can use the prepackaged thin-sliced meats located in the cold deli section. Or you can move.

3 ounces deli-sliced turkey breast
2 large slices sourdough bread
butter, softened

2 slices processed Swiss cheese
   (Kraft Singles)
salt
2 slices bacon, cooked
2 slices tomato

ON THE SIDE
French fries   *Pickles*

1. Heat a skillet or frying pan over medium heat. Grill the stack of turkey breast in the pan without separating the stack until the meat is golden brown on both sides.
2. While the turkey is browning, butter one side of each slice of sourdough bread. Place one slice of bread in the pan, buttered side down.

3. Place the 2 slices of Swiss cheese on the unbuttered side of the bread grilling in the pan.
4. Put the stack of turkey breast slices on the Swiss cheese. Sprinkle with a bit of salt.
5. Place the cooked bacon on the turkey breast.

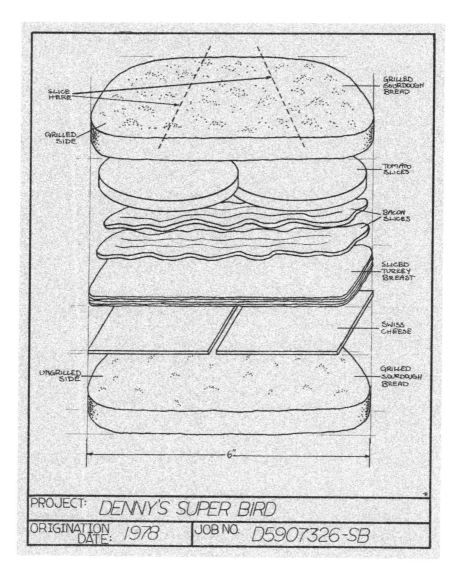

6. Stack the tomato slices on the bacon next.
7. Top off the sandwich with the remaining slice of sourdough bread. Be sure to place the bread with the unbuttered side facing the tomato slices.
8. When the slice of bread on the bottom has grilled until golden brown, carefully flip the sandwich over to grill the other slice.
9. After about 2 minutes, when the bread has grilled to a golden brown, remove the sandwich from the pan and slice the sandwich twice with a sharp knife, creating 3 equal-size pieces. Serve with French fries and pickles, if desired.

- SERVES 1 (CAN BE DOUBLED).

• • • •

HOOTERS BUFFALO CHICKEN WINGS

MENU DESCRIPTION: *"Nearly world famous. Often imitated, hardly ever duplicated."*

"Hooters is to chicken wings what McDonald's is to hamburgers," claims promotional material from the company. True, the six fun-loving midwestern businessmen who started Hooters in Clearwater, Florida, on April Fool's Day in 1983 chose a classic recipe for chicken wings as their feature item. But while some might say it's the Buffalo Wings that are their favorite feature of Hooters, others say it's the restaurant chain's trademark Hooters girls—waitresses casually attired in bright orange short-shorts and skin-tight T-shirts. Apparently it's a combination that works.

Today there are nearly 200 Hooters across the United States serving more than 150 tons of chicken wings every week. I've tasted lots of chicken wings, and I think these are some of the best wings served in any restaurant chain today. The original dish can be ordered in 10-, 20- or 50-piece servings; or if you want to splurge, there's the "Gourmet Chicken Wing Dinner" featuring 20 wings and a bottle of Dom Perignon champagne, for only $125. To further enhance the Hooters experience when you serve these messy wings, throw a whole roll of paper towels on the table, rather than napkins, as they do in the restaurants.

vegetable oil for frying
1/4 cup butter
1/4 cup Crystal Louisiana Hot Sauce
   or Frank's Red Hot Cayenne
   Sauce
dash ground pepper

dash garlic powder
1/2 cup all-purpose flour
1/4 teaspoon paprika
1/4 teaspoon cayenne pepper
1/4 teaspoon salt
10 chicken wing pieces

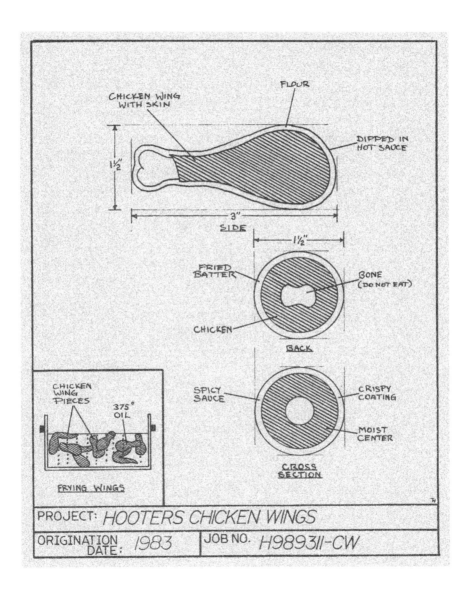

CHICKEN WING
WITH SKIN

FLOUR

DIPPED IN
HOT SAUCE

1½"

3"
SIDE

1½"

FRIED
BATTER

BONE
(DO NOT EAT)

CHICKEN

BACK

CHICKEN
WING
PIECES

375°
OIL

SPICY
SAUCE

CRISPY
COATING

MOIST
CENTER

CROSS
SECTION

FRYING WINGS

PROJECT: *HOOTERS CHICKEN WINGS*

ORIGINATION
DATE: *1983*

JOB NO. *H989311-CW*

1. Heat oil in a deep fryer to 375ºF. You want just enough oil to cover the wings entirely—an inch or so deep at least.
2. Combine the butter, hot sauce, ground pepper, and garlic powder in a small saucepan over low heat. Heat until the butter is melted and the ingredients are well-blended.
3. Combine the flour, paprika, cayenne pepper, and salt in a small bowl.
4. If the wings are frozen, be sure to defrost and dry them. Put the wings into a large bowl and sprinkle the flour mixture over them, coating each wing evenly. Put the wings in the refrigerator for 60 to 90 minutes. (This will help the breading to stick to the wings when fried.)
5. Put all the wings into the hot oil and fry them for 10 to 15 minutes or until some parts of the wings begin to turn dark brown.
6. Remove the wings from the oil to a paper towel to drain. But don't let them sit too long, because you want to serve the wings hot.
7. Quickly put the wings into a large bowl. Add the hot sauce and stir, coating all of the wings evenly. You could also use a large plastic container (such as Tupperware) with a lid for this. Put all the wings inside the container, add the sauce, put on the lid, then shake. Serve with bleu cheese dressing and celery sticks on the side.

- SERVES 3 TO 5 AS AN APPETIZER.

• • • •

HOOTERS
BUFFALO SHRIMP

☆ ✌ 💣 ✏ ☯ ✂ ☞

MENU DESCRIPTION: *"It don't get no batter than this."*

With the double-entendre name and female servers (many of whom, off-duty, are models), Hooters has become a company with critics. Several years ago a group of Hooters Girls in Minneapolis sued the company on grounds of sexual harassment, saying that the uniforms featuring shorts and tight T-shirts or tank tops were demeaning. Ultimately, the women dropped the suit. But more recently, the Equal Employment Opportunity Commission ordered the company to hire men on the foodservice staff. Hooters countered with a sarcastic million-dollar advertising campaign featuring a mustachioed man named "Vince" dressed in Hooters Girl getup. Once again, that suit was dropped.

Vice president of marketing Mike McNeil told *Nation's Restaurant News,* "Hooters Girls are actually wearing more clothing than what most women wear at the gym or the beach. It's part of the concept. I don't think the world would be a better place if we had guys be Hooters Girls." You may agree or disagree, but the fact is that Hooters is currently the country's thirteenth largest dinner house chain and one of the fastest growing, with an increasing number of diners discovering Buffalo Shrimp, a delicious spin-off of Buffalo Chicken Wings.

vegetable oil for frying
1/4 cup butter
1/4 cup Crystal Louisiana Hot Sauce
    or Frank's Red Hot Cayenne
    Sauce
dash ground pepper

dash garlic powder
1/8 teaspoon paprika
12 uncooked large shrimp
1 egg, beaten
1/2 cup milk
1 cup all-purpose flour

1. Heat oil in a deep fryer to 375ºF. You want the oil deep enough to cover the shrimp completely.
2. Combine the butter, hot sauce, ground pepper, garlic powder,

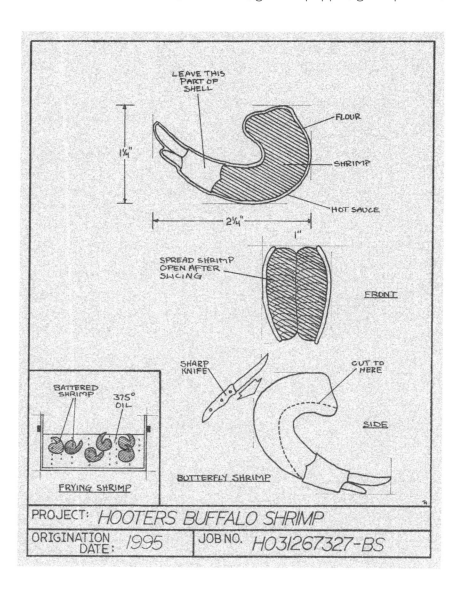

and paprika in a small saucepan over low heat. Heat until the butter is melted and the ingredients are well blended.

3. Prepare the shrimp by cutting off the entire shell, leaving only the last segment of the shell and the tailfins. Remove the vein from the back and clean the shrimp. Then, with a paring knife, cut a deeper slice where you removed the vein (down to the tail), so that you can fan the meat out. Be careful not to cut too deep. This will butterfly the shrimp.

4. Combine the egg with the milk in a small bowl. Put the flour into another bowl.

5. Dredge each shrimp in the milk mixture, then coat it with the flour. Make sure each shrimp is evenly coated. When you have coated all of the shrimp with flour, let them sit for about 10 minutes in the refrigerator before frying.

6. Fry the shrimp in the hot oil for 7 to 10 minutes or until the tip of each tail begins to turn dark brown. Remove the shrimp from the oil to paper towels briefly, to drain.

7. Quickly put the shrimp into a large bowl, add the hot sauce and stir, coating each shrimp evenly. You could also use a large plastic container with a lid for this. Put all the shrimp inside, add the sauce, put on the lid, then gently turn the container over a few times to coat all of the shrimp. Serve with wedges of lemon on the side.

• SERVES 3 TO 4 AS AN APPETIZER.

•   •   •   •

HOOTERS
PASTA SALAD

MENU DESCRIPTION: *"Rotini, cukes, tomatoes, scallions and vinaigrette dressing on the side."*

On the back of each menu at this popular dinner house chain is the "Hooters Saga"—a tongue-in-cheek tale of the restaurant's origin. The story claims that the chain's founders, referred to as "the Hooters Six," were arrested shortly after opening the first Hooters restaurant "for impersonating restauranteurs (sic). There were no indictments," the story explains. "But the stigma lingers on."

Even though the "saga" claims the building for the first Hooters restaurant was originally going to be used as a "giant walk-in dumpster," each Hooters outlet is designed to look like a Florida beachhouse. And whether it's December or July, day or night, you'll notice the trademark multicolored Christmas lights are always on.

Since Hooters is more than just Buffalo wings and shrimp, I thought I'd include a clone for a newer item on the menu. You'll love the tasty tri-color pasta salad tossed with tomatoes, cucumbers, and green onion, and a delicious vinaigrette. Use this Top Secret version of the pink vinaigrette dressing on a variety of salads or sub sandwiches, or even as a marinade.

VINAIGRETTE DRESSING

²/₃ cup vegetable oil
¹/₃ cup red wine vinegar
1 ¹/₂ tablespoons sugar
1 tablespoon Grey Poupon Dijon
    mustard
2 teaspoons minced shallot
1 teaspoon lemon juice
¹/₂ teaspoon dried thyme

¹/₄ teaspoon dried parsley flakes
¹/₄ teaspoon garlic powder
¹/₈ teaspoon salt
¹/₈ teaspoon coarsely ground black
    pepper
¹/₈ teaspoon dried basil
¹/₈ teaspoon dried oregano
dash onion powder

4 quarts water
1 pound rainbow rotini or
    tri-color radiatore (red, green,
    and white colors)
1 to 2 teaspoons vegetable oil
1 large or 2 medium tomatoes

1 green onion
$1/4$ cup minced cucumber
salt
green leaf lettuce (optional, for
    garnish)

1. Make the dressing: Use an electric mixer to combine all of the dressing ingredients in a bowl. Mix on high speed for about a minute or so until the dressing becomes thick and creamy. Put the dressing in a sealed container and store it in the refrigerator until ready to toss with the chilled pasta.
2. Bring 4 quarts of water to a boil over high heat and add the pasta. Cook for 12 to 14 minutes, until tender, then drain it.
3. Spray the pasta with a gentle stream of cold water to help cool it off. Drizzle the oil over the cooling pasta to keep it from sticking together. Gently toss the pasta, then put it into a covered container and let it cool in the refrigerator for 30 minutes or so.
4. While the pasta is cooling down, prepare the vegetables: remove the seeds and soft pulp from the tomato(es) before dicing; use only the green part of the green onion (or scallions); and be sure to mince the cucumber into very small pieces.
5. When the pasta is no longer warm, add the diced tomato, green onion, and cucumber. Sprinkle salt over the pasta salad to taste and put it back in the refrigerator until well chilled.
6. When the pasta has chilled, spoon it onto plates and place the vinaigrette dressing on the side. For a cool garnish like that served in the restaurant, spread some leaves of green leaf lettuce onto each plate, then spoon the pasta onto the lettuce. You may also toss the salad with the dressing ahead of time rather than serving it on the side. But don't do this too far in advance or the pasta tends to soak up the dressing.

• SERVES 4 AS A LUNCH OR LIGHT DINNER.

TIDBITS

Although I didn't detect it in the original vinaigrette dressing for this pasta salad, for best flavor I recommend substituting 1/2 clove of minced or grated garlic into the blend, for the 1/4 teaspoon of garlic powder.

LONE STAR
STEAKHOUSE & SALOON
BLACK BEAN SOUP

This restaurant boasts a unique "Texas roadhouse" ambiance. When you walk into any Lone Star restaurant, the first thing you'll notice is the crackling of peanut shells beneath your feet. When you're seated you get your own free bucket of peanuts to munch on, and you just flip the shells onto the wood plank floors. Western music plays over the speakers, and every hour or so the wait staff breaks into a funky little honky tonk line dance next to your table while the crunching peanut shells add a unique percussion element.

The spicy black bean soup is a popular item on the Lone Star menu. Here's a way to make a version of your own that can be served as an appetizer or as a meal in itself. It's great with a garnish of freshly diced red onion, jalapeños, and sour cream on top.

2 15-ounce cans black beans
1/4 cup diced red onion
2 teaspoons chopped pickled
   jalapeño slices ("nacho slices")
1 teaspoon sugar

1 teaspoon cider or wine vinegar
2 cloves garlic, minced
1/4 teaspoon salt
1/4 teaspoon cayenne pepper
1/2 teaspoon chili powder

GARNISH
4 teaspoons chopped red onion

6 to 8 jalapeño slices
1 tablespoon sour cream

1. Pour the canned beans along with the liquid into a medium saucepan. Add the remaining soup ingredients and mix.
2. Bring the soup to a boil, then reduce the heat to low and simmer, covered, for about 1 hour, adding water if necessary or until it's as thick as you like.
3. Serve each bowl of soup with a garnish of red onion, jalapeño slices, and sour cream arranged carefully in the center of the soup.

• SERVES 4 AS AN APPETIZER, 2 AS AN ENTREE.

TIDBITS

This soup is also very good with a bit of chopped fresh cilantro added to it while simmering and/or as a garnish. You may want to try some shredded Cheddar or Monterey Jack cheese on top as well.

•　•　•　•

LONE STAR STEAKHOUSE & SALOON TEXAS RICE

☆　　✌　　💣　　✏　　☯　　✂　　☞

The best selling menu items at the Lone Star Steakhouse & Saloon are the mesquite grilled steaks. The USDA choice-graded steaks are hand-cut fresh daily and displayed in a glass meat counter that is visible from the dining area of each restaurant. Customers are encouraged to view the meat for themselves and personally select the steak they wish to eat.

Even though much of the beef, chicken, and fish served at the restaurant is mesquite grilled, you may not have the equipment to cook your meat that way. Never fear, you can still have this popular and tasty side dish alongside another entree or steak cooked up any way you like. Rice this good goes with just about anything.

2 cups beef stock or canned beef
　　broth
　　1 cup uncooked long grain
　　parboiled or converted (**not**
　　instant or quick) white rice
　　1 tablespoon vegetable oil

1/3 cup diced white onion
3 to 4 mushrooms, sliced
1/2 cup frozen peas
1/4 teaspoon chili powder
1/4 teaspoon salt

1. Bring the beef stock to a boil over high heat in a medium saucepan.
2. Add the rice to the stock, cover the pan, reduce heat to low, and simmer for 20 minutes.

3. When the rice has cooked for about 10 minutes, heat the oil in a skillet over medium heat.
4. When the oil is hot, add the onion and mushrooms to the pan and sauté for 5 minutes.
5. When the rice is done, pour it into the skillet with the mushrooms and onion. Turn the heat to medium/low and add the frozen peas, chili powder, and salt to the rice. Heat the mixture, stirring often, for 3 to 4 minutes or until the peas are tender.

- SERVES 2 AS A SIDE DISH.

TIDBITS

It's important that you use converted or parboiled rice for this recipe, and others that call for white rice. Sure, this type of rice may take longer to cook than instant rice, but all its nutrients and taste haven't been stripped out—which is exactly what happens in the process that creates the popular quick-cooking, 5-minute stuff. You don't need that junk. Converted rice is one of the best rices to use in cooking because it doesn't get too mushy or sticky, and the grains don't easily split open.

• • • •

LONE STAR STEAKHOUSE & SALOON SWEET BOURBON SALMON

MENU DESCRIPTION: *"Fresh salmon filet, marinated and mesquite grilled."*

It is said that Americans eat an estimated 63 pounds of beef per capita, and we get a lot of it in chain restaurants. But for those of you who want something other than beef, Lone Star has additional selections including the Sweet Bourbon Salmon.

Don't worry if you can't mesquite grill your salmon, it's the sweet bourbon marinade that makes this dish so tasty. Not only is this marinade good on salmon, but on other fish and chicken as well. If you do happen to use a charcoal grill and have some mesquite smoking chips on hand, soak a handful of chips in water for a couple hours and then arrange them on the red-hot coals. This will give your salmon a taste even closer to the original.

SWEET BOURBON MARINADE

1/4 cup pineapple juice
2 tablespoons soy sauce
2 tablespoons brown sugar
1 teaspoon Kentucky bourbon

1/4 teaspoon cracked black
    pepper
1/8 teaspoon garlic powder
1/2 cup vegetable oil

2 8-ounce salmon
    fillets

2 teaspoons snipped fresh
    chives

1. Combine the pineapple juice, soy sauce, brown sugar, bourbon, pepper and garlic powder in a medium bowl. Stir to dissolve the sugar. Add the oil.
2. Be sure all of the skin is removed from the salmon. Place the fillets in a shallow dish and pour the bourbon marinade over them, saving a little to brush on the fish as it cooks. Put a lid over the fish and refrigerate for at least an hour. A few hours is even better.
3. Preheat your barbecue or stovetop grill over medium/high heat.
4. Cook the fish for 5 to 7 minutes per side or until each fillet is cooked all the way through. Regularly brush the fillets with the marinade.
5. Arrange the fillets on each plate with the chives sprinkled over the top.

• SERVES 2 AS AN ENTREE.

• • • •

MARIE CALLENDER'S CHICKEN POT PIE

MENU DESCRIPTION: *"Tender chunks of chicken with seasonings and vegetables."*

All the Marie Callender's restaurants try to maintain a homestyle ambiance, kind of like being at Grandma's house for dinner. The wallcoverings reflect styles of the thirties and forties and are complemented by dark mahogany-stained, wood-paneled walls and brass fixtures. You'll also find old-fashioned furnishings, many of them throwbacks to the forties, the time of this restaurant chain's founding fifty years ago.

The menu, which features meatloaf, pot roast, and country fried steak, reflects a satisfying homestyle cuisine that today is all too rare. If you wondered whether a company that is known for its great dessert pies could make a great pot pie ... it can.

For this recipe, try to use small 16-ounce casserole dishes that measure 4 or 5 inches across at the top. Any casserole dishes that come close to this size will probably work; the yield will vary depending on what size dishes you decide to use.

CRUST
1 1/2 cups all-purpose flour
3/4 teaspoon salt
2 egg yolks

3 tablespoons ice water
2/3 cup cold butter

FILLING
1 cup sliced carrots (3 carrots)
1 cup sliced celery (1 stalk)
2 cups frozen peas
1 cup chopped white onion
4 boneless, skinless chicken breast
    halves

4 tablespoons butter
5 tablespoons all-purpose flour
2 1/2 cups chicken broth
2/3 cup milk
1/2 teaspoon salt
dash pepper
1 egg, beaten

1. Prepare the crust by sifting together the flour and salt in a medium bowl. Make a depression in the center of the flour with your hand.
2. Put the yolks and ice water into the depression. Slice the butter into tablespoon-size portions and add it into the flour depression as well.
3. Using a fork, cut the wet ingredients into the dry ingredients. When all of the flour is moistened, use your hands to finish combining the ingredients. This will ensure that the chunks of butter are well blended into the dough. Roll the dough into a ball, cover it with plastic wrap and put it into the refrigerator for 1 to 2 hours. This will make the dough easier to work with.
4. When the dough has chilled, preheat the oven to 425°F and start on the filling by steaming the vegetables. Steam the carrots and celery for 5 minutes in a steamer or a saucepan with a small amount of water in the bottom. Add the frozen peas and onions and continue to steam for an additional 10 to 12 minutes or until the carrots are tender.
5. Prepare the chicken by poaching the breasts in lightly salted boiling water for 8 to 10 minutes.
6. In a separate large saucepan, melt the butter over medium heat, remove from the heat, then add the flour and whisk together until smooth. Add the chicken broth and milk and continue stirring over high heat until the mixture comes to a boil. Cook for an additional minute or so until thick, then reduce the heat to low.
7. Cut the poached chicken into large bite-size chunks and add them to the sauce. Add the salt and a dash of pepper.
8. Add the steamed vegetables to the sauce and simmer the mixture over medium/low heat for 4 to 5 minutes.
9. As the filling simmers, roll out the dough on a floured surface. Use one of the casserole dishes you plan to bake the pies in as a guide for cutting the dough. The filling will fit four 16-ounce casserole dishes perfectly, but you can use just about any size single-serving casserole dishes or oven-safe bowls for this recipe. Invert one of the dishes onto the dough and use a knife to cut around the rim. Make the cut about a half-inch larger all

of the way around to give the dough a small "lip," which you will fold over when you cover the pie. Make four of these.

10. Spoon the chicken and vegetable filling into each casserole dish and carefully cover each dish with the cut dough. Fold the edge of the dough over the edge of each dish and press firmly so that the dough sticks to the outer rim. Brush some beaten egg on the dough on each pie.

11. Bake the pies on a cookie sheet for 30 to 45 minutes or until the top crust is light brown.

• SERVES 4.

•   •   •   •

MARIE CALLENDER'S
BANANA CREAM PIE

☆   ✌   💣   ✎   ☯   ✂   ☞

MENU DESCRIPTION: *"Fresh ripe bananas in our rich vanilla cream, topped with fresh whipped cream or fluffy meringue."*

Bakers get to work by 5 A.M. at Marie Callender's to begin baking over 30 varieties of pies. Huge pies. Pies that weigh nearly three pounds apiece. The fresh, creamy, flaky, delicious pies that have made Marie Callender's famous in the food biz. On those mornings about 250 pies will be made at each of the 147 restaurants. Modest, I suppose, when compared with Thanksgiving Day when the stores can make up to 3,500 pies each.

For now though, we'll start with just one—banana cream pie with flaky crust, whipped cream, and slivered almonds on top. This recipe requires that you bake the crust unfilled, so you will have to use a pie weight or other oven-safe object to keep the crust from puffing up. Large pie weights are sold in many stores, or you can use small metal or ceramic weights (sold in packages) or dried beans on the crust which has first been lined with aluminum foil or parchment paper.

1/4 cup butter	1/4 teaspoon salt
1/4 cup shortening	1 egg yolk
1 1/4 cups all-purpose flour	2 tablespoons ice water
1 tablespoon sugar	1/2 teaspoon vinegar

FILLING

2/3 cup sugar	4 egg yolks, beaten
1/4 cup cornstarch	1 tablespoon butter
1/2 teaspoon salt	2 teaspoons vanilla
2 3/4 cups whole milk	2 ripe bananas, sliced

TOPPING

I can whipped cream   *¹/₄ cup slivered almonds*

1. Beat together the butter and shortening until smooth and creamy and chill until firm.
2. Sift together the flour, sugar, and salt in a medium bowl.

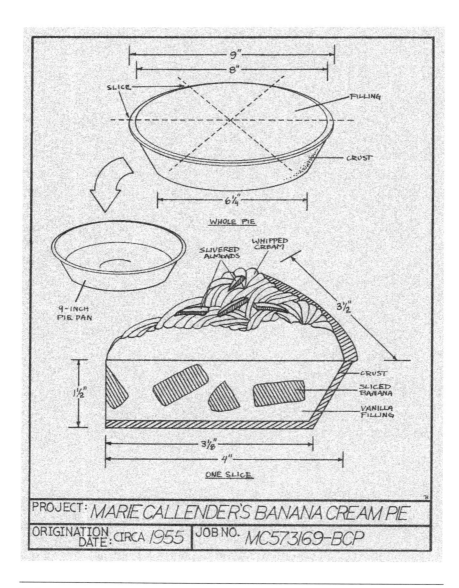

PROJECT: *MARIE CALLENDER'S BANANA CREAM PIE*

ORIGINATION DATE: CIRCA *1955*   JOB NO. *MC573169-BCP*

3. Using a fork, cut the butter and shortening into the dry ingredients, until the mixture has a consistent texture. Mix egg yolk, ice water, and vinegar into the dough, then form it into a ball and refrigerate it for 1 hour so that it will be easier to work with.

4. Preheat the oven to 450°F. When the dough has chilled, roll it out and press it into a 9-inch pie plate.

5. Press parchment paper or aluminum foil into the crust and weight the crust down with a ceramic pie weight or another pie pan filled with dried beans. This will prevent the crust from puffing up and distorting. Bake for 15 minutes, then remove the weight or pan filled with beans and prick the crust with a fork to allow steam to escape. Bake for another 5 to 10 minutes, or until the crust is golden brown. Let the crust cool.

6. Make the filling by sifting together the sugar, cornstarch, and salt into a medium saucepan.

7. Blend the milk, eggs, and butter in a medium bowl, then add the mixture to the dry ingredients and cook over medium heat stirring constantly for 6 to 8 minutes or until the mixture boils and thickens, then cook for 1 minute more.

8. Remove the filling from the heat, and mix in the vanilla.

9. Put plastic wrap on the surface of the filling and let it cool to about room temperature. The plastic wrap will prevent the top of the filling from becoming gummy.

10. When the filling has cooled, remove the plastic wrap and add the sliced bananas. Stir.

11. Pour the filling into the pie shell and chill for a couple of hours before serving. Slice across the pie 3 times to make 6 large slices. Serve each slice topped with fresh whipped cream and slivered almonds.

- SERVES 6.

•   •   •   •

PIZZA HUT
TRIPLEDECKER PIZZA

MENU DESCRIPTION: *"We start with a thin layer of crust, then we lay down a luscious layer of our six-cheese blend and seal it in with another thin layer of crust. We pile on your favorite Pizza Hut toppings, more cheese and bake it to gooey perfection."*

You might be as surprised as I was to learn that Pizza Hut uses 2.5 percent of all the milk produced in the U.S. every year for the cheese used on the pizzas. We're talking about a lot of pizzas here—1.3 million served every day. The cheese production alone requires a herd of 250,000 dairy cows producing at full capacity 365 days a year!

Certainly even more overworked cows had to be recruited to produce the additional cheese needed for this gooey new creation. This special pizza is made with two crispy cracker-like crusts that have a hidden layer of six cheeses cooked between them. Because this pizza requires two crusts, Pizza Hut created a dough that does not rise as much as the dough used in their other pizzas. This version has been adapted from a classic recipe for soda crackers. The finished product is surely the perfect pizza for people who think they just don't get enough cheese in their diet.

CRUST

¾ teaspoon yeast
1 cup warm water (105 degrees to 115 degrees F)
3¾ cups all-purpose flour

2 teaspoons salt
½ teaspoon baking soda
3 tablespoons shortening
¼ cup milk

SAUCE

1 15-ounce can tomato sauce
1/4 teaspoon dried oregano
1/4 teaspoon dried basil leaves
1/4 teaspoon dried thyme
1/4 teaspoon garlic powder
1/4 teaspoon salt
1/8 teaspoon ground black pepper
1 bay leaf
1/2 teaspoon lemon juice
dash onion powder

SIX-CHEESE BLEND

1/3 cup shredded Cheddar cheese
1/3 cup shredded Monterey Jack
   cheese
1/2 cup shredded mozzarella cheese

2 tablespoons shredded provolone
1 tablespoon grated Parmesan
   cheese
1 tablespoon grated Romano cheese

1 1/2 cups shredded mozzarella
   cheese

TOPPINGS (YOUR CHOICE OF . . .)

pepperoni slices, chopped onions, sliced mushrooms, sliced black olives, sliced
   jalapeños ("nacho slices"), sliced green peppers, pineapple chunks,
   Italian sausage, sliced tomatoes, sliced ham, anchovies

1. To prepare the crust, dissolve the yeast with the warm water in a small bowl or measuring cup and let it sit for 5 minutes.
2. Sift the flour, salt, and baking soda together in a large bowl.
3. Cut the shortening into the flour and mix the ingredients together with your hands until the shortening is reduced to tiny pea-size pieces.
4. Make an indention in the flour and pour in the milk and yeast mixture. Using a fork, stir the liquid around in the center, slowly drawing in more flour as you stir. When all of the flour is moistened and you can no longer stir with a fork, use your hands to combine the ingredients into a ball.
5. On a lightly floured surface, knead the dough with the heel of

your hands. Continue kneading until the dough is smooth and silky, about 10 minutes.

6. Form the dough into a ball and put it into a large bowl covered with plastic wrap. Let the dough rise in a warm place for about 2 hours. After 2 hours, place the covered container into the refrigerator to rise overnight. Take the dough out of the refrig-

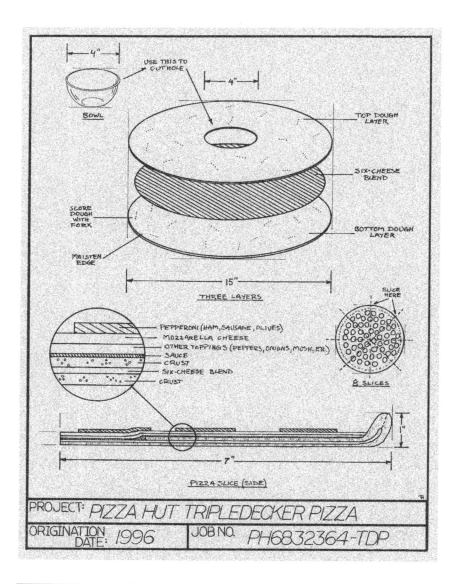

PROJECT: PIZZA HUT TRIPLEDECKER PIZZA

ORIGINATION DATE: 1996   JOB NO. PH6832364-TDP

erator 2 hours before you plan to cook the pizza so that the dough can warm up to room temperature.

7. You may want to make the pizza sauce a day ahead as well, at the same time as you prepare the dough. Combine all of the ingredients in a small saucepan over medium heat until it bubbles. Reduce the heat and simmer for about 1 hour. When the sauce is cool, store it in the refrigerator.

8. Preheat the oven to 475°F. Divide the dough in half, and form the two halves into balls. On a floured surface roll out each of the dough balls until they form thin 15-inch circles. Use a fork to poke the dough several times on the surface. This will keep the crust from bubbling. Place one of the crusts on a pizza pan that has been well-greased or sprinkled with cornmeal.

9. Combine the six cheeses to make the blend for the second layer. Sprinkle the cheese blend evenly over the pizza crust in the pan. Leave about a half-inch margin around the outside edge of the dough. Moisten the dough by brushing some water around the outside edge in that margin.

10. While the top pizza dough sits on a hard, floured surface, use an inverted bowl with a 4-inch diameter as a guide to cut a 4-inch circle out of the center of the dough. This is to keep the crusts from separating at the tip of each pizza slice when cut. Carefully place the dough on top of the cheese layer and crimp the edges together. Bend the crust up to form a lip. Brush some olive oil just on that lip all of the way around the pizza.

11. Spread the pizza sauce over the surface of the top pizza dough layer to the lip around the edge.

12. Sprinkle any vegetable toppings (or pineapple) on the pizza sauce. Sprinkle the 1½ cups mozzarella cheese over the pizza to the lip around the edge. Place any meat toppings or the olives on top of the cheese.

13. Bake the pizza for 12 to 15 minutes.

14. Slice the pizza 4 times through the center, making 8 slices.

- SERVES 3 TO 4.

• • • •

PLANET HOLLYWOOD PIZZA BREAD

MENU DESCRIPTION: *"Fresh baked on premises, sliced into eight pieces, brushed with garlic butter, Parmesan cheese, mozzarella and basil, topped with chopped plum tomatoes and herbed olive oil."*

In 1988, London-born restaurant mogul Robert Ian Earl joined with movie producer Keith Barrish and a gaggle of celebrities including Arnold Schwarzenegger, Sylvester Stallone, Bruce Willis, and Demi Moore to start a Hollywood-themed restaurant that is on its way to becoming his most successful venture yet. In 1991, a gala star-studded affair in New York City celebrated the opening of the world's first Planet Hollywood.

But even the coolest theme restaurant won't fly if the food doesn't please. Earl told *Nation's Restaurant News,* "People don't eat themes—no concept in the world can succeed for long unless it also delivers great food at the right price." So Planet Hollywood has created a menu of delicious dishes rivaling food from national chains that don't have a theme to lean on.

The Pizza Bread appetizer comes highly recommended by Planet Hollywood servers. The "bread" is actually just pizza dough, rolled thin, with a light layer of cheese, basil, and tomato on top; then it's baked in a special pizza oven at the restaurant. Since most of us don't have these ovens at home, this recipe has been designed for a conventional gas or electric oven.

1 12-inch thin-crust uncooked pizza dough (see Tidbits)
1/2 teaspoon garlic salt
1 1/2 tablespoons butter, melted
1 cup shredded mozzarella cheese

2 tablespoons coarsely chopped fresh basil
1 small tomato, chopped (use a Roma or plum tomato if available)
2 tablespoons grated Parmesan cheese

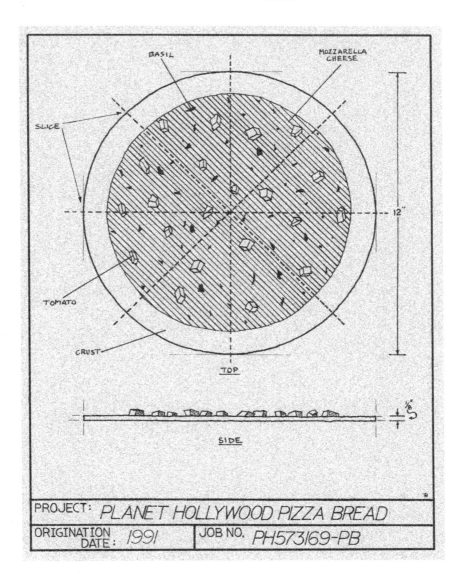

PROJECT: *PLANET HOLLYWOOD PIZZA BREAD*

ORIGINATION DATE: *1991*   JOB NO. *PH573169-PB*

1. Preheat the oven to 475⁰F.
2. If you are making your own crust, roll out the dough to a 12-inch diameter.
3. Mix the garlic salt with the butter.
4. Use a brush to coat the entire crust with garlic butter.
5. Spread half of the mozzarella cheese over the crust.
6. Spread the basil over the cheese.
7. Spread the remaining mozzarella over the basil.
8. Sprinkle the tomato over the cheese.
9. Bake for 8 to 10 minutes or until the surface begins to turn brown.
10. Remove the pizza bread from the oven and sprinkle the fresh Parmesan over it.
11. Slice into 8 pieces through the middle, like a pizza, and serve hot.

• SERVES 2 TO 4 AS AN APPETIZER.

TIDBITS

For the dough you can use the recipe for pizza dough from page 62, or a canned tube of pizza dough (such as Pillsbury), or an instant dough mix. You will need only about 1 cup of dough after rising, which is about half a tube of the Pillsbury-type dough. Of course, I highly recommend making the dough from scratch if you have time. There's nothing in a box or can that tastes as good as the home-made stuff.

•   •   •   •

PLANET HOLLYWOOD
CHICKEN CRUNCH

MENU DESCRIPTION: *"A basket of tender chicken breaded with Cap'n Crunch and seasonings, served with Creole mustard sauce."*

The Orlando, Florida Planet Hollywood, which had its big opening in 1994, pulls in yearly sales receipts totaling around $50 million, making it the highest volume restaurant in America. If you've never tried the Chicken Crunch at Planet Hollywood, you're missing a treat. Sliced chicken breast fingers are coated with a crunchy, slightly sweet breading combination of Cap'n Crunch cereal and cornflake crumbs. The chicken is then deep-fried to a golden brown and served with a tasty dipping sauce made from mayonnaise, horseradish, and Dijon mustard. You've probably tasted nothing like it.

CREOLE MUSTARD SAUCE

2 tablespoons Grey
    Poupon Country Dijon mustard
3 tablespoons mayonnaise

1 teaspoon yellow mustard
1 teaspoon cream-style horseradish
1 teaspoon honey

vegetable oil for frying
2 boneless, skinless chicken breast
    halves
2 cups Cap'n Crunch cereal
1/2 cup cornflake crumbs
1/2 teaspoon onion powder

1/2 teaspoon garlic powder
1/2 teaspoon salt
1/4 teaspoon white pepper
1 egg, beaten
1 cup milk

1. Preheat oil in a deep pan or deep fryer to 375⁰F. You want to use enough oil to completely cover the chicken 1 to 2 inches deep.
2. Combine all of the ingredients for the Creole mustard sauce in a small bowl and chill the sauce while the chicken is prepared.

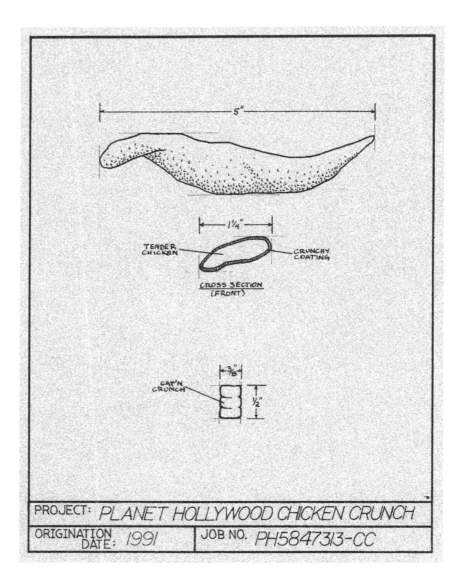

5"

1¼"

TENDER CHICKEN

CRUNCHY COATING

CROSS SECTION (FRONT)

CAP'N CRUNCH

⅜"

½"

PROJECT: PLANET HOLLYWOOD CHICKEN CRUNCH

ORIGINATION DATE: 1991

JOB NO. PH5847313-CC

3. Cut each chicken breast, lengthwise, into 5 long slices (chicken fingers).
4. Smash the Cap'n Crunch into crumbs using a food processor, or put the cereal into a plastic bag and start pounding.
5. Combine the cereals, onion powder, garlic powder, salt, and pepper in a medium bowl.
6. Combine the egg with the milk in a separate bowl.
7. Dredge each piece of chicken in the milk mixture, then completely coat it with the dry mixture. Do this for all the chicken before frying.
8. When the oil is hot, fry the chicken for 4 to 6 minutes or until golden to dark brown and crispy. Remove to paper towels or a rack to drain. Serve hot with Creole mustard sauce on the side for dipping.

• SERVES 2 TO 4 AS AN APPETIZER OR SNACK.

• • • •

PLANET HOLLYWOOD
POT STICKERS

☆   ✌   ●   ✎   ☯   ✂   ☞

MENU DESCRIPTION: *"Six pot stickers filled with fresh ground turkey meat seasoned with ginger, water chestnuts, red pepper and green onions. They are fried and served in a basket with spicy hoisin."*

Planet Hollywood is known for the film and television memorabilia displayed throughout the restaurants. Some of the items on display behind thick Plexiglas include the genie bottle from *I Dream of Jeannie*, Val Kilmer's bat suit from *Batman Forever*, Tom Hanks' costume from *Forrest Gump*, Judy Garland's dress from The Wizard of Oz, and the painting from the set of the television show *Friends*. In addition to the memorabilia is a wall at the entrance to each restaurant that displays handprints in plaster from the likes of Mel Gibson, Jimmy Stewart, Harrison Ford, Demi Moore, Samuel L. Jackson, Paul Newman, Goldie Hawn, Patrick Swayze, and many others.

Pot stickers are a popular Asian dumpling that can be fried, steamed, or simmered in a broth. Planet Hollywood has customized its version to make them crunchier than the traditional dish, and it's a tasty twist. Since hoisin sauce would be very difficult to make from scratch, you can use a commercial brand found in most stores.

<table>
<tr><td>¹/₄ pound ground turkey</td><td>¹/₄ teaspoon salt</td></tr>
<tr><td>¹/₂ teaspoon minced fresh ginger</td><td>¹/₈ teaspoon garlic powder</td></tr>
<tr><td>1 teaspoon minced green onion</td><td>¹/₂ teaspoon soy sauce</td></tr>
<tr><td>1 teaspoon minced water chestnuts</td><td>¹/₂ teaspoon ground black pepper</td></tr>
<tr><td>¹/₄ teaspoon crushed red pepper
    flakes (no seeds)</td><td>1 egg, beaten
vegetable oil for frying</td></tr>
</table>

1. In a small bowl, combine all the ingredients except the egg, wrappers, and oil. Add 1 tablespoon of the beaten egg. Save the rest of the egg for later. Preheat oil in a deep fryer or a deep saucepan to 375ºF. Use enough oil to cover the pot stickers—1 to 2 inches should be enough.

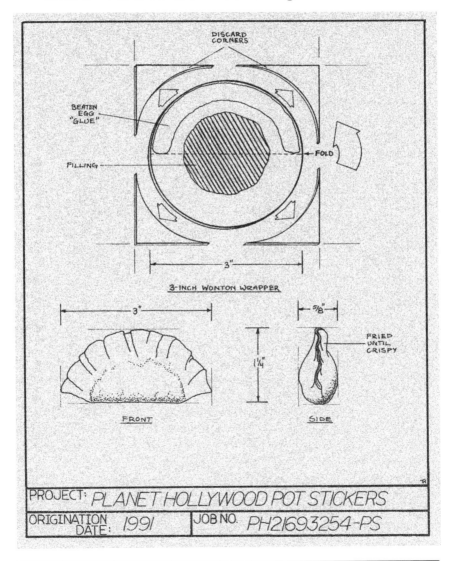

DISCARD CORNERS

BEATEN EGG "GLUE"

FILLING

FOLD

3"

3-INCH WONTON WRAPPER

3"

5/8"

FRIED UNTIL CRISPY

1¼"

FRONT

SIDE

PROJECT: *PLANET HOLLYWOOD POT STICKERS*

ORIGINATION DATE: *1991*   JOB NO. *PH21693254-PS*

2. Invert a small bowl or glass with a 3-inch diameter on the center of a wonton wrapper and cut around it to make a circle. Repeat for the remaining wrappers.
3. Spoon ½ tablespoon of the turkey filling into the center of one wrapper. Brush a little beaten egg around half of the edge of the wrapper and fold the wrapper over the filling. Gather the wrapper as you seal it, so that it is crinkled around the edge. Repeat with the remaining ingredients.
4. Deep-fry the pot stickers, six at a time, in the hot oil for 3 to 6 minutes or until they are brown. Drain on a rack or paper towels. Serve with the hoisin sauce for dipping. If you want a spicier sauce, add some more crushed red pepper or cayenne pepper to the sauce.

• SERVES 3 TO 6 AS AN APPETIZER OR SNACK.

TIDBITS

If you can't find wonton wrappers, you can also use eggroll wrappers for this recipe. Eggroll wrappers are much bigger, so you will be wasting more of the dough when you trim the wrappers to 3-inch-diameter circles. But in a pinch, this is a quick solution.

Pot sticker wrappers can also be found in some supermarkets, but I've found the wonton wrappers and eggroll wrappers, when fried, taste more like the restaurant version.

•　•　•　•

T.G.I. FRIDAY'S CALIFORNIA CHARGRILLED TURKEY SANDWICH

☆　　✌　　💣　　✏　　☯　　✂　　☞

MENU DESCRIPTION: *"Chargrilled all-white meat turkey burger, served on a toasted whole wheat bun with lettuce, tomatoes, alfalfa sprouts, onions and avocado."*

Noting the success of the first T.G.I. Friday's in New York City, a group of fun-loving Dallas businessmen opened the first franchise store. The investors decorated their Dallas T.G.I. Friday's with fun antiques and collectibles gathered from around the countryside—and now all of the Friday's are decorated that way. Six months after the opening of the Dallas location, waiters and waitresses began doing skits and riding bicycles and roller skates around the restaurant. That's also when the now defunct tradition of ringing in every Friday evolved. Thursday night at midnight was like a New Year's Eve party at T.G.I. Friday's, with champagne, confetti, noisemakers, and a guy jumping around in a gorilla suit as if he had a few too many espressos.

Here's a favorite of burger lovers who don't care where the beef is. It's an alternative to America's most popular food with turkey instead of beef, plus some alfalfa sprouts and avocado to give it a "California" twist.

HONEY MUSTARD SAUCE

1/4 cup mayonnaise	1 tablespoon honey
1 tablespoon yellow mustard (like French's)	1/2 teaspoon sesame oil
	1/2 teaspoon distilled vinegar

1 pound ground turkey (all-white
    meat if available)
salt
pepper
4 whole wheat hamburger buns
soft butter

4 romaine lettuce leaves
1/2 cup alfalfa sprouts
    (a handful)
1 medium tomato, sliced
1 to 2 slices white onion
1 ripe avocado, sliced

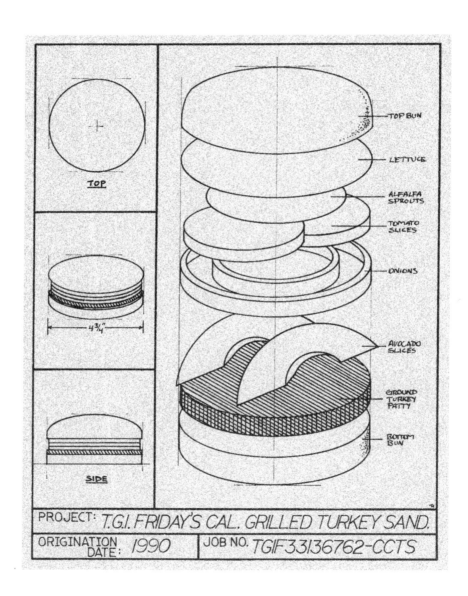

TOP

SIDE

4 3/4"

TOP BUN
LETTUCE
ALFALFA
SPROUTS
TOMATO
SLICES
ONIONS
AVOCADO
SLICES
GROUND
TURKEY
PATTY
BOTTOM
BUN

PROJECT: T.G.I. FRIDAY'S CAL. GRILLED TURKEY SAND.

ORIGINATION DATE: 1990

JOB NO. TGIF33136762-CCTS

1. Prepare the barbecue or preheat the stovetop grill.
2. Combine the mayonnaise, mustard, honey, oil, and vinegar in a small bowl. Cover and keep refrigerated until later.
3. Divide the ground turkey into four even portions and on wax paper pat out four ½-inch-thick patties with the same diameter as the buns.
4. Grill these patties for 6 to 8 minutes per side or until done. Be sure to salt and pepper both sides of each patty.
5. Prepare the buns by lightly buttering the face of the tops and bottoms, and then grilling them in a hot skillet until brown.
6. The sandwich is served "open face" so that the customer can put the hot side and the cold side together at the table (remember the McD.L.T?). Build the cold side of the sandwich by inverting the top bun and stacking the ingredients on it in the following order from the bottom up:
    a. top bun (face up)
    b. lettuce leaf
    c. alfalfa sprouts
    d. 1 to 2 tomato slices
    e. 2 onion rings (from the separated slices)
    f. 2 avocado slices
7. Arrange the bottom bun on the same plate. Add the hot ground turkey patty on the face of the bun and serve with the honey mustard dressing on the side.

- SERVES 4 AS AN ENTREE.

TIDBITS

Some tasty variations of this sandwich include adding slices of cooked bacon, or substituting barbecue sauce for the honey mustard.

• • • •

T.G.I. FRIDAY'S SPICY CAJUN CHICKEN PASTA

☆ ✌ 💣 ✎ ☯ ✂ ☞

MENU DESCRIPTION: *"Fettuccine tossed with sautéed chicken, mushrooms, onions and red and green peppers in Friday's own spicy, tomato Creole sauce."*

There are over 360 T.G.I. Friday's restaurants in 44 states and 22 countries, all serving this Cajun-style chicken pasta. This dish is a bit like a jambalaya except the rice has been replaced with pasta.

Use a large pan for this recipe, and note that for the chicken stock or broth, you can also use a chicken bouillon cube dissolved in boiling water.

This recipe makes two large restaurant-size portions, but could easily serve a family of four.

4 tablespoons (½ stick) butter
1 green bell pepper, chopped
    (1 cup)
1 red bell pepper, chopped
    (1 cup)
½ white onion, sliced and quartered
    (1 cup)
1 clove garlic, pressed
2 boneless, skinless chicken breast
    halves
2 teaspoons olive oil
1 medium tomato, chopped
4 to 6 mushrooms, sliced
    (1 ¼ cup)

1 cup chicken stock or
    1 chicken bouillon cube dissolved
    in 1 cup boiling water
salt
¼ teaspoon cayenne pepper
¼ teaspoon paprika
¼ teaspoon white pepper
¼ teaspoon dried thyme
4 to 6 quarts water
1 12-ounce box fettuccine
2 teaspoons chopped fresh parsley

1. Melt 2 tablespoons of the butter in a large skillet over medium/high heat.
2. Sauté the bell peppers, onions, and garlic in the butter for 8 to 10 minutes or until the vegetables begin to soften slightly.
3. As the vegetables are cooking, cut the chicken breasts into bite-size pieces.
4. Prepare a medium-size pan over high heat with the olive oil. When the pan is hot, add the chicken and cook, stirring, for 5 to 7 minutes or until the chicken shows no pink.
5. When the vegetables are soft (about 10 minutes) add the chicken to the pan.
6. Add the tomatoes, mushrooms, chicken stock, 1/4 teaspoon salt, cayenne pepper, paprika, white pepper, and thyme and continue to simmer for 10 to 12 minutes until it thickens.
7. In the meantime bring the water to a boil in a large pot. If you like, add a half tablespoon of salt to the water. Cook the fettuccine in the boiling water until done. This will take 10 to 12 minutes.
8. When the noodles are done, drain them and add the remaining 2 tablespoons of butter. The butter should melt quickly on the hot noodles. Toss the noodles to mix in the butter.
9. Serve the dish by dividing the noodles in half onto two plates. Divide the chicken and vegetable sauce evenly and spread it over the top of the noodles on each plate. Divide the parsley and sprinkle it over each serving.

- SERVES 2 AS A LARGE ENTREE.

TIDBITS

If you want a thicker sauce, combine 1/2 teaspoon arrowroot or corn-starch with 2 tablespoons of white wine in a small bowl and stir to dissolve. Remove the pan from the heat before adding this thickener, stir it in, then put it back on the heat.

• • • •

T.G.I. FRIDAY'S
FRIDAY'S SMOOTHIES

MENU DESCRIPTION: *"Healthful, nonalcoholic frozen fruit drinks."*
  "GOLD MEDALIST: *Coconut and pineapple, blended with grenadine, strawberries and bananas."*
  "TROPICAL RUNNER: *Fresh banana, pineapple and pina colada mix frozen with crushed ice."*

From the "obscure statistics" file, T.G.I. Friday's promotional material claims the restaurant was the first chain to offer stone-ground whole wheat bread as an option to its guests. It was also the first chain to put avocados, bean sprouts, and Mexican appetizers on its menu.

Also a first: Friday's Smoothies. In response to growing demand for nonalcoholic drinks, T.G.I. Friday's created smoothies, a fruit drink now found on many other restaurants' menus. Here are recipes to clone two of the nine fruit blend varieties. Great on a sizzling afternoon.

GOLD MEDALIST

8 ounces frozen strawberries (not in
     syrup—do not defrost)
1 banana
1 cup pineapple juice

2 tablespoons coconut cream
1/4 cup grenadine
1 cup ice
2 fresh strawberries
     (for garnish)

1. Pour all of the ingredients except the 2 fresh strawberries in the order listed into a blender and blend on high speed for 15 to 30 seconds or until all the ice is crushed and the drink is smooth.
2. Garnish each drink with a fresh strawberry.

TROPICAL RUNNER

1 banana

1 8-ounce can crushed pineapple
   with juice

1/2 cup liquid pina colada mix

1/2 cup orange sherbet

2 cups ice

1. Cut the banana in half and slice two 1/4-inch slices from the middle of the banana and set the two slices aside for garnish.
2. Put the rest of banana and the remaining ingredients into a blender in the order listed. Blend on high speed for 15 to 30 seconds, or until the drink is smooth and creamy.
3. Add 1 banana slice to the top of each drink as a garnish.

• Each recipe serves 2

TIDBITS

You've probably already thought of this, but these drinks make tasty cocktails too. Just add a little rum or vodka, and about 1/2 cup more ice, before blending.

• • • •

A&W
ROOT BEER

☆ ✌ 💣 ✏ ☯ ✂ ☞

On a hot summer afternoon in 1919, Roy Allen came up with a plan. He set up a roadside stand to sell cool drinks to spectators of a Veterans Day Parade in Lodi, California. For a nickel, thirsty parade-goers could knock back a tall glass of what would eventually become America's favorite root beer. The success of Allen's unique blend of roots, herbs, and berries led to three root beer concessions in Sacramento, California, all featuring carhop service—the first of the drive-in fast-food chains. Allen expanded his business further in 1922 when he formed a partnership with entrepreneur Frank Wright. This led to the name that would become famous, A&W, the country's best-selling root beer. In 1993 Cadbury Schweppes PLC, a British candy and beverage company, bought A&W Brands, Inc., for $334 million.

The root beer you'll make here is a simplified version of Roy Allen's method from the early 1900s. Instead of harvesting roots, herbs, and berries, you have the luxury of using a root beer concentrate that can be found in most grocery stores.

3/4 cup granulated sugar
3/4 cup hot water
1 liter cold seltzer water

1/2 teaspoon plus 1/8 teaspoon root beer concentrate (McCormick is best)

1. Dissolve the sugar in the hot water.
2. Add the root beer concentrate and let cool.

3. Combine the root beer mixture with the cold seltzer water, drink immediately, or store in refrigerator in tightly covered container.

• MAKES 5 CUPS.

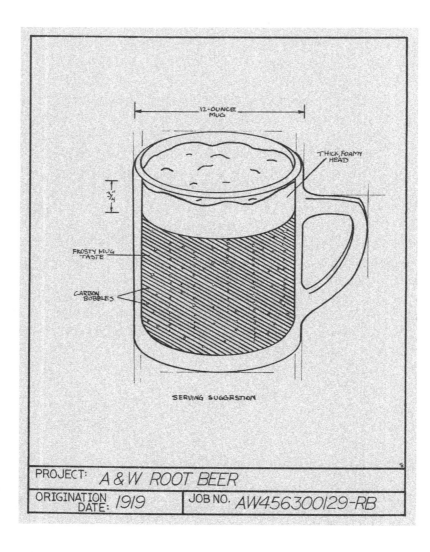

SERVING SUGGESTION

PROJECT: A & W ROOT BEER

ORIGINATION DATE: 1919   JOB NO. AW456300129-RB

JAMBA JUICE
STRAWBERRIES WILD

☆   🖐   💣   ✏   ☯   ✂   ☞

One of the most popular smoothie combinations around is strawberry-banana. This clone imitates Jamba's version, which adds apple juice and vanilla frozen yogurt to the mix. Look for the strawberry nectar in the juice aisle and warm up the blender.

¾ cup apple juice
¾ cup Kern's strawberry nectar
⅔ cup frozen whole strawberries
1 sliced banana

2 scoops fat-free vanilla frozen yogurt
1 cup ice

Combine all ingredients in a blender and blend on high speed until all the ice is crushed and the drink is smooth.

• MAKES 1 24-OUNCE DRINK.

• • • •

LIPTON BRISK
ICED TEA

Here's a great technique for re-creating the lemony zing in a can of Brisk Iced Tea that'll make those angry little celebrity puppets in the commercials even angrier. Kool-Aid lemonade drink mix has the perfect mixture of citric acid and lemon juice solids to help us effortlessly clone this one over and over again. Puppets don't scare us.

3 Lipton tea bags (regular size)
I cup plus 2 tablespoons granulated
    sugar

½ teaspoon Kool-Aid lemonade
    unsweetened drink mix

1. Bring 2 quarts of water to a boil in a large saucepan. Add the tea bags and remove the pan from the heat. Let the tea steep for at least an hour.
2. Pour the granulated sugar and Kool-Aid drink mix into a 2-quart pitcher. Add the tea and stir so that the sugar dissolves. Add additional water if necessary to bring the tea to the 2-quart mark on the pitcher. Chill well before serving.

• MAKES 2 QUARTS.

• • • •

MCDONALD'S MCFLURRY

These 16-ounce desserts-in-a-cup are made with McDonald's soft-serve ice cream and one of several crumbled sweet additives. Duplicating soft-serve ice cream at home comes easy using regular vanilla ice cream (not French vanilla), a little whole milk, and a frozen bowl to do the mixing. You might also want to freeze the glass that you plan to serve this in to ensure the ice cream is served up creamy yet firm, rather than melted and soupy.

BUTTERFINGER

2 cups vanilla ice cream
¼ cup milk

⅔ Butterfinger candy bar

1. Freeze a medium glass or ceramic bowl in the freezer for at least 30 minutes. Freeze the Butterfinger candy bar (in a plastic bag) as well, along with the 16-ounce glass you plan to use.
2. When the bowl is frozen, first break your candy bar (while it's still in the bag) into little pieces with the handle of a butter knife.
3. Pour the ice cream and milk into the frozen bowl and stir well until smooth and creamy.
4. Add the candy bar pieces and stir, then pour into the frozen 16-ounce glass and serve with a spoon.

• MAKES 1 16-OUNCE DESSERT.

M&M'S

2 cups vanilla ice cream
¼ cup milk

¼ cup (1 mega-tube) M&M's Minis

1. Freeze a medium glass or ceramic bowl in the freezer for at least 30 minutes. While you're at it put the 16-ounce glass you plan to use in there as well.
2. When the bowl is frozen, pour the ice cream and milk into the frozen bowl and stir well until smooth and creamy.
3. Add the M&M's and stir, then pour it all into the frozen 16-ounce glass and serve with a spoon.

- MAKES 1 16-OUNCE DESSERT.

OREO COOKIE

2 cups vanilla ice cream
¼ cup milk

3 Oreo cookies

1. Freeze a medium glass or ceramic bowl in the freezer for at least 30 minutes. While you're at it put the 16-ounce glass you plan to use in there as well.
2. When the bowl is frozen, crumble the cookies (in a plastic bag) into little pieces with your fist or the handle of a butter knife.
3. Pour the ice cream and milk into the frozen bowl and stir well until smooth and creamy.
4. Add the Oreo cookie pieces and stir, then pour it all into the frozen 16-ounce glass and serve with a spoon.

- MAKES 1 16-OUNCE DESSERT.

REESE'S

2 cups vanilla ice cream
¼ cup milk

2 Reese's Peanut Butter Cups
  (1 package)

1. Freeze a medium glass or ceramic bowl in the freezer for at least 30 minutes. Freeze the peanut butter cups in a plastic bag, and while you're at it put the 16-ounce glass you plan to use in there as well.
2. When the bowl is frozen, break the peanut butter cups (while still in the bag) into little pieces with the handle of a butter knife.
3. Pour the ice cream and milk into the frozen bowl and stir well until smooth and creamy.
4. Add the candy pieces and stir, then pour into the frozen 16-ounce glass and serve with a spoon.

• Makes 1 16-ounce dessert.

• • • •

MINUTE MAID
ALL NATURAL LEMONADE

Minute Maid is credited with creating the modern orange juice industry by marketing the first frozen concentrated orange juice in 1946. Today the company is owned by The Coca-Cola Company and sells juices, punches, and fruit drinks in countries all over the world. Minute Maid also sells one of the most recognized brands of lemonade, made from lemon concentrate. You can easily duplicate the taste of the drink at home, but since this *TSR* version is made with fresh lemons, it might just edge out the real thing in a side-by-side taste test.

½ cup fresh-squeezed lemon juice
   (from 2 to 3 lemons)
3¼ cups water

¼ cup plus 3 tablespoons granulated
   sugar

Combine the lemon juice with the water and sugar in a 1-quart pitcher. Stir or shake the pitcher vigorously until all the sugar is dissolved. Cover and chill.

• MAKES 1 QUART.

•   •   •   •

ORANGE JULIUS
BANANA JULIUS

☆   ✌   💣   ✏   ☯   ✂   ☞

It may be called Banana Julius, but there's also a little orange juice in there. Make sure your bananas are ripe for this clone so you get a nice sweet drink with the perfect thickness.

½ cup orange juice
3 tablespoons pasteurized egg white
   or egg substitute
1 teaspoon vanilla

¼ cup sugar
2 medium ripe bananas
3 cups ice

1. Combine all ingredients except bananas and ice in a blender and blend on high speed for 15 seconds or until sugar is dissolved.
2. Add bananas and ice and blend until ice is crushed. Pour into two 16-ounce glasses, add a straw and serve.

• MAKES 2 REGULAR-SIZE DRINKS.

• • • •

ORANGE JULIUS
STRAWBERRY-BANANA
CLASSIC SMOOTHY

☆　　✌　　💣　　✏　　☯　　✂　　☞

As the trend for fruit smoothies developed in the 1990s, the Orange Julius company didn't want to be left out. After all, Orange Julius developed what was the first smoothies on the block with the original Orange Julius blended drink back in 1926. But as thicker smoothie drinks of more complex blends became popular, Orange Julius set out to put its own twist on the fruity beverage by using a special additive called "coconut-almond compound" (and then trademarked a unique spelling of the word "smoothie" using a "Y"). In addition to a scoop of the compound that's added to the original Orange Julius drinks, servers add a scoop of this new powder to the drink. In that secret powder are some thickening agents such as powdered egg whites and flavors that include coconut and almond. So, here now is how you can clone your own version of the most popular flavor of the chain's Classic Smoothie using common coconut syrup and almond extract as part of your own secret "compound."

½ cup orange juice
3 tablespoons pasteurized egg white
　　or egg substitute
1 teaspoon vanilla
¼ cup sugar
¼ cup milk

¼ cup coconut syrup (such as Coco
　　Lopez)
¼ teaspoon almond extract
2 medium ripe bananas
1 10-ounce box frozen strawberries
　　in syrup, thawed
3 cups ice

1. Combine all ingredients except banana, strawberries, and ice in a blender and blend on high speed for 15 seconds or until sugar is dissolved.
2. Add banana, strawberries and ice and blend until ice is crushed. Pour into two 16-ounce glasses, add a straw, and serve.

• Makes 2 regular-size drinks.

• • • •

ORANGE SLICE

To make your own version of the syrup for this orange soda that comes to us from the Pepsi-Cola Company, you need to combine a simple syrup recipe with two popular versions of dry orange drink mix: Kool-Aid orange unsweetened drink mix and Tang. But unlike the real thing that "contains no juice," your homemade version includes a bit of real orange juice solids that come powdered into every scoop of Tang mix. After you make the syrup, be sure to let it cool in the refrigerator before you combine it with cold soda water to make a perfect finished product.

1 cup granulated sugar
1 cup corn syrup
1 0.15-ounce package Kool-Aid
   orange unsweetened drink mix

1 tablespoon Tang orange drink mix
1 1/4 cups boiling water

8 cups cold soda water

1. Combine sugar, corn syrup, and drink mix powders in a medium pitcher or bowl. Add boiling water and stir until sugar has dissolved and syrup is clear. Cover and chill this syrup for several hours until cold.
2. To make the soda, add 1/3 cup of cold syrup to 1 cup of cold soda water (1 to 3 ratio). Stir gently, drop in some ice, and serve.

• MAKES 8 13-OUNCE SERVINGS.

STARBUCKS CARAMEL MACCHIATO

☆   ✌   💣   ✏   ☯   ✂   ☞

If you've got an espresso/cappuccino machine, you're well on your way to re-creating a top-choice Starbucks coffee drink. For the caramel part, you can use any caramel sauce that you find in the grocery store near the ice-cream toppings. Pick your favorite. Just note that to make this recipe work best, you'll only need 3 table-spoons of a richer caramel sauce (like the stuff Starbucks uses), but more like 4 tablespoons of a lighter sauce (such as fat-free Smuckers). For the vanilla syrup you can use the bottled syrups, such as those made by Torani, or just whip up your own clone from scratch. By the way, if you want to make this clone super accurate, pick up bottles of the authentic vanilla syrup and caramel sauce sold in Starbucks stores.

VANILLA SYRUP

2 cups water
1 1/2 cups granulated sugar
3/4 teaspoon vanilla extract

1/2 cup fresh espresso
8 ounces milk, steamed with foam
3 to 4 tablespoons caramel sauce

1. You can use vanilla syrup from a bottle for the drink or make your own vanilla syrup following this Top Secret Recipe: Simply combine 2 cups water and 1 1/2 cups sugar in a medium saucepan and bring to a boil. Reduce heat and simmer for 5 minutes, then add 3/4 teaspoon vanilla extract. Remove from heat and cool. Store in a covered container.

2. To make your coffee drink, add two tablespoons of vanilla syrup to a 16-ounce glass. Add ½ cup fresh brewed espresso followed by 8 ounces of steamed milk.
3. Add 3 to 4 tablespoons caramel sauce to the drink. Stir before drinking.

• MAKES ONE 16-OUNCE DRINK (GRANDE SIZE).

•   •   •   •

STARBUCKS
GINGERBREAD LATTE

☆ ✌ 💣 ✏ ☯ ✂ ☞

As the winter holidays come around, so too does this incredible latte from Starbucks. Into the coffee house's basic latte recipe go a few pumps of special gingerbread-flavored syrup, and we soon experience the combined sensation of munching on a gingerbread cookie while sipping hot, milky java. Nice! To re-create the experience at home, holidays or not, all we have to do is make our own gingerbread syrup with a few common ingredients. When the syrup is done, simply brew some espresso in your espresso machine, steam some hot milk, and throw it all in cup. Top off your latte with whipped cream and a dash of nutmeg as they do at the store, and you'll fool anyone with this hot little clone. By the way, this recipe is for a single grande-size latte, but you'll have enough syrup left over for as many as seven drinks.

GINGERBREAD SYRUP

2 cups water
1 ½ cups granulated sugar
2½ teaspoons ground ginger
½ teaspoon ground cinnamon

½ teaspoon vanilla extract

½ cup fresh espresso
8 ounces milk, steamed (with a little foam)

GARNISH

whipped cream

ground nutmeg

1. Make the gingerbread syrup by combining water, sugar, ginger, cinnamon, and vanilla in a medium saucepan. Be sure the pan is not too small or the mixture could easily bubble over.
2. Bring mixture to a boil, then reduce heat and simmer syrup, uncovered, for 15 minutes. Remove the syrup from the heat when it's done and slap a lid on it.
3. Make a double shot of espresso ($\frac{1}{2}$ cup), using an espresso machine. Use the machine to steam 8 ounces of milk, or heat up the milk in the microwave if your machine does not foam and steam milk.
4. Make your latte by first adding $\frac{1}{2}$ cup espresso to a 16-ounce cup. Add $\frac{1}{4}$ cup gingerbread syrup, followed by the steamed milk. Stir.
5. Top off the drink with a dollop of whipped cream and a sprinkle of nutmeg.

• MAKES 1 16-OUNCE DRINK (GRANDE SIZE).

•   •   •   •

STARBUCKS MOCHA COCONUT FRAPPUCCINO

☆ ✌ ● ✎ ☯ ✂ ☞

Here's one of Starbucks' newest delights that's like a cold Mounds bar in a cup with a caffeine kick thrown in for extra buzzing. Find shredded coconut in the baking aisle and toast ½ cup of it (Store the leftover coconut in the fridge.). You'll use most of the toasted coconut in the blender, but save a little for the garnish when the drinks are done.

½ cup shredded coconut
¾ cup cold double-strength coffee
1 cup low-fat milk

⅓ cup Hershey's chocolate syrup
3 tablespoons granulated sugar
2 cups ice

GARNISH
whipped cream

1. Preheat oven to 300ºF. Spread shredded coconut on a baking sheet and toast coconut in the oven. Stir the coconut around every 10 minutes or so for even browning. After 25 to 30 minutes the shredded coconut should be light brown. Allow to cool.
2. Make double-strength coffee by brewing with twice the coffee required by your coffee maker. That should be 2 tablespoons of ground coffee per each cup of coffee. Chill before using.

3. To make the drinks, combine cold coffee, milk, $\frac{1}{3}$ cup of the toasted coconut, $\frac{1}{3}$ cup chocolate syrup, and sugar in a blender. Blend for 15 to 20 seconds to dissolve sugar. Add ice and blend until ice is crushed and the drink is smooth. Pour drinks into two 16-ounce glasses. Garnish each drink with whipped cream, a drizzle of chocolate, and a pinch of some of the remaining toasted coconut. Add a straw to each one.

• MAKES 2 16-OUNCE DRINKS (GRANDE SIZE).

• • • •

STARBUCKS TAZOBERRY TEA

☆ ✌ ☄ ✐ ☯ ✂ ☞

Check out the menu board at any Starbucks and you'll find this frozen drink described as a blend of raspberry and other fruit juices plus Starbucks' own Tazo brand tea. We've discovered that those other fruit juices include white grape juice, aroniaberry, cranberry, and blackberry. Since aroniaberry juice is next to impossible to track down in a local supermarket, we'll have to make a taste-alike drink with a combination of just the other, more important flavors. Grab the raspberry syrup and a jar of seedless blackberry jam made by Knott's Berry Farm, and brew up a little tea. Starbucks uses Tazo black tea for the drink, but you can use the more common Lipton tea bags. You will only use ⅓ cup of the tea for this 1-serving recipe, so you'll have plenty left over for additional servings, or for a quick iced tea fix.

4 cups water
1 tea bag
¼ cup Ocean Spray cranberry/
    raspberry juice
2 tablespoons concentrated white
    grape juice, thawed

2 tablespoons Knott's Berry Farm
    raspberry syrup
1 tablespoon Knott's Berry Farm
    seedless blackberry jam
1 teaspoon lemon juice
2 cups ice

1. First brew the tea by bringing 4 cups of water to a rapid boil. Turn off the heat, drop in the tea bag, and let the tea steep for an hour or so. Remove the tea bag and put the tea into the refrigerator to chill.

2. When the tea is cold, make your drink by pouring juices, raspberry syrup, blackberry jam, and ⅓ cup of tea into a blender.
3. Add 2 cups of ice and blend on high speed for 20 to 30 seconds or until the drink is smooth and all ice has been crushed.

• MAKES 1 16-OUNCE SERVING.

TAZOBERRY & CREAM

Some folks like their Tazoberry a little creamier. It's an easy variation that includes adding just 2 tablespoons of cream to the blender with the other ingredients in the recipe above. Blend as described in Step 3, and top the drink off with whipped cream if you've got it.

•   •   •   •

T.G.I. FRIDAY'S
TROPICAL OASIS
SMOOTHIE

I remember when the menu at T.G.I. Friday's used to include over half a dozen smoothies, but in many Friday's restaurants today the list has been trimmed to just the top few sellers. This is a clone for one of those three favorites. The other two—Gold Medalist and Tropical Runner—are cloned in the restaurant section of this book.

¼ cup pineapple juice
¼ cup papaya juice
½ cup canned peaches
1 scoop orange sherbet
½ cup ice

GARNISH
orange slice
maraschino cherry

1. Combine all ingredients in a blender and mix on high speed until smooth.
2. Pour into a 14-ounce glass, add an orange slice and maraschino cherry on a toothpick. Serve with a straw.

• MAKES 1 DRINK.

• • • •

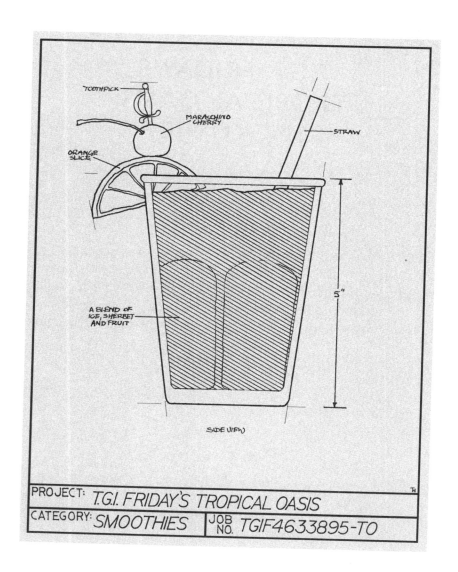

TOOTHPICK

MARASCHINO CHERRY

STRAW

ORANGE SLICE

A BLEND OF ICE, SHERBET AND FRUIT

5"

SIDE VIEW

PROJECT: *T.G.I. FRIDAY'S TROPICAL OASIS*

CATEGORY: *SMOOTHIES*   JOB NO. *TGIF4633895-TO*

T.G.I. FRIDAY'S NOVEMBER SEA BREEZE FLING

Not only does the restaurant still serve some of the tastiest cocktails and mixed drinks, but Friday's also has one of the best darn selections of custom non-alcoholic drinks in the business. The smoothies and shakes at Friday's are all excellent, as are the designer sodas called "Flings." These are hand-mixed soda beverages made in a fashion reminiscent of old-time soda fountains. Juices and sweeteners are mixed with cold soda water and served elegantly over ice—you can't go wrong with one of these. The Fling cloned here uses cranberry juice, apple juice, simple syrup, and sweet & sour mix.

1 ½ ounces cranberry juice
1 ½ ounces apple juice
1 ½ ounces sweet & sour mix

½ ounce simple syrup
1 ½ ounces club soda

GARNISH
lime wedge

1. Fill a 14-ounce glass with ice.
2. Pour juices, sweet & sour mix, and simple syrup into a shaker and shake well.

3. Pour drink over the ice, add a lime wedge and the club soda on top, and serve with a straw.

- MAKES 1 DRINK.

•   •   •   •

T.G.I. FRIDAY'S STRAWBERRY SURPRISE FLING

This version of a Friday's Fling is more tropical than the preceding recipe and doesn't require simple syrup. When you're ready to be flung, get some of the sweetened sliced strawberries out of the freezer and start thawing.

2 tablespoons frozen sweetened
    sliced strawberries, thawed
1 ½ ounces pineapple juice
1 ½ ounces papaya juice
1 ½ ounces apple juice

1 ½ ounces club soda

GARNISH
1 fresh strawberry

1. Fill a 14-ounce glass with ice.
2. Pour strawberries, with syrup, and juices into a shaker and shake well.
3. Pour drink over the ice, and add a fresh strawberry to the rim of the glass. Splash the club soda over the top and serve with a straw.

• MAKES 1 DRINK.

•   •   •   •

WENDY'S FROSTY

First served at Wendy's in 1969, the Frosty continues as a favorite in fast food shakes, even if it only comes in chocolate flavor. This clone recipe is an improved version of the recipe that appears in the first book, *Top Secret Recipes*. I've designed this for just a one-person serving and have reduced the chocolate in the shake so that it's more like the real thing served today. I find the smaller yield also helps to make the thing blend better.

½ cup milk
4 teaspoons Nesquik chocolate
    drink mix

2 cups vanilla ice cream

Combine all of the ingredients in a blender. Blend on medium speed, stopping to stir several times with a long spoon, if necessary, to help the ingredients blend well.

• MAKES 1 SERVING.

•   •   •   •

YOO-HOO MIX-UPS

A while back when I was rummaging through my pantry I came upon several bottles of flavored Yoo-hoo that I'd scored from Wal-Mart and tucked away for over a year. Each of the bottles was covered with a little dust and needed a pretty fierce shaking, but the contents were very well preserved and quite tasty. After some web browsing of a few unofficial Yoo-hoo web sites, I discovered these previously worshipped "Mix-Ups" varieties of the famous chocolate drink had since been put to rest. Now, after a little work in the top secret underground lab, I've come up with a way to clone the flavor of this "dead product" that's no longer obtainable outside of the ethereal food-world afterlife.

CHOCOLATE-BANANA

¾ cup nonfat dry milk
3 tablespoons Nesquik chocolate
   drink mix

1½ cups cold water
1½ teaspoons sugar
½ teaspoon banana extract

CHOCOLATE-MINT

¾ cup nonfat dry milk
3 tablespoons Nesquik chocolate
   drink mix
1½ cups cold water

1 teaspoon sugar
dash mint extract (less than
   ⅛ teaspoon)

CHOCOLATE-STRAWBERRY

¾ cup nonfat dry milk
3 tablespoons Nesquik chocolate
  drink mix

1 ½ cups cold water
1 tablespoon sugar
1 ½ teaspoons strawberry extract

Combine all ingredients for flavor of your choice in a container or jar with a lid. Shake until dry milk is dissolved. Drink immediately or chill in refrigerator.

• MAKES 1 14-OUNCE DRINK.

• • • •

BAILEY'S ORIGINAL IRISH CREAM

Bailey's launched its Irish Cream Liqueur in 1974, after years of development. The cream liqueur is based on an old Irish recipe using all-natural ingredients, including cream that is produced just for the Bailey's company. In fact, because the product line has become so successful, Bailey's accounts for one-third of Ireland's entire milk production. More than 4,000 farmers supply the 40 million gallons of milk used annually in producing cream for the liqueur. Bailey's now ranks number one among all liqueur brands in the world.

1 cup light cream (<u>not</u> heavy cream)
one 14-ounce can Eagle sweetened
   condensed milk
1 2/3 cups Irish whiskey
1 teaspoon instant coffee

2 tablespoons Hershey's chocolate
   syrup
1 teaspoon vanilla extract
1 teaspoon almond extract

1. Combine all the ingredients in a blender set on high speed for 30 seconds.
2. Bottle in a tightly sealed container and refrigerate. The liqueur will keep for at least 2 months if kept cool. Be sure to shake the bottle well before serving.

• MAKES 4 CUPS.

TIDBITS

If you can't find light cream, use half-and-half or whole milk (rather than heavy cream, which will tend to separate).

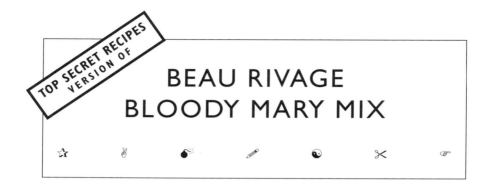

BEAU RIVAGE
BLOODY MARY MIX

Why make a clone recipe for an obscure bloody mary mix from a Biloxi, Mississippi, casino? Because I've had every major bloody mary mix brand on the market and none can compare to this one. With other mixes I find myself doctoring up the drink with additional Tabasco or salt or Worcestershire sauce. That's sure not the case here. This mix tastes great right out of the bottle, and it doesn't even contain horseradish, which is commonly found in good bloody marys. Make this one soon and keep it handy.

1 6-ounce can tomato paste
2 cups water
1 12-ounce can V-8 vegetable juice
⅓ cup distilled white vinegar

¼ cup Worcestershire sauce
2 teaspoons Lawry's seasoned salt
1¼ teaspoons ground black pepper
½ teaspoon Tabasco

Combine all ingredients in a pitcher and stir well. Combine with vodka to make bloody mary cocktails.

• MAKES 1 QUART.

• • • •

DEKUYPER
THRILLA VANILLA
FRENCH VANILLA LIQUEUR

Just as with the real thing, this clone of the unique vanilla liqueur from DeKuyper can be mixed with cola over ice, or with 1 part vanilla liqueur to 2 parts raspberry liqueur for another tasty tipple. Also try splashing some of it into the shaker with your favorite vodka for a sweet vanilla-tini.

1 1/4 cups very hot water
3/4 cup granulated sugar
1 cup 80-proof vodka

1 teaspoon McCormick vanilla
    butter & nut flavoring

1. Dissolve sugar in the hot water.
2. Add vodka and flavoring, and stir well. Store in a sealed container.

• MAKES 2 2/3 CUPS.

• • • •

DISARONNO AMARETTO

The story behind this one is that for several months artist Bernardino Luini worked closely with a model to help him paint a fresco of the Madonna in Saronno, Italy. As the months passed the girl, whose name has since been forgotten, fell in love with Bernardino. To show her feelings for him, the girl gave Bernardino a gift of sweet almond-flavored liqueur she made from the trees growing in her garden. The year was 1525, and that bottle is said to have been the first DiSaronno Amaretto. The recipe was passed down through the ages, until late in the eighteenth century when the liqueur went into commercial production.

Reenact the legend by giving someone a bottle of your own version of the famous liqueur, whether they paint you on a wall or not.

½ cup granulated sugar
¼ cup dark brown sugar
¾ cup very hot water
½ cup corn syrup

1 ½ cups 80-proof vodka
1 tablespoon almond extract
1 teaspoon vanilla extract

1. Combine the water with the sugars in a medium glass pitcher or bowl. Stir until the sugar is dissolved. Add corn syrup and stir well.
2. Add vodka and flavorings and stir well. Store in a sealed container.

• MAKES 3 CUPS.

GRAND MARNIER LIQUEUR

In 1880s France, oranges were quite rare and exotic. So when Louis Alexandre Marnier-Lopostolle traveled to the Caribbean in search of ingredients, he came back with bitter oranges to combine with his family's fine cognac. While other orange-flavored liqueurs such as triple sec and curaçao are mixed with a neutral alcohol base, Grand Marnier took it to the next level with a more complex flavor that makes it today's top-selling French liqueur.

Now you too can combine cognac with real orange to make a home version of this tasty (and pricey) stuff. By using an inexpensive cognac that costs around 18 to 20 dollars a bottle, you can create a clone cousin of the real thing that normally sells for 28 to 32 dollars a bottle. All you need, in addition to the cognac, is some sugar, an orange, and a little patience.

2 cups cognac
1 medium orange

⅔ cup granulated sugar

1. Pour the cognac into a 2-cup jar with a lid.
2. Peel and section the orange, then slice each of the orange sections in half lengthwise, and add them to the jar along with the sugar.
3. Cover jar and shake until the sugar is dissolved.
4. Store the jar at room temperature for at least 2 weeks, then strain the orange slices and pulp from the liquid. Use as you would the real thing, for sipping or in mixed drinks.

• MAKES 2 CUPS.

HIRAM WALKER
CRÈME DE BANANA
LIQUEUR

In the Cocktails section you'll find many recipes that require banana-flavored liqueur, a very common ingredient at the bars these days. Here's how to make some from scratch for your top secret concoctions if you don't feel like fetching the real thing.

¾ cup very hot water
¾ cup granulated sugar
1 cup 80-proof vodka

¼ teaspoon imitation banana extract
1 drop yellow food coloring

1. Combine the hot water with the sugar in a small pitcher. Stir until sugar is dissolved.
2. Add vodka, banana extract, and food coloring and stir well. Cool to room temperature before using. Store in a sealed container.

• MAKES 2 CUPS.

• • • •

HIRAM WALKER
CRÈME DE CACAO
LIQUEUR

The chocolate taste in this liqueur comes from cocoa most commonly used for baking. After storing this liqueur for a week or so, we'll strain it through a coffee filter or a wire strainer that's been lined with paper towels to remove most of the cocoa. Sediment is not cool in liqueurs. Our finished product won't be quite as clear as the real thing, but the taste should be right there.

¾ cup very hot water
¾ cup plus 1 tablespoon granulated
   sugar

1 cup 80-proof vodka
2 tablespoons cocoa
½ teaspoon vanilla extract

1. Dissolve the sugar in the hot water.
2. Add the vodka, cocoa, and vanilla. Stir well. Store in a covered container for at least a week. Shake the liqueur every day or two.
3. Strain the liqueur through a coffee filter or paper towel–lined strainer into a bowl or pitcher. Store in a covered container.

- MAKES 2 CUPS.

• • • •

HIRAM WALKER CRÈME DE MENTHE LIQUEUR

☆　✌　💣　✏　☯　✂　☞

The popular mint liqueur is quick to make at home, and we'll even make it a deep, dark green like the real thing with 45 drops (or ½ teaspoon) of green food coloring. As for the mint flavoring, be sure to get "peppermint" extract, not "mint" extract.

½ cup very hot water
⅔ cup plus 1 tablespoon
   granulated sugar

1 cup 80-proof vodka
¾ teaspoon peppermint extract
45 drops green food coloring
   (½ teaspoon)

1. Dissolve the sugar in the hot water.
2. Add the vodka, peppermint extract, and food coloring. Store in a sealed container.

- MAKES 2 CUPS.

•　•　•　•

MARA
SIMPLE SYRUP

Simple syrup will sometimes be needed to mix great-tasting drinks that require additional sweetening. Use enough of the clone recipes for cocktails in this book and you'll eventually need to use some simple syrup.

½ cup hot water   *½ cup sugar*

Stir ingredients together until sugar is dissolved.

- MAKES APPROX. 7 OUNCES.

• • • •

MR & MRS T
BLOODY MARY MIX

☆   ✌   💣   ✏   ☯   ✂   ☞

Here's a way to clone the famous and very popular bloody mary mix from that couple with a letter for a last name. It's a simple-to-make blend of tomato juice and spices with some prepared horse-radish and canned jalapeño juice thrown in for a "spicier, zestier" drink. Mix this with vodka over ice and you've got a delicious cock-tail. But if you're not in the mood to get zoinked, this clone recipe is also a great way to kick up your tomato juice, just for drinking straight.

1 46-ounce can tomato juice
4 tablespoons lime juice
3 tablespoons juice from canned
    jalapeños (nacho slices)
3 tablespoons vinegar
2 tablespoons sugar

2 teaspoons prepared horseradish
1/4 teaspoon salt
1/4 teaspoon pepper
1/8 teaspoon onion powder
dash garlic

1. Combine all ingredients in a 2-quart pitcher. Store covered in the refrigerator.
2. Directions for mixing a drink, as per the original mix: "Add 3 parts Mr & Mrs T Rich & Spicy Bloody Mary Mix to 1 part vodka, gin, rum or tequila, over ice. Mr & Mrs T Rich & Spicy Bloody Mary Mix is also delicious by itself. Simply pour over ice and serve."

• MAKES 52 OUNCES.

•   •   •   •

MR & MRS T
SWEET & SOUR MIX

This clone recipe makes a little more of the popular sweet & sour mixer than you'll get in the 34-ounce plastic bottles at the store. So now when you crave that frosty margarita or snappy whiskey sour and don't have any sweet & sour mix on hand, you can whip together a batch of your own. Just mix this stuff, as you would the brand-name sweet & sour mix, in your favorite cocktails and party libations.

3 cups hot water
¾ cup bottled lime juice
½ cup corn syrup

¼ cup granulated sugar
¼ cup bottled lemon juice
1 drop yellow food coloring

Combine all ingredients in a 2-quart pitcher and mix until sugar is dissolved. Store covered in refrigerator.

• MAKES 40 OUNCES.

• • • •

CALIFORNIA PIZZA KITCHEN TUSCAN HUMMUS

Nowhere could I find the "Tuscan white bean," or any mention of it in research materials. But there it is in the California Pizza Kitchen menu description for this delicious hummus. Could this just be the chain's fancy way of describing garbanzo beans, otherwise known as chickpeas? After all, garbanzos are the only beans used for any traditional hummus recipe, and they seemed to work perfectly in this low-fat re-creation of the chain's tasty appetizer. Just be sure you have a good food processor to puree all the ingredients. If you have trouble finding sesame tahini in your supermarket, check out your local health food store. And while you're there, see if you can spot those Tuscan white beans.

1 15-ounce can garbanzo beans
  (strain and keep ¼ cup of liquid)
¼ cup liquid from the can
¼ cup fresh lemon juice
3 tablespoons sesame tahini
2 teaspoons minced garlic

1 teaspoon granulated sugar
¾ teaspoon white pepper
½ teaspoon salt
¼ teaspoon cumin
⅛ teaspoon cayenne pepper
⅛ teaspoon paprika

OPTIONAL GARNISH
2 tablespoons chopped Roma
  tomatoes

pinch fresh basil
pinch chopped fresh garlic

1. Dump the entire contents of the can of garbanzo beans into a strainer set over a bowl. Let the beans sit for a little while so that all of the liquid drips into the bowl.
2. Dump the beans and ¼ cup of the liquid from the bowl into a food processor.
3. Add the remaining ingredients to the food processor, and puree the mixture until completely smooth—about a minute or so.
4. Spoon the hummus into a covered container and chill for at least 2 hours so that the flavors can develop. When serving, you may wish to garnish the hummus with a couple tablespoons of chopped Roma tomatoes mixed with a dash of chopped fresh basil and garlic. Serve with warm, sliced pita bread or your choice of chips or crackers.

- MAKES 1¾ CUPS.

Nutrition Facts

SERVING SIZE—2 TABLESPOONS	FAT (PER SERVING)—2.5G
TOTAL SERVINGS—14	CALORIES (PER SERVING)—48

•　•　•　•

CALIFORNIA PIZZA KITCHEN GRILLED EGGPLANT CHEESELESS PIZZA

When PepsiCo shelled out $100 million for a 67 percent share of the trendy pizza chain back in 1992, founders Lawrence Flax and Richard Rosenfield thought they had it made. Unfortunately, the company behind Pizza Hut found expanding the more upscale eatery an unfamiliar struggle. The company expanded too quickly (Planet Hollywood, anyone?), and as costs began to dwarf sales figures, fresh ingredients were replaced with cheaper frozen products. Customers noticed, and sales took a nosedive. By 1996, PepsiCo decided to bail.

The following year, PepsiCo's share of the chain was picked up by New York investment firm Rosser, Sherrill & Co. Fresh ingredients returned to the kitchens, and the size of the pizzas was increased without adjusting the price. Sales once again blossomed, and the chain was on its way back to turning its first profit since 1991.

Here's a great pizza to clone if you need to take a little time off from delicious-yet-fat-filled mozzarella cheese. With the marinated, grilled eggplant and tasty honey-wheat dough, you won't even miss that gooey white stuff. Be sure to start this one a day before you plan to eat it. The dough needs that long to rise in the fridge for just the right California Pizza Kitchen–like consistency.

HONEY-WHEAT DOUGH

⅓ cup plus 1 tablespoon warm
    water (105 to 115 degrees F)
1 tablespoon honey
¾ teaspoon yeast

⅔ cup bread flour
⅓ cup whole wheat flour
½ teaspoon salt
½ tablespoon olive oil

TOPPING

1 ½ tablespoons soy sauce
1 tablespoon olive oil
⅛ teaspoon cayenne pepper
⅛ teaspoon garlic powder
⅛ teaspoon cumin
½ eggplant, sliced lengthwise ¼ inch
    thick

¼ medium red onion, sliced into thin
    rings (about ½ cup)
1 teaspoon minced fresh cilantro
1 ½ to 2 cups fresh spinach, chopped
    into thin strips
⅓ cup reconstituted sun-dried
    tomatoes,* sliced into strips

OPTIONAL

fat-free vinaigrette

1. Prepare the pizza dough by combining the water with the honey and yeast in a small bowl or measuring cup. Stir until the yeast is dissolved, then let the mixture sit for 5 minutes until the surface turns foamy. (If it doesn't foam, either the yeast was too old or the water was too hot. Try again.) Sift the flours and salt together in a medium bowl. Make a depression in the flour and pour the olive oil and yeast mixture into it. Use a fork or spoon to stir the liquid, gradually drawing in more flour as you stir, until all the ingredients are combined. At this point you will have to use your hands to blend the dough until it is smooth and to form it into a ball. Knead the dough with the heels of your hands on a lightly floured surface for 10 minutes or until the texture of the dough is smooth and elastic. Form the dough back into a ball, coat it lightly with oil, and place it into a clean bowl covered with plastic wrap. Keep the dough in a warm place for about 2 hours to allow the dough to double in size.

*Heat a couple cups of water to boiling in the microwave. Add 6 to 8 sun-dried tomato slices to the water and let them sit for about ½ hour. Remove the slices and drain on paper towels until you need them.

Punch the dough down and put it back into the covered bowl and back into the refrigerator overnight. Take the dough from the refrigerator 1 to 2 hours before you plan to build the pizza so that the dough can warm up to room temperature.

2. When you're ready to make your pizza, preheat the oven to 500ºF. If you have a pizza stone, now's the time to use it.
3. Preheat barbecue grill to high temperature.
4. Combine the soy sauce with 1 tablespoon of olive oil, cayenne pepper, garlic powder, and cumin in a small bowl.
5. Brush the entire surface of each eggplant slice with this soy sauce mixture. Make sure you have some left over.
6. Grill the eggplant slices for 2 to 3 minutes per side, then remove them from the grill to cool.
7. On a lightly floured surface, form the pizza dough into a circle with an approximately 10-inch diameter. Be sure to form a lip around the edge.
8. Brush the top surface of the pizza dough with the remaining soy sauce mixture.
9. Arrange the red onion slices over the pizza dough.
10. The eggplant slices go on the pizza next, then toss the pizza into the oven on a pizza pan, or directly onto a pizza stone. Bake for 10 to 12 minutes or until the crust is light brown and crispy. Pop any bubbles in the crust that may form as the pizza bakes.
11. Remove the pizza from the oven and sprinkle cilantro over the top.
12. Slice the pizza into 6 even slices with a sharp pizza wheel.
13. Sprinkle the thinly chopped spinach over the top of the pizza.
14. Sprinkle the sun-dried tomato strips over the top.
15. Serve pizza with the optional vinaigrette on the side.

- MAKES 1 10-INCH PIZZA.

Nutrition Facts

SERVING SIZE—3 SLICES	FAT (PER SERVING)—8G
TOTAL SERVINGS—2	CALORIES (PER SERVING)—380

• • • •

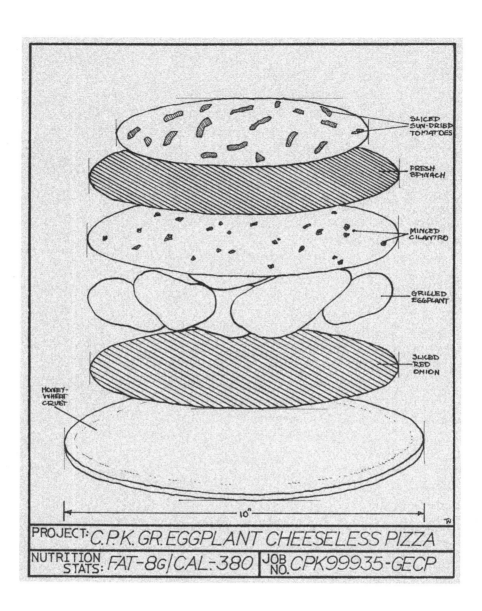

SLICED SUN-DRIED TOMATOES

FRESH SPINACH

MINCED CILANTRO

GRILLED EGGPLANT

SLICED RED ONION

HONEY-WHEAT CRUST

10"

PROJECT: C.P.K. GR. EGGPLANT CHEESELESS PIZZA

NUTRITION STATS: FAT-8g / CAL.-380

JOB NO. CPK99935-GECP

CHEVYS
FRESH SALSA

Chevys's concept of Fresh Mex® has made it one of the best Mexican restaurant chains in the country. You won't find any cans of food in the kitchen since every item on the menu is made daily with fresh ingredients. The restaurant claims it makes its heart-shaped tortillas each day, and this delicious, smoky salsa every hour. You can certainly taste that freshness in the salsa, along with the unique mesquite flavors that come from the restaurant's mesquite-fire grill.

For this clone you won't need a mesquite grill, just some mesquite liquid smoke flavoring and a hot barbecue grill. Oh, and you'll also need a food processor to get the right consistency. The original contains chipotle peppers, which is just another name for smoked red jalapeños. But if you get tired of hunting for the red jalapeños in your local supermarkets, just grab the green ones. They'll work fine. You'll need a total of ten peppers, which may seem like a lot, but their heat is tamed considerably when you grill 'em.

6 medium tomatoes
olive oil
10 jalapeños (red is best)
¼ medium Spanish
    onion
2 cloves garlic

2 tablespoons chopped fresh cilantro
2 teaspoons salt
2 tablespoons white vinegar
1 ½ teaspoons mesquite-flavored
    liquid smoke

1. Preheat your barbecue grill to high temperature.
2. Remove any stems from the tomatoes, then rub some oil over each tomato. You can leave the stems on the jalapeños for now.
3. Place the tomatoes on the grill when it's hot. After about 10 minutes, place all of the jalapeños onto the grill. In about 10 minutes you can turn the tomatoes and the peppers. When nearly the entire surface of the peppers has charred black, you can remove them from the grill. The tomatoes will turn black partially, but when the skin begins to come off they're done. Put the peppers and tomatoes on a plate and let them cool.
4. When the tomatoes and peppers have cooled, remove most of the skin from the tomatoes and place them into a food processor. Pinch the stem off the end of the peppers and place them into the food processor as well. Don't include the liquid left on the plate. Toss that out.
5. Add the remaining ingredients to the food processor and puree on high speed for 5 to 10 seconds or until the mixture has a smooth consistency.
6. Place the salsa into a covered container and chill for several hours or overnight while the flavors develop.

- MAKES 2 CUPS.

Nutrition Facts

SERVING SIZE—2 TABLESPOONS	FAT (PER SERVING)—0G
TOTAL SERVINGS—16	CALORIES (PER SERVING)—10

•   •   •   •

GARDENBURGER
FIRE-ROASTED VEGETABLE
VEGGIE PATTY

☆ ✌ 💣 ✏ ☯ ✂ ☞

Paul Wenner started his company in 1985 when he developed a meatless hamburger from leftovers at his vegetarian restaurant. Even though his Gardenburger was a hit, Paul was forced to close the restaurant due to dwindling sales. On the bright side, this gave Paul more free time to develop and sell his delicious puck-shaped plant patty. Today, Paul's Gardenburger brand is thriving, with an estimated fifty million patties served in restaurants, cafeterias, and concession stands in 1998 alone.

To make this clone, you'll need a food processor and a hot barbecue grill. And if you're looking for an interesting way to serve it, the manufacturer suggests you slap the veggie patty onto some focaccia bread and top it off with marinara sauce, grilled squash, and a little Parmesan cheese.

1 head garlic
olive oil
2 tablespoons bulgur wheat
2/3 cup cooked brown rice
1/4 red bell pepper
1 ear yellow sweet corn
1/4 red onion
1/2 small tomato
1 pound white button mushrooms, quartered
1 cup diced white onion

1/2 cup rolled oats
2/3 cup reduced-fat mozzarella cheese (2% fat)
1/4 cup Kraft Parmesan cheese
2 tablespoons fat-free cottage cheese
1 1/4 teaspoons salt
1/2 teaspoon garlic powder
1/2 teaspoon paprika
1/2 teaspoon onion powder
dash ground black pepper
2 egg whites

3 tablespoons cornstarch
2 tablespoons cornmeal
2 teaspoons minced sun-dried
  tomatoes (marinated and
  drained)

2 teaspoons lemon juice
2 teaspoons juice from
  canned jalapeños
  (nacho slices)

1. Preheat your oven to 325°F.
2. To roast the garlic, cut about ½ inch off the top of the garlic head. Cut the roots so that the garlic will sit flat. Remove most of the papery skin from the garlic, but leave enough so that the cloves stay together. Place the head of garlic in a small casserole dish or baking pan, drizzle about a tablespoon of olive oil over it, and cover it with a lid or foil. Bake for 1 hour. Remove the garlic from the oven and let it cool until you can handle it.
3. Add ¼ cup of boiling water to the bulgur wheat in a small bowl or measuring cup and let it sit for about 1 hour. Prepare the brown rice according to the directions on the package.
4. To fire-roast the vegetables, use a barbecue grill preheated to medium. Rub olive oil on ¼ of a red bell pepper, an ear of corn, ¼ of a red onion, and ½ of a small tomato. Place the vegetables on the hot grill with the skin of the pepper and tomato facing toward the flame. Turn the corn and red onion as they cook. Grill for 30 minutes or until vegetables are tender. The skin of the red bell pepper should turn black so that it can be quickly peeled off. Also remove the skin from the tomato. (If you don't have a grill, you can roast the vegetables in your oven set to high broil for around 15 to 20 minutes. Face the skin of the tomato and pepper toward the heat and be sure to turn the corn and red onion as they cook.) Dice the pepper, onion, and tomato when cool. Keep separate.
5. Steam the quartered mushrooms for 10 minutes or until tender. Remove the mushrooms from your steamer and replace them with the white onion. Steam the diced onion for 10 minutes or until the pieces become translucent. Keep these two ingredients separate and set aside.
6. Add ½ cup of water to the rolled oats and let them soak for at least 10 minutes, until soft.

7. Drain any excess water from the bulgur wheat and oats, then combine the grains with the steamed mushrooms, rice, cheeses, corn, and spices in a food processor and pulse 4 or 5 times until the ingredients are chopped but not pureed. You want a coarse texture with some identifiable chunks of grain, mushrooms, corn, and cheese.

8. Pour the mixture into a bowl with the remaining ingredients and mix well.

9. Preheat the oven to 300ºF and set a large skillet over medium/low heat.

10. Spray the skillet with a light coating of olive oil cooking spray. Measure ½ cup at a time of the patty mixture into the pan and shape with a spoon into a 3¾-inch patty that is approximately ½ inch thick. Cook the patties in batches for 2 to 4 minutes per side, or until light brown on the surface.

11. When all of the patties have been cooked in the skillet, arrange them on a lightly sprayed baking sheet and bake for 20 to 25 minutes in the oven. Be sure to turn them over halfway through the cooking time. You can serve the patties immediately or freeze them, like the originals, when they have cooled.

12. If you freeze the patties like the originals, you can reheat them several ways. Refer to step #9 on page 37 for heating instructions.

- MAKES 8 PATTIES.

Nutrition Facts

SERVING SIZE—1 PATTY	FAT (PER SERVING)—3G
TOTAL SERVINGS—8	CALORIES (PER SERVING)—150

• • • •

HIRAM WALKER
ANISETTE LIQUEUR

For centuries anise has been a key ingredient in distilled spirits, and it is the most widely used flavor for drinks in countries surrounding the Mediterranean. Today it's used as the key flavoring ingredient in ouzo, sambuca, raki, Pernod, and a host of other international aperitifs and liqueurs. The availability of anise extract (found near the vanilla in most supermarkets) makes home cloning this popular brand of anisette liqueur an easy project.

½ cup very hot water
⅔ cup granulated sugar

1 cup 80-proof vodka
¼ teaspoon anise extract

1. Dissolve sugar in the hot water.
2. Add vodka and anise extract. Store in sealed container.

• MAKES 2 CUPS.

• • • •

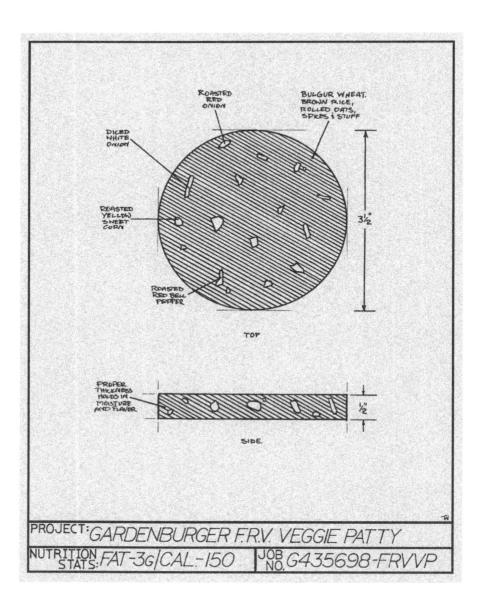

ROASTED
RED
ONION

BULGUR WHEAT,
BROWN RICE,
ROLLED OATS,
SPICES & STUFF

DICED
WHITE
ONION

ROASTED
YELLOW
SWEET
CORN

ROASTED
RED BELL
PEPPER

3½"

TOP

PROPER
THICKNESS
HOLDS IN
MOISTURE
AND FLAVOR

½"

SIDE

PROJECT: *GARDENBURGER F.R.V. VEGGIE PATTY*

NUTRITION STATS: *FAT-3g/CAL.-150*   JOB NO. *G435698-FRVVP*

GARDENBURGER SAVORY MUSHROOM VEGGIE PATTY

☆　　　✌　　　💣　　　✎　　　☯　　　✂　　　☞

Chef Paul Wenner fathered a hot product when he ground up those leftover vegetables at his restaurant and formed them into the shape of a hamburger patty. When Paul got out of the restaurant business, he peddled the meatless patties out of his van under the name Wholesome & Hearty Foods. In 1992, when his company went public, the stock shot up to $30 from $3 on rumors that McDonald's was planning to sell the veggie patties under the golden arches. When those rumors proved to be false, the stock came crashing down quicker than sales figures for the McLean Deluxe. Later, the name of the company was changed to Gardenburger, and new products, such as the Savory Mushroom Veggie Patty, were developed.

For this clone, you'll need to track down three types of mushrooms: the common white button, brown (or crimini), and portobello. You'll also need a food processor to mash everything up real good.

2 tablespoons bulgur wheat
⅔ cup cooked brown rice
6 ounces white button mushrooms, quartered
6 ounces brown Italian mushrooms (crimini), quartered
4 ounces portobello mushroom (1 small cap), quartered

1 cup diced white onion (about ½ cup steamed)
½ cup rolled oats
⅔ cup reduced-fat mozzarella cheese (2% fat)
2 tablespoons shredded Gorgonzola cheese

2 tablespoons fat-free cottage cheese
1¼ teaspoons salt
1 teaspoon onion powder
½ teaspoon garlic powder
dash ground black pepper
2 egg whites

3 tablespoons cornstarch
1 tablespoon all-purpose flour
2 teaspoons soy sauce
2 teaspoons brown sugar
2 teaspoons molasses

1. Add ¼ cup of boiling water to the bulgur wheat in a small bowl or measuring cup and let it sit for about 1 hour. Prepare the brown rice according to the directions on the package.
2. Steam the quartered mushrooms for 10 minutes or until tender. Remove the mushrooms from your steamer and replace them with the onion. Steam the diced onion for 10 minutes or until the pieces become translucent. Keep the mushrooms separate from the onions and set them aside.
3. Add ½ cup of water to the rolled oats and let them soak for at least 10 minutes, until soft.
4. Drain any excess water from the bulgur wheat and oats, then combine the grains with the steamed mushrooms, rice, cheeses, and spices in a food processor and pulse 4 or 5 times until the ingredients are chopped but not pureed. You want a coarse texture with some identifiable chunks of grain, mushrooms, and cheese.
5. Pour the mixture into a bowl with the remaining ingredients and mix well.
6. Preheat the oven to 300°F and set a large skillet over medium/low heat.
7. Spray the skillet with a light coating of olive oil cooking spray. Measure ½ cup of the patty mixture at a time into the pan and shape with a spoon into a 3¾-inch patty that is approximately ½ inch thick. Cook the patties in batches for 2 to 4 minutes per side or until light brown on the surface.
8. When all of the patties have been cooked in the skillet, arrange them on a lightly sprayed baking sheet and bake for 20 to 25 minutes in the oven. Be sure to turn them over halfway through the cooking time. You can serve the patties immediately or freeze them, like the originals, when they have cooled.

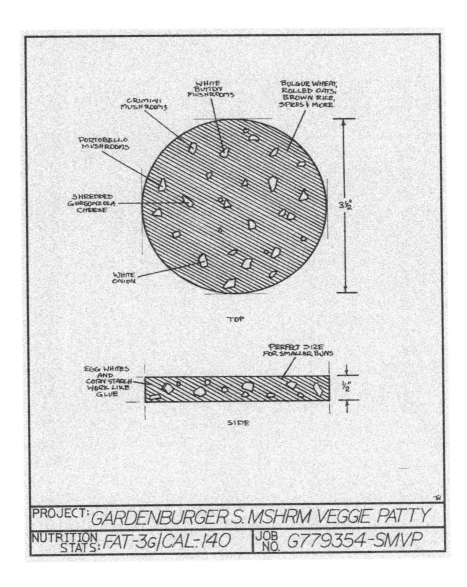

CRIMINI MUSHROOMS

WHITE BUTTON MUSHROOMS

BULGUR WHEAT, ROLLED OATS, BROWN RICE, SPICES & MORE

PORTOBELLO MUSHROOMS

SHREDDED GORGONZOLA CHEESE

3½"

WHITE ONION

TOP

PERFECT SIZE FOR SMALLER BUNS

EGG WHITES AND CORN STARCH WORK LIKE GLUE

½"

SIDE

PROJECT: *GARDENBURGER S. MSHRM VEGGIE PATTY*	
NUTRITION STATS: *FAT-3g/CAL.-140*	JOB NO. *G779354-SMVP*

9. If you freeze the patties, you can reheat them several ways. Refer to step #9 on page 37 for heating instructions.

- MAKES 8 PATTIES.

Nutrition Facts

SERVING SIZE—1 PATTY   FAT (PER SERVING)—3G

TOTAL SERVINGS—8   CALORIES (PER SERVING)—140

• • • •

EL POLLO LOCO
SALSA

Along with your order from this 250-unit Western U.S. chain, comes a delicious, yet simple to clone, fat-free salsa. If you don't have a food processor, never fear. You can also make the salsa by hand, with a large, sharp knife and some steady-handed, energetic, calorie-burning mincing action. Keep your head down, legs slightly spread, and watch the fingers. You don't want the salsa too red.

2 medium tomatoes, quartered
½ fresh jalapeño pepper, stem and
   seeds removed

2 leaves fresh cilantro
¼ teaspoon salt

Combine all the ingredients in a food processor. Pulse 3 to 5 times on low speed until the vegetables are well chopped. Be careful that you don't overchop and puree the ingredients. Pour everything, including the liquid, into a medium bowl. Cover and chill for several hours.

- Makes 1 cup.

Nutrition Facts
Serving size—1 ounce
Total servings—8

Fat (per serving)—0g
Calories (per serving)—6

• • • •

ENTENMANN'S LIGHT LOW-FAT GOURMET CINNAMON ROLLS

☆ ✌ 💣 ✏ ☯ ✂ ☞

You say you like your cinnamon rolls oversize? Then this is the clone recipe for you. You'll find this method is very similar to the previous recipe, but it makes rolls almost twice the size, and there ain't no raisins. Otherwise, the recipe still uses the same filling formula, with Wondra flour to keep it from liquefying. And like the other recipe, the icing here includes our good friend, fat-free cream cheese, to create a smooth consistency while keeping the goopy fat grams at bay.

ROLLS

2 teaspoons yeast
1/2 cup warm water
1/4 cup sugar
1 2/3 cups bread flour

1/2 teaspoon baking powder
1/4 teaspoon salt
2 tablespoons shortening, melted
3 tablespoons egg substitute

FILLING

1/4 cup fat-free butter-flavored
    spread
1/3 cup light brown sugar

2 tablespoons Wondra flour
2 teaspoons cinnamon

ICING

1/2 cup powdered sugar
2 tablespoons fat-free cream cheese

2 to 3 drops vanilla extract
dash salt

1. Dissolve the yeast in the warm water. When the yeast is dissolved, add the sugar and stir until it is dissolved as well. In about 5 minutes, foam will form on the surface. (If foam does not form, your yeast may be too old or the water may be too hot. Try again.)
2. In a large bowl, mix the flour, baking powder, and salt together.
3. Melt the shortening in the microwave, set on high, for about 1 minute. Add the melted shortening, egg substitute, and yeast mixture to the flour and stir by hand until all ingredients are combined. Use your hands to knead the dough for about 5 minutes, then form it into a ball and put it into a covered bowl in a warm spot for 1 to 1½ hours or until it doubles in size.
4. Roll dough out onto a floured surface so that it is a rectangle measuring 18 inches long and 12 inches wide.
5. Use a spatula to spread the butter-flavored spread evenly over the surface of the dough. Combine the brown sugar, Wondra flour, and cinnamon in a small bowl. Spread this mixture evenly over the surface of the dough.
6. Starting from the top edge, roll the dough down until it forms a long roll. Cut off the ends, then slice the dough into 8 even slices and arrange them, cut side down, in a 9 x 13-inch greased baking pan or dish. Cover the pan with plastic wrap and let the rolls rise again for 1 to 1½ hours in a warm place.
7. Preheat oven to 400°F.
8. Remove the plastic from the pan and bake the rolls for 18 to 22 minutes or until brown.
9. As rolls bake, combine the icing ingredients in a medium bowl with an electric mixer. Mix on high speed for about 1 minute.
10. When rolls are cool, spread icing over the top of each one. Cover the baking dish and store the rolls at room temperature until you are ready to serve them.

- MAKES 8 ROLLS.

Nutrition Facts

SERVING SIZE—½ ROLL	FAT (PER SERVING)—2 G
TOTAL SERVINGS—16	CALORIES (PER SERVING)—160

• • • •

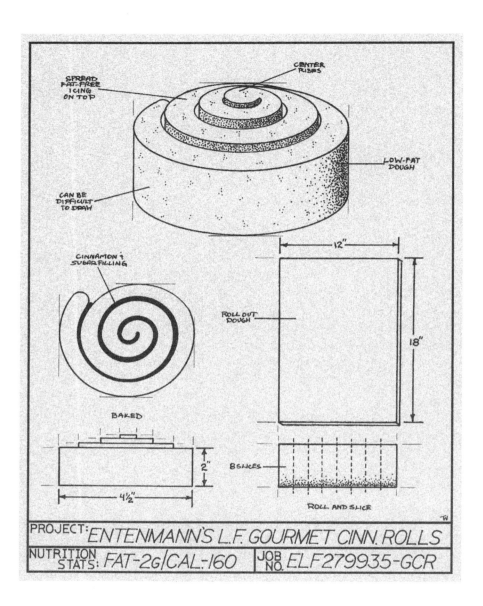

SPREAD FAT-FREE ICING ON TOP

CENTER RISES

LOW-FAT DOUGH

CAN BE DIFFICULT TO DRAW

CINNAMON & SUGAR FILLING

ROLL OUT DOUGH

12"

18"

BAKED

2"

4½"

8 SLICES

ROLL AND SLICE

TW

PROJECT: *ENTENMANN'S L.F. GOURMET CINN. ROLLS*

NUTRITION STATS: *FAT-2g/CAL.-160*   JOB NO. *ELF279935-GCR*

GARDENBURGER CLASSIC GREEK VEGGIE PATTY

In June of 1998, Gardenburger was on a roll. Bolstered by booming sales of its Original Veggie Burger, the company introduced three new varieties of its popular meatless patties: Classic Greek, Fire-Roasted Vegetable, and Savory Mushroom. Since all three sounded so good, I thought we'd just clone the lot of 'em right here in the following pages. The first one, the Classic Greek Veggie Patty, includes calamata olives, feta cheese, and spinach to give it a distinctively Mediterranean flavor, yet with only three grams of fat per serving.

2 tablespoons bulgur wheat
1 cup cooked brown rice
½ pound white button mushrooms, quartered
⅔ cup diced white onion
¼ cup diced red onion
½ cup rolled oats
¼ cup canned white beans, drained
⅔ cup reduced-fat mozzarella cheese (2% fat)
¼ cup crumbled feta cheese

2 tablespoons fat-free cottage cheese
2 tablespoons frozen chopped spinach, thawed
4 pitted calamata olives
1 teaspoon salt
½ teaspoon onion powder
½ teaspoon garlic powder
¼ teaspoon parsley
¼ teaspoon paprika
dash ground black pepper
3 egg whites
2 tablespoons cornstarch

1. Add ¼ cup of boiling water to the bulgur wheat in a small bowl or measuring cup and let it sit for about 1 hour. Now is a good time to prepare the brown rice according to the directions on the package.

2. Steam the quartered mushrooms for 10 minutes or until tender. Remove the mushrooms from your steamer, and replace them with the onions. Steam the diced onions for 10 minutes or until the pieces become translucent. Keep the steamed mushrooms and onions separate and set them aside.

3. Add ½ cup of water to the rolled oats and let them soak for at least 10 minutes, until soft.

4. Drain any excess water from the bulgur wheat and oats, then combine the grains with the steamed mushrooms, rice, beans, cheeses, spinach, olives, and spices in a food processor and pulse 3 to 4 times until the ingredients are chopped but not pureed. You want a coarse texture with some identifiable chunks of grain, mushrooms, beans, cheese, and olives.

5. Pour the mixture into a bowl with the remaining ingredients and mix well.

6. Preheat the oven to 300ºF and set a large skillet over medium/low heat.

7. Spray the skillet with a light coating of olive oil cooking spray. Measure ½ cup at a time of the patty mixture into the pan and shape with a spoon into a 3¾-inch patty that is approximately ½ inch thick. Cook the patties in batches for 2 to 4 minutes per side, or until light brown on the surface.

8. When all of the patties have been cooked in the skillet, arrange them on a lightly sprayed baking sheet and bake for 20 to 25 minutes in the oven. Be sure to turn them over halfway through the cooking time. You can serve the patties immediately or freeze them, like the original, when they have cooled.

9. If you freeze the patties, you can reheat them several ways. Simply spray a light coating of olive oil cooking spray on each side and heat each patty in a pan over medium heat for 3 to 4 minutes per side until it is hot in the center. You can also use a grill to prepare the patties. Just be sure to spray each frozen patty with the oil, and be sure the flames are low. Cook for 3 to 4 minutes per side. Those are the best cooking methods;

however, you can also prepare a frozen patty by microwaving it for 30 to 35 seconds, then turn the patty over and zap it for another 30 to 35 seconds. Finally, you can heat a frozen patty in the microwave for 30 to 35 seconds, then place the partially defrosted patty in a toaster or toaster oven and cook it on medium heat until it's hot in the center.

• MAKES 8 PATTIES.

Nutrition Facts

SERVING SIZE—1 PATTY   FAT (PER SERVING)—3G
TOTAL SERVINGS—8   CALORIES (PER SERVING)—150

• • • •

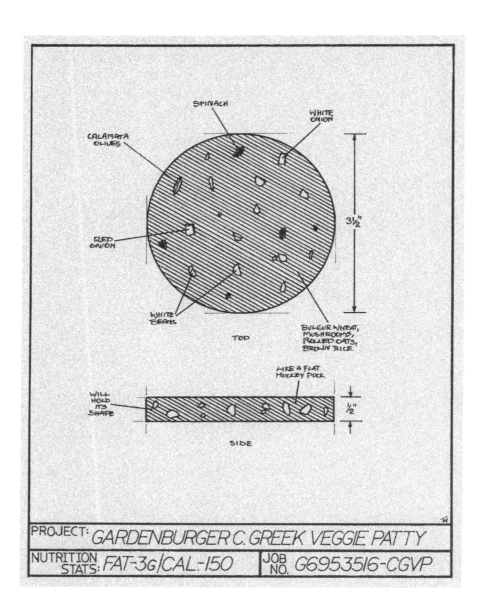

SPINACH

WHITE ONION

CALAMATA OLIVES

3½"

RED ONION

WHITE BEANS

BULGUR WHEAT, MUSHROOMS, ROLLED OATS, BROWN RICE

TOP

LIKE A FLAT HOCKEY PUCK

WILL HOLD ITS SHAPE

½"

SIDE

PROJECT: *GARDENBURGER C. GREEK VEGGIE PATTY*

NUTRITION STATS: *FAT-3g/CAL.-150*

JOB NO. *G6953516-CGVP*

GARDENBURGER
ORIGINAL VEGGIE PATTY

In the early eighties, at his Gardenhouse restaurant, Chef Paul Wenner created a unique meatless patty to replace hamburgers. The patty, which contained mushrooms, brown rice, onions, oats, and low-fat cheeses, was dubbed the Gardenburger and quickly became a hit. Soon, Wenner closed his restaurant and began to concentrate on marketing his meatless, low-fat creation to a hungry, health-conscious America. Today Gardenburger patties can be found in more than 35,000 food service outlets around the world, and more than 20,000 stores.

Now you can make a surprisingly accurate clone of the real thing with the same type of ingredients Wenner uses. Most of the ingredients can be found at your local supermarket, although you may have to go to a health food store for the bulgur wheat. And if you jog over there, you can burn off what little calories you gain from this amazing kitchen clone.

2 tablespoons bulgur wheat
1 pound mushrooms, quartered
    (4 cups steamed)
1 cup diced onion (½ cup steamed)
½ cup rolled oats
⅔ cup cooked brown rice
½ cup shredded low-fat mozzarella
    cheese

2 tablespoons shredded low-fat
    cheddar cheese
2 tablespoons low-fat cottage cheese
½ teaspoon salt
½ teaspoon garlic powder
dash pepper
2 tablespoons cornstarch
olive oil cooking spray

1. Add ¼ cup boiling water to the bulgur wheat in a small bowl and let it sit for about 60 minutes. The wheat will swell to about double in size.

2. Steam the quartered mushrooms for 10 minutes or until tender, then remove them from your steamer, and replace with the onion. Steam the diced onion for 10 minutes or until the pieces are translucent. Keep these two ingredients separate, and set aside.

3. Add ½ cup of water to the oats and let them soak for about 10 minutes, until soft.

4. Drain any excess water from the bulgur wheat and oats, then combine the grains with the steamed mushrooms, rice, cheeses, and spices in a food processor and pulse 4 or 5 times until ingredients are chopped fine, but not pureed. You want a coarse texture with some identifiable chunks of grain, mushroom, and cheese.

5. Pour the mixture into a bowl with the steamed onion and cornstarch, and mix well.

6. Preheat the oven to 300ºF and set a large skillet over medium/low heat.

7. Spray the skillet with a light coating of olive oil cooking spray. Measure ½ cup at a time of the patty mixture into the pan and shape with a spoon into a 3¾-inch patty that is approximately ½-inch thick. Cook the patties in batches for 2 to 4 minutes per side, or until light brown on the surface.

8. When all of the patties have been cooked in the skillet, arrange them on a lightly sprayed baking sheet and bake for 20 to 25 minutes in the oven. Be sure to turn them over halfway through the cooking time. You can serve the patties immediately, or freeze them, like the original, when they have cooled.

9. If you freeze the patties, you can reheat them several ways. Simply spray a light coating of olive oil cooking spray on each side and heat each patty in a pan over medium heat for 3 to 4 minutes per side until it is hot in the center. You can also use a grill to prepare the patties. Just be sure to spray each frozen patty with the oil, and be sure the flames are low. Cook for 3 to 4 minutes per side. Those are the best cooking methods; however, you can also prepare a frozen patty by microwaving it

for 30 to 35 seconds, then turning the patty over and zapping it for another 30 to 35 seconds. Finally, you can heat a frozen patty in the microwave for 30 to 35 seconds, then place the partially defrosted patty in a toaster or toaster oven and cook it on medium heat until it's hot in the center.

- MAKES 6 VEGGIE PATTIES.

TIDBITS

If your food processor is too small to hold all of the ingredients, simply divide the ingredients and process one half at a time, or cut the recipe in half. Bulgur wheat can be found in most health food stores, and even some supermarkets carry it.

Nutrition Facts

SERVING SIZE—1 PATTY   FAT (PER SERVING)—3G
TOTAL SERVINGS—6   CALORIES (PER SERVING)—135

• • • •

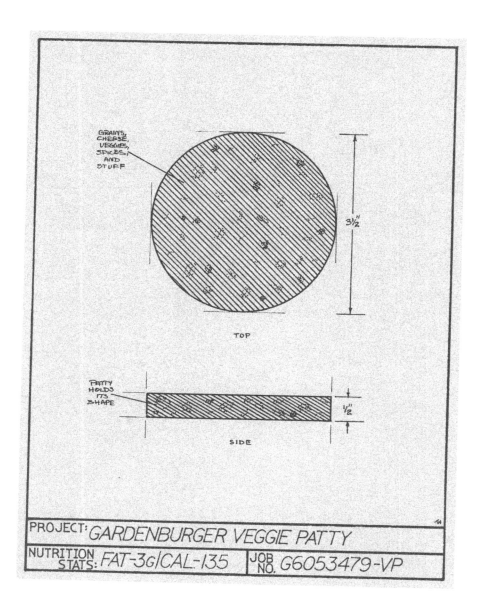

GRAINS,
CHEESE,
VEGGIES,
SPICES,
AND
STUFF

3½"

TOP

PATTY
HOLDS
ITS
SHAPE

½"

SIDE

PROJECT: *GARDENBURGER VEGGIE PATTY*

NUTRITION STATS: *FAT-3g/CAL-135*   JOB NO. *G6053479-VP*

330

HEALTHY CHOICE
TRADITIONAL PASTA SAUCE

☆   ✌   💣   ✐   ☯   ✂   ☞

It was a heart attack that inspired Charles M. Harper of ConAgra Foods to come up with a new product line. In 1988, the Healthy Choice brand introduced frozen dinners with reduced fat, sodium, and cholesterol. Hundreds of other products followed through the '90s, including this fat-free pasta sauce, which hit stores in 1992. It's a cinch to make and goes great on any pasta, pizza, or meatball sandwich. If it's a chunky sauce you're looking for, check out the next recipe.

2 10¾-ounce cans tomato puree
1 cup water
½ teaspoon dried minced garlic
1 teaspoon dried minced onion
5 teaspoons granulated sugar
½ teaspoon salt

1 tablespoon lemon juice
¼ teaspoon dried parsley
⅛ teaspoon dried thyme
¼ teaspoon dried basil
¼ teaspoon dried oregano
dash ground black pepper

1. Combine all of the ingredients in a medium saucepan over medium/high heat and bring to a boil.
2. Reduce heat to low and simmer for 1 to 1½ hours or until sauce is thick.

- MAKES 2½ CUPS.

Nutrition Facts
SERVING SIZE—½ CUP
TOTAL SERVINGS—5

FAT (PER SERVING)—0G
CALORIES (PER SERVING)—50

• • • •

HEALTHY CHOICE CHUNKY TOMATO, MUSHROOM & GARLIC PASTA SAUCE

☆　　　✌　　　💣　　　✏　　　☯　　　✂　　　☞

Healthy Choice was one of the first low-fat brands to hit the stores. The *Wall Street Journal* reported in 1993, "When Healthy Choice dinners first arrived in stores, big competitors were caught off guard: nothing quite like it had ever been marketed on a large scale." But nowadays the competition ain't so lean. You'll find more than a dozen brands devoted to the same low-fat, healthy claims in stores, all fighting it out for shelf space and market share.

If you like your marinara sauce with big chunks of veggies in it, then this is the one you'll want to make. The canned tomatoes, plus fresh mushrooms, onion, and garlic make for a thicker sauce that works great over your favorite pasta creation.

2 10¾-ounce cans tomato
　　puree
1 cup water
1 cup chopped canned
　　tomatoes
¾ cup sliced white button
　　mushrooms
2 teaspoons minced garlic
¼ cup minced white onion

5 teaspoons granulated
　　sugar
½ teaspoon salt
4 teaspoons lemon juice
¼ teaspoon dried parsley
⅛ teaspoon dried thyme
¼ teaspoon dried basil
¼ teaspoon dried oregano
dash ground black pepper

1. Combine all of the ingredients in a medium saucepan over medium/high heat and bring to a boil.
2. Reduce heat to low and simmer for 1 to 1½ hours or until sauce is thick.

- MAKES 2½ CUPS.

Nutrition Facts

SERVING SIZE—½ CUP   FAT (PER SERVING)—0G

TOTAL SERVINGS—5   CALORIES (PER SERVING)—45

• • • •

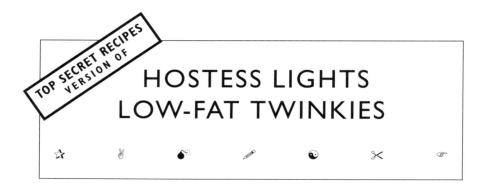

HOSTESS LIGHTS
LOW-FAT TWINKIES

Howdy Doody peddled them on his 1950s TV show. Archie Bunker got one in his lunchbox every day. Even President Jimmy Carter was a fan, supposedly ordering a Twinkie vending machine installed in the White House. Yes, Twinkies are an American favorite. And if the oblong little snack cake isn't being eaten, it's being talked about; usually by talk show hosts joking about the snack food's supposedly long shelf life.

The crème-filled cakes we know today are not exactly the same as the early Twinkies. When the snack cake was first conceived by Hostess plant manager James Dewar in 1930, it was as a way to use the cake pans for the strawberry "Little Short Cake Fingers," which sat idle for all but the six-week strawberry season. The filling in those original cakes was flavored with bananas, and they were called "Twinkle Fingers." But when bananas got scarce during World War II the filling was changed to the vanilla flavor we know today, and the name was shortened to "Twinkies."

The latest reformulation of the Twinkie came in 1990, when a low-fat version was first introduced. Now Twinkie lovers could have their cakes and eat 'em too, with only half the fat of the original.

You should know that these clones are twice the size of the Hostess version, with the fat and calories double as well. By weight, however, this clone's nutrition stats are right on track with the original.

CAKE

1 cup egg substitute
1 egg white
1⅔ cups sugar
½ teaspoon vanilla
⅛ teaspoon lemon extract

2 cups unsifted cake flour
1 tablespoon baking powder
½ teaspoon salt
½ cup fat-free milk
1½ teaspoons vegetable oil

12 12 x 12-inch pieces of
    aluminum foil

nonstick cooking spray

FILLING

¼ teaspoon salt
2 teaspoons water
1 7-ounce jar marshmallow crème

⅓ cup shortening
2 tablespoons powdered sugar
¼ teaspoon vanilla

1. Preheat the oven to 325⁰F.
2. In a large glass or metal bowl (copper is best—don't use plastic), beat together the egg substitute egg white until thick and lemon-colored. Add sugar, vanilla, and lemon extract and beat until smooth.
3. In another bowl, mix together the flour, baking powder, and salt.
4. Fold the dry mixture into the wet. Don't overmix.
5. In a small microwave-safe bowl, combine the fat-free milk with the oil. Heat this mixture in the microwave on high for 1½ minutes, or until it is very hot, but not boiling.
6. Fold the hot milk mixture into the batter. Do not beat and don't overmix.
7. Prepare the cake molds by folding each square of foil in half and then in half again, so that each piece is a 6-inch square. Wrap each of these foil pieces around a spice bottle. Fold the ends and leave the side open, so that when the foil is removed it makes a small pan (see diagram on page 67). Spray the inside of each mold with nonstick cooking spray. Then, arrange the molds in one or two baking dishes so that they can't tip over when baking.
8. Fill each mold about halfway with batter. Bake the cakes for

25 to 30 minutes or until the tops of the cakes turn light brown. Remove the cakes from the oven, and when they have cooled enough to touch, peel the foil off of each one and place them flat side (the top when baking) down onto wax paper or a cooling rack.

9. As the cakes cool, prepare the filling by combining ¼ teaspoon salt with 1 teaspoon water in a small microwave-safe bowl or cup. Microwave for 10 to 20 seconds on high, then stir until the salt is dissolved.

10. Beat the marshmallow crème with the shortening in a medium bowl with an electric mixer until smooth and fluffy. Add the powdered sugar, salt, water, and vanilla and beat well.

11. When the cakes have cooled, use a toothpick to poke three holes along the flat side of the cake (the top when baking). Swirl the toothpick around inside the cake to make room for the filling.

12. Squirt crème filling into each of the three holes in each of the cakes. Be careful not to overfill the cakes or you will have a sticky explosion that must be eaten immediately.

- MAKES 12 SNACK CAKES.

TIDBITS

If you want the cake to be yellow, like the original, you will have to be selective when choosing egg substitute. Scramblers brand egg substitute seems to make the cake the deepest yellow. Or, if you don't use Scramblers, you can add a couple drops of yellow food coloring. These snack cakes are best if eaten within a couple days of filling.

Nutrition Facts

SERVING SIZE—1 SNACK CAKE   FAT (PER SERVING)—3G
TOTAL SERVINGS—12   CALORIES (PER SERVING)—280

• • • •

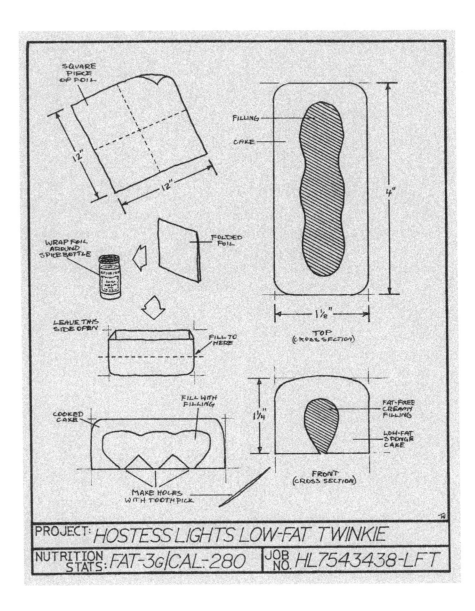

SQUARE
PIECE
OF FOIL

12"

12"

FILLING

CAKE

4"

1½"

TOP
(CROSS SECTION)

WRAP FOIL
AROUND
SPICE BOTTLE

FOLDED
FOIL

LEAVE THIS
SIDE OPEN

FILL TO
HERE

FAT-FREE
CREAMY
FILLING

LOW-FAT
SPONGE
CAKE

1¼"

FRONT
(CROSS SECTION)

COOKED
CAKE

FILL WITH
FILLING

MAKE HOLES
WITH TOOTHPICK

PROJECT: *HOSTESS LIGHTS LOW-FAT TWINKIE*

NUTRITION
STATS: *FAT-3g/CAL-280*

JOB
NO. *HL7543438-LFT*

KEEBLER REDUCED-FAT PECAN SANDIES

☆　　✌　　💣　　✏　　☯　　✂　　☞

The full-fat version of these delicious discs are the top-selling short-bread cookies in the United States. It's no wonder the baked-goods giant elected to introduce a reduced-fat version in 1994. You'll find this clone as easy to make as any other cookie recipe, but with much less fat in the crispy finished product.

1/3 cup shortening
1 cup powdered sugar
1/2 teaspoon baking soda
1/2 teaspoon vanilla
1/4 teaspoon salt
1/8 teaspoon coconut extract
2 tablespoons buttermilk

1 1/2 cups sifted all-purpose flour
1/4 teaspoon baking powder
1/4 cup finely chopped pecans

1. Preheat oven to 325°F.
2. With an electric mixer, cream together the shortening, sugar, baking soda, vanilla, salt, coconut extract, and buttermilk in a large bowl.
3. Combine flour and baking powder in another bowl.
4. Pour the dry ingredients into the wet ingredients and mix well.
5. Add pecans and mix until incorporated.
6. Roll dough into 1-inch balls and press them down onto an ungreased cookie sheet. Flatten the dough slightly with your fingers, and bake for 15 to 18 minutes or until cookies are light brown.

• MAKES 30 COOKIES.

Nutrition Facts

SERVING SIZE—1 COOKIE   FAT (PER SERVING)—3G

TOTAL SERVINGS—30   CALORIES (PER SERVING)—80

• • • •

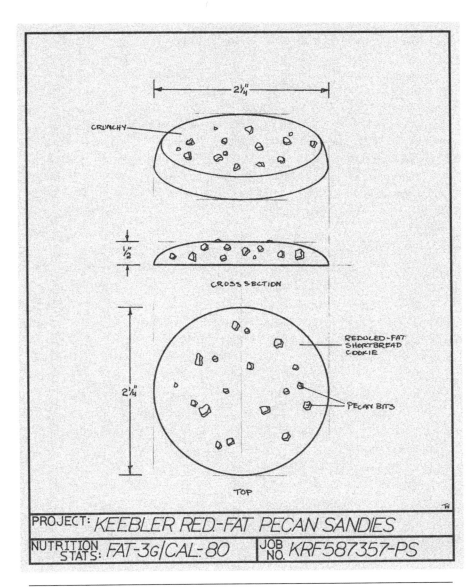

2¼"

CRUNCHY

½"

CROSS SECTION

REDUCED-FAT
SHORTBREAD
COOKIE

2¼"

PECAN BITS

TOP

PROJECT: *KEEBLER RED.-FAT PECAN SANDIES*

NUTRITION STATS: *FAT-3G/CAL.-80*   JOB NO. *KRF587357-PS*

KELLOGG'S LOW-FAT FROSTED BROWN SUGAR CINNAMON POP-TARTS

☆ ✌ 💣 ✏ ☯ ✂ ☞

Not even Tony the Tiger is a match for the world's most beloved toaster pastries. While Kellogg's Frosted Flakes is the best-selling cereal in the U.S., Pop-Tarts are an even bigger seller for the food manufacturer, with $330 million in sales in 1996. The two-to-a-pack rectangular snacks were born in 1964, when Kellogg's followed a competitor's idea for breakfast pastries that could be heated through in an ordinary toaster. With the company's experience in cereals and grains it was able to create pastries in a variety of flavors. Pop-Tarts have always dominated the toaster pastry market, but in the first half of the 1990s Nabisco was coming on strong with its own toaster pastries called Toastettes. Toastettes became so appealing to consumers because the package held eight pastries, while Pop-Tarts still had six to a box. In June of 1996, Kellogg's added two more Pop-Tarts to each box without changing the price, and Toastettes sales quickly dropped by 45 percent.

Another move against competitor Nabisco came that same year when Kellogg's introduced its new line of low-fat Pop-Tarts. Nabisco had earlier introduced low-fat toaster pastries in its Snack-Well's line, but the Kellogg's low-fat version of its popular product once again dominated.

This recipe makes eight clones, or a box's worth of the toaster pastries. Be sure to roll the dough very flat when preparing the pastries, and toast them on the very lowest setting of your toaster. Watch the pastries closely and pop 'em up if the frosting begins to turn brown.

DOUGH

2 tablespoons shortening
1/3 cup powdered sugar
3 tablespoons low fat
   (1 percent fat) buttermilk
1 tablespoon light corn syrup
1/2 teaspoon baking soda

rounded 1/4 teaspoon salt
scant 1/8 teaspoon baking powder
1 2/3 cups all-purpose flour
   (plus about 1/4 cup
   reserved for rolling dough)
3 tablespoons water

FILLING

3 tablespoons dark brown sugar
3 tablespoons sugar
3 tablespoons all-purpose flour

dash cinnamon
dash salt

1 egg white, beaten

FROSTING

1 tablespoon dark brown sugar
4 teaspoons fat-free milk
1 1/4 cups powdered sugar

dash salt
dash cinnamon

1. In a large bowl combine the shortening, powdered sugar, buttermilk, corn syrup, baking soda, salt, and baking powder using an electric mixer.
2. Add the flour and mix by hand to incorporate.
3. Mix in the water by hand, then use your hands to form the dough into a ball. Cover and set aside.
4. To make the filling, combine the ingredients in a small bowl and whisk together. Set aside.
5. To build the pastries, divide the dough in half, then roll one half out onto a floured surface, using additional flour on the rolling pin to prevent the dough from sticking. Roll the dough to no more than 1/16-inch thick. Use a knife or pizza wheel to cut the dough into four 3 x 8-inch rectangles.
6. Brush the beaten egg white over the entire surface of one half of each rectangle. Sprinkle a rounded 1/2 tablespoon of the filling over the surface of the brushed half of the pastry, being sure to leave a margin of about 1/4-inch from the edge of the dough all of the way around. Fold the other side of the dough

over onto the filling. Press down on the edge of the dough all of the way around with the tines of a fork to seal it. Use the fork to poke several holes in the top of the pastry. Fill the remaining three dough rectangles, and then repeat the process with the remaining half portion of dough.

7. Arrange the pastries on a lightly greased cookie sheet and bake in a preheated 350ºF oven 8 to 10 minutes. The pastries should be only very light brown, not dark brown (the pastries will be reheated and browned in a toaster before eating, like the real thing). Remove the pastries from the oven and cool completely.

8. Make the frosting by combining the brown sugar and milk in a small bowl. Microwave on half power for 10 to 20 seconds and stir until the sugar is dissolved. Add the remaining ingredients and stir well until smooth.

9. Spread a thin layer of the frosting over the top of each pastry and allow it to dry. Now leave the pastries out so that they dry completely. Overnight is best.

10. To reheat the pastries, toast them in a toaster oven or toaster on the lightest setting only. Watch carefully so that the pastries do not burn.

- SERVES 8.

Nutrition Facts

SERVING SIZE—1 PASTRY   FAT (PER SERVING)—3G
TOTAL SERVINGS—8   CALORIES (PER SERVING)—219

• • • •

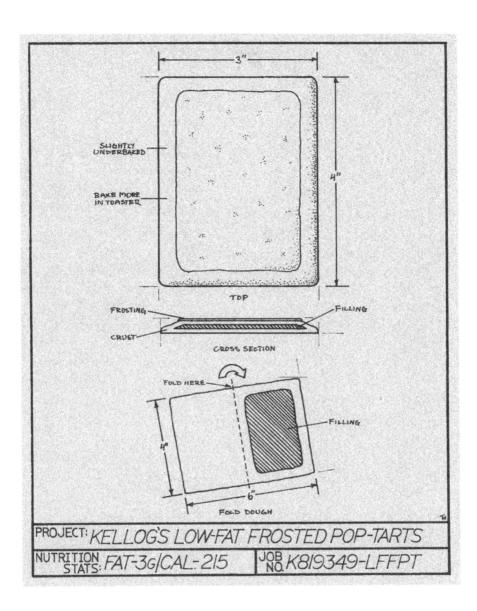

3"

4"

SLIGHTLY
UNDERBAKED

BAKE MORE
IN TOASTER

TOP

FROSTING

FILLING

CRUST

CROSS SECTION

FOLD HERE

FILLING

4"

6"

FOLD DOUGH

PROJECT: *KELLOGS LOW-FAT FROSTED POP-TARTS*

NUTRITION STATS: *FAT-3g/CAL.-215*

JOB NO. *K819349-LFFPT*

KRAFT FREE
CATALINA DRESSING

In 1958, Kraft became one of the first companies to introduce low-calorie salad dressings, with dietetic versions of Italian, French, Bleu Cheese, and Thousand Island dressings. Then, in 1990, Kraft scored another series of hits with its line of fat-free dressings. Today, fat-free and low-fat dressings are just about as popular and diverse as the full-fat varieties.

Here's a TSR clone recipe to create a fat-free dressing like the popular Catalina variety from the innovative food conglomerate. Where the fat should be, cornstarch and gelatin help thicken the dressing and give it a pleasing texture that will ensure you don't even miss those big-time fat grams of the traditional stuff.

1 cup water
⅓ cup sugar
⅓ cup white vinegar
3 tablespoons tomato paste

1 teaspoon cornstarch
½ teaspoon Knox unflavored gelatin
¾ teaspoon salt
dash garlic powder

1. Combine all the ingredients in a saucepan and stir to dissolve the gelatin and cornstarch.
2. Set the pan over medium heat until the mixture begins to boil. Boil for 1 minute, stirring often, then remove the pan from the heat, cover it, and let it cool.
3. Pour the dressing into a covered container and refrigerate it for several hours or overnight until chilled.

- MAKES 1 CUP.

Nutrition Facts

SERVING SIZE—2 TABLESPOONS   FAT (PER SERVING)—0G

TOTAL SERVINGS—8   CALORIES (PER SERVING)—40

•   •   •   •

KRAFT FREE
CLASSIC CAESAR DRESSING

☆   ✌   💣   ✏   ☯   ✂   ☞

Thanks to fat-free mayonnaise and low-fat buttermilk, we can make a homegrown version of this popular fat-free Kraft creation. You might at first say, "Wait a minute ... how can this be fat-free when there's buttermilk and two kinds of grated cheese in there?" Yes, indeed, those products do contain fat. But, as long as a serving of the finished product contains less than ½ gram of fat—as it does here—it's considered fat-free. Be sure to give yourself plenty of time to allow this dressing to chill in the refrigerator for several hours before serving.

I tablespoon sugar
½ teaspoon salt
2 tablespoons hot water
½ cup fat-free mayonnaise
2 tablespoons low-fat buttermilk
   (I percent fat)
4 teaspoons white vinegar

2 teaspoons grated Romano
   cheese
2 teaspoons grated Parmesan
   cheese
dash coarse ground black pepper
dash dried oregano
dash garlic powder

1. Dissolve the sugar and salt in a small bowl with the hot water. Set aside.
2. Combine the remaining ingredients in a medium bowl and stir well.
3. Add the water/sugar/salt mixture to the other ingredients and stir once more to combine. Place the dressing in a covered container in the refrigerator and chill for several hours.

- MAKES A LITTLE OVER ¾ CUP.

TIDBITS

If the dressing seems too thick, just add some more water, a table-spoon at a time, until it has the desired consistency.

Nutrition Facts

SERVING SIZE—2 TABLESPOONS   FAT (PER SERVING)—0G
TOTAL SERVINGS—7   CALORIES (PER SERVING)—35

• • • •

KRAFT FREE THOUSAND ISLAND DRESSING

Once upon a time we drenched our salads with generous portions of popular dressings such as this one and considered it a healthy pre-entrée course. Just two tablespoons of the full-fat version of Thousand Island dressing packs about 10 grams of fat, and we normally use about ¼ cup on a salad. That's 20 grams of fat in our bellies, before the main course has even started. Yikes! But, today we know better. So, never fear, a *Top Secret Recipe* is here. And you won't get even one gram of fat from a serving of this TSR formula that clones the most popular fat-free Thousand Island dressing on the supermarket shelves.

1 tablespoon sugar
⅛ teaspoon salt
2 tablespoons hot water
½ cup fat-free mayonnaise
2 tablespoons ketchup

1 tablespoon white vinegar
2 teaspoons sweet pickle relish
1 teaspoon finely minced white onion
dash black pepper

1. Dissolve the sugar and salt in the hot water in a small bowl.
2. Combine the remaining ingredients with the water mixture. Stir well.
3. Place the dressing in a covered container and refrigerate it for several hours so that the flavors blend.

• MAKES ABOUT 1 CUP.

If the dressing seems too thick, just add some more water, a tablespoon at a time, until it has the desired consistency.

Nutrition Facts

SERVING SIZE—2 TABLESPOONS	FAT (PER SERVING)—0G
TOTAL SERVINGS—6	CALORIES (PER SERVING)—40

•   •   •   •

KRAFT LIGHT DELUXE MACARONI & CHEESE DINNER

☆　　✌　　💧　　✒　　☯　　✂　　☞

The difference between the "deluxe" version of Kraft's Macaroni & Cheese Dinner and the original is the cheese. The deluxe dinner has an envelope of cheese sauce, while the original dinner, introduced to the nation back in 1937, comes with powdered cheese. The original Kraft Macaroni & Cheese Dinner is the most popular packaged dinner product around, and one of the top six best-selling of all dry goods sold in the supermarket—probably because it only takes about 7 minutes to prepare, and a box costs just 70 cents. And who doesn't like macaroni and cheese? But it's the deluxe version—the more expensive version—with its pouch of gooey, yellow cheese sauce, which Kraft reformulated as a reduced-fat product in 1997. The new version boasts 50 percent less fat and 10 percent fewer calories than the deluxe original, and tastes just as good. So here's a simple clone that requires you to get your hands on Cheez Whiz Light, reduced-fat cheddar cheese, and elbow macaroni. Then you're on your way to an amazing clone of what cartoon Texan Hank Hill from the TV show *King of the Hill* refers to as "veggies."

8 cups water
1¾ cups uncooked elbow macaroni
⅓ cup reduced-fat
　　(2 percent milk) shredded
　　cheddar cheese

½ cup Cheez Whiz Light
1 tablespoon whole milk
½ teaspoon salt

1. Bring 8 cups (2 quarts) of water to a boil over high heat in a large saucepan. Add the elbow macaroni to the water and cook for 10 to 12 minutes or until tender, stirring occasionally.
2. As the macaroni boils, prepare the sauce by combining the cheddar cheese, Cheez Whiz, and milk in a small saucepan over medium/low heat. Stir the cheese mixture often as it heats, so that it does not burn. Add the salt. When all of the cheddar cheese has melted and the sauce is smooth, cover the pan and set it aside until the macaroni has cooked.
3. When the macaroni is ready, drain the water off, but do not rinse the macaroni.
4. Using the same pan you prepared the macaroni in, combine the macaroni with the cheese sauce and mix well.

• SERVES 4.

TIDBITS

If you would like your macaroni and cheese to have a color that is similar to the happy, fluorescent orange tint of the original, you can add a little paprika—about ⅛ teaspoon—to the cheese sauce just before you remove it from the heat.

Nutrition Facts

SERVING SIZE—1 CUP   FAT (PER SERVING)—5G
TOTAL SERVINGS—4   CALORIES (PER SERVING)—290

• • • •

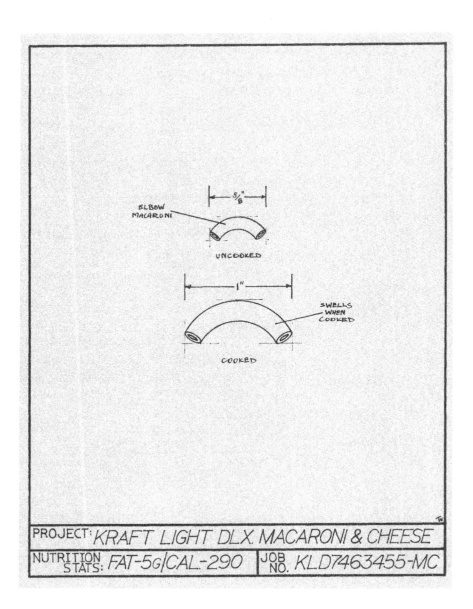

ELBOW
MACARONI

⅝"

UNCOOKED

1"

SWELLS
WHEN
COOKED

COOKED

PROJECT: *KRAFT LIGHT DLX. MACARONI & CHEESE*

NUTRITION
STATS: *FAT-5g/CAL.-290*

JOB
NO. *KLD7463455-MC*

NABISCO REDUCED-FAT CHEESE NIPS

☆   ✌   ●   ✏   ◉   ✂   ☞

In the last several years, since 1992, Nabisco has taken great effort to produce reduced-fat versions of all the popular products created by the food giant. This product loyalty–retaining move is just good business. According to one Nabisco spokesperson, "We want to bring back the people who have enjoyed our products, but went away for health and diet reasons." Indeed, that's exactly what we see happening, as customers are now grabbing for all those boxes with the green on them. The box for these cheesy crackers is indeed splashed with green and has big letters at the top that say: "Reduced Fat: 40% less fat than original Cheese Nips."

The secret ingredient for this clone of the popular little square crackers is the fat-free cheese sprinkles by Molly McButter. One 2-ounce shaker of the stuff will do it, and you won't use it all. Just keep in mind that cheese powder is pretty salty, so you may want to go very easy on salting the tops of the crackers.

1 cup sifted all-purpose flour
   (plus about 1/2 cup for kneading
   and rolling)
1 teaspoon baking soda
1/4 teaspoon baking powder

nonstick cooking spray

1/2 cup Molly McButter fat-free
   cheese sprinkles
2 1/2 tablespoons shortening
1/3 cup plus 1 tablespoon low-fat
   buttermilk (1 percent fat)

1/2 teaspoon salt (optional for tops)

1. Sift together 1 cup of flour, the baking soda, baking powder, and cheese sprinkles in a large bowl.
2. Cut in the shortening with a fork and knife with a crosswise motion until the dough is broken down into rice-size pieces. The mixture will still be very dry.
3. Stir in the buttermilk with a fork until the dough becomes very moist and sticky.
4. Sprinkle a couple tablespoons of the reserved flour over the dough and work it in until the dough can be handled without sticking, then turn it out onto a floured board, being sure to reserve ¼ cup of flour for later. Knead the dough well for 60 to 90 seconds, and be sure the flour is incorporated. Wrap the dough in plastic wrap and chill for at least one hour.
5. Preheat the oven to 325°F. Spray a light coating of cooking spray on a baking sheet.
6. Remove the dough from the refrigerator and use the remaining reserved flour to dust a rolling surface. Roll about one-third of the dough to about 1/16-inch thick. Trim the edges square (a pizza slicer works great for this), then transfer the dough to the baking sheet. Use the rolling pin to transfer the dough. Simply pick up one end of the dough onto the rolling pin, and roll the dough around it. Reverse the process onto the baking sheet to transfer the dough.
7. Use a pizza slicer to cut across and down the dough, creating 1-inch square pieces. Use the blunt end of a skewer or a cut toothpick to poke a hole in the center of each piece.
8. Sprinkle a very light coating of salt over the top of the crackers (this is optional—the crackers will already be quite salty) and bake for 8 to 10 minutes. Mix the crackers around like Scrabble tiles (so those on the edge don't burn) and bake for another 3 to 5 minutes, or until some are just barely turning a light brown. Repeat the rolling and baking process with the remaining dough.

- MAKES APPROXIMATELY 300 CRACKERS.

Serving size—31 crackers   Fat (per serving)—3.5g
Total servings—about 10   Calories (per serving)—105

• • • •

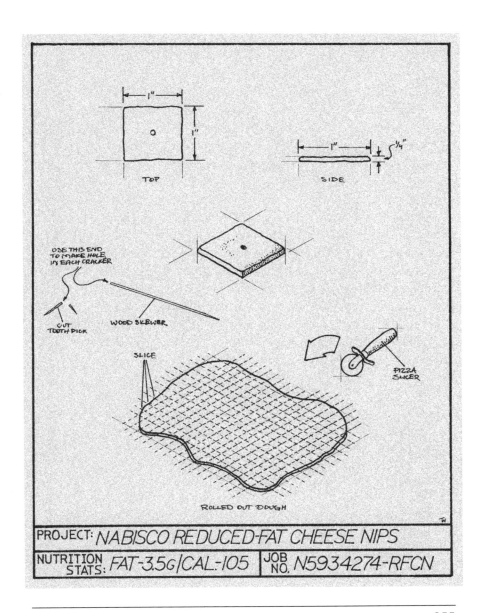

PROJECT: *NABISCO REDUCED-FAT CHEESE NIPS*

NUTRITION STATS: *FAT-3.5G/CAL.-105*   JOB NO. *N5934274-RFCN*

NABISCO SNACKWELL'S CHOCOLATE CHIP COOKIES

☆   ✌   💣   ✏   ☯   ✂   ☞

Nabisco debuted its first six SnackWell's line of products in 1992 to rave reviews and more than impressive sales. The company was having a very hard time keeping up with the extraordinary demand, and customers would find empty shelves in the supermarkets where SnackWell's cookies were once stacked. That supply problem would eventually be addressed in a series of humorous commercials, featuring the shelf-stocking "Cookie Man" who was attacked by ravenous women in search of the fast-selling products. The ads' announcer told everyone not to worry, that the products would soon be on the way to the stores.

Today, supply has caught up with demand, and the stores seem to be able to keep plenty of the products in stock, including the bite-size chocolate chip cookies, which can be cloned with this recipe. The cookies are easily made so small by rolling the dough into long, plastic-wrapped logs, which you then chill, slice, and bake.

1 egg white
¼ cup sugar
1 tablespoon brown sugar
1 tablespoon corn syrup
1 tablespoon shortening
1 ½ tablespoons egg
   substitute

¾ cup all-purpose flour
¼ teaspoon plus a pinch
   of salt
¾ teaspoon baking soda
½ teaspoon baking powder
½ cup mini chocolate chips

1. Preheat the oven to 325°F.
2. Beat the egg white until thick.
3. Add the granulated sugar to the egg white and continue beating until the mixture forms soft peaks.
4. While beating, add the brown sugar, corn syrup, shortening, and egg substitute.
5. In a separate bowl, combine the flour, salt, baking soda, and baking powder.
6. Combine the dry mixture with the wet and mix well. Add the chocolate chips and incorporate them into the dough.
7. Divide the dough in half, then roll each portion into a long, thin log about the same diameter as a nickel and wrap each in plastic wrap. Put the dough into the refrigerator and chill it for a couple hours (you may also use the freezer for roughly half the time if you're in a hurry).
8. When the dough has thoroughly chilled, remove each log of dough from the plastic wrap and cut into ¼-inch-thick slices. Place slices on a cookie sheet coated lightly with nonstick spray about ½-inch apart, and bake for 10 to 12 minutes or until the cookies turn light brown.

- MAKES 12 DOZEN BITE-SIZE COOKIES.

Nutrition Facts

SERVING SIZE—13 COOKIES FAT (PER SERVING)—3.3G
TOTAL SERVINGS—11 CALORIES (PER SERVING)—105

• • • •

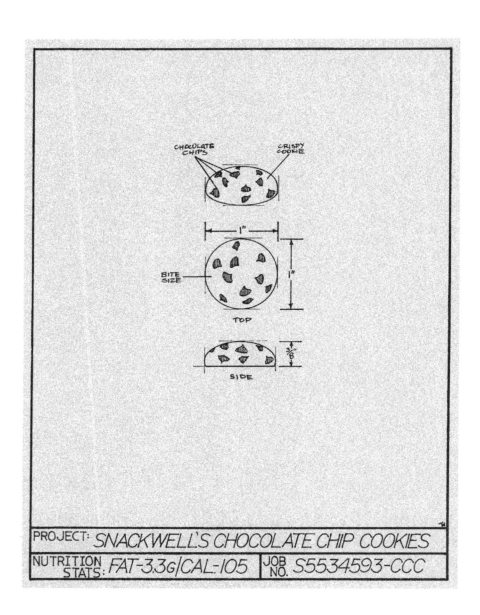

CHOCOLATE CHIPS

CRISPY COOKIE

1"

BITE SIZE

1"

TOP

SIDE

3/8"

PROJECT: *SNACKWELL'S CHOCOLATE CHIP COOKIES*

NUTRITION STATS: *FAT-3.3g/CAL-105*

JOB NO. *S5534593-CCC*

NABISCO SNACKWELL'S GOLDEN SNACK BARS

☆ ✌ ● ✏ ◉ ✂ ☞

Bite into one of these chewy cake bars and you won't believe that it's so low in fat. That's because we replace a lot of the fat you would find in most cakes with sweetened condensed milk, and some egg substitute. That gives us room to throw some shortening in there and still keep the fat count at less than 2 grams per serving, just like the real thing. Also, take note of the technique used to give the snack bars that sugar-crystal coating on the top and bottom of the bars, just as you will find on the original SnackWell's creation.

2 egg whites
I cup plus 5 tablespoons
    sugar
2 tablespoons corn syrup
3 tablespoons shortening
1/4 cup sweetened condensed skim
    milk
1/4 cup egg substitute

3 tablespoons low-fat
    (2 percent) milk
1 1/2 teaspoons vanilla
1/4 teaspoon lemon extract
1 1/2 cups all-purpose flour
I teaspoon salt
1/4 teaspoon baking soda
nonstick cooking spray

1. Preheat the oven to 350ºF.
2. In a large bowl, whip the egg whites with an electric mixer until they become thick. Do not use a plastic bowl for this.
3. Add I cup of sugar to the egg whites and continue to beat until the mixture forms soft peaks.
4. Add the corn syrup, shortening, condensed milk, egg substitute,

low-fat milk, vanilla, and lemon extract to the mixture while beating.

5. In a separate bowl, combine the flour, salt, and baking soda.
6. While beating the wet mixture, slowly add the dry ingredients.
7. Lightly grease a 9 x 13-inch pan with a light coating of nonstick cooking spray. Be sure to coat the sides as well as the bottom of the pan. Dump about 3 tablespoons of sugar into the pan, then tilt and shake the pan so that a light layer of sugar coats the entire bottom of the pan and about halfway up the sides. Pour out the excess sugar.
8. Pour the batter into the pan, spreading it evenly around the inside. Sprinkle a light coating of sugar—about two tablespoons—over the entire top surface of the batter. Gently shake the pan from side to side to evenly distribute the sugar over the batter. Bake for 25 to 28 minutes or until the cake begins to pull away from the sides of the pan.
9. Remove the cake from the oven and turn it out onto a cooling rack. When the cake has cooled, place it onto a sheet of wax paper on a cutting board and slice across the cake 6 times, creating 7 even slices. Next cut the cake lengthwise twice, into thirds, creating a total of 21 snack bars. When the bars have completely cooled, store them in a resealable plastic bag or an airtight container.

- MAKES 21 SNACK BARS.

Nutrition Facts
SERVING SIZE—1 BAR
SERVINGS—21

TOTAL FAT (PER SERVING)—1.8G
CALORIES (PER SERVING)—113

• • • •

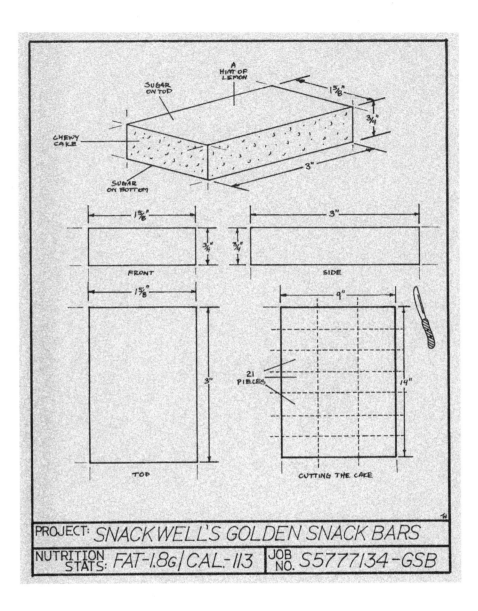

SUGAR
ON TOP

A
HINT OF
LEMON

1⅝"

¾"

CHEWY
CAKE

3"

SUGAR
ON BOTTOM

1⅝"

¾"

¾"

3"

FRONT

SIDE

1⅝"

9"

3"

21
PIECES

14"

TOP

CUTTING THE CAKE

PROJECT: *SNACKWELL'S GOLDEN SNACK BARS*

NUTRITION STATS: *FAT-1.8g / CAL-113*

JOB NO. *S5777134-GSB*

RED LOBSTER
LEMON-PEPPER GRILLED
MAHI-MAHI

☆   ✌   💣   ✎   ☯   ✂   ☞

The Red Lobster menu describes this dish as: "A mild-tasting fillet sprinkled with lemon-pepper seasoning, plus rice." Simple enough. And, if you keep the butter to a minimum, this clone becomes a naturally low-fat meal. Most of the butter will melt away from the fish when grilling, and mahi-mahi has hardly any fat in it. The liquid smoke is here to give the fish a flavor similar to that served in the restaurant, and I find Jane's brand of lemon-pepper seasoning the best to use here, if you can find it. Add some rice on the side— either brown or converted—some steamed veggies, and you've got yourself an incredibly guilt-free meal.

1 ½ pounds mahi-mahi fillets,
    skinned
1 tablespoon water
2 to 3 drops liquid smoke

1 tablespoon butter, melted
1 teaspoon lemon-pepper seasoning
    (Jane's is best)

1. Preheat the barbecue or indoor grill to high heat.
2. Cut the mahi-mahi into four equal portions. Be sure to remove the skin.
3. Combine the water and liquid smoke in a small bowl. Brush this solution over the entire surface of each piece of fish.
4. Brush the melted butter over the entire surface of each piece of fish.

5. Sprinkle a generous portion of the lemon-pepper seasoning on the top of each piece of fish, then grill the fish with this side down on the grill. Sprinkle the remaining seasoning over the top of each piece.

6. Grill the fish for 5 to 6 minutes per side, then serve hot with rice.

• SERVES 2.

Nutrition Facts

SERVING SIZE—2 FILLETS

TOTAL SERVINGS—2

FAT (PER SERVING)—5G

CALORIES (PER SERVING)—340

• • • •

RED LOBSTER
NANTUCKET BAKED COD

☆　✌　💣　✏　☯　✂　☞

Here's another Red Lobster selection that is a simple, healthy choice for your next kitchen-cloned meal. The menu described it as: "A flaky, white fish, baked with fresh tomatoes & Parmesan, served with rice." Much of the butter will slip away from the fish, and you will get a very small amount of fat from the Parmesan cheese; but at a total of 6 grams of fat per serving, this is still a very low-fat choice for lunch or dinner. Serve this dish with rice and some steamed veggies, and save the fat grams for dessert.

SPICE BLEND

1/4 teaspoon salt	dash black pepper
1/4 teaspoon paprika	dash cayenne pepper

1 1/2 pounds fresh cod fillet	2 small tomatoes, thinly sliced
1 tablespoon butter, melted	2 tablespoons grated Parmesan
lemon juice	cheese

1. Combine the spices in a small bowl and set aside.
2. Preheat the oven to 425ºF. Cut the fish into 4 equal portions (2 per serving), and arrange the fillets in a 9 x 13-inch baking dish or pan.
3. Melt the butter in a small bowl in the microwave for 10 to 20 seconds. Brush the top of each fillet with butter, drizzle a little lemon juice on the fish, then sprinkle the spice blend evenly over the top of each fillet.
4. Arrange 2 to 3 tomato slices over the top of each fillet.

5. Sprinkle grated Parmesan cheese over each tomato slice. Each slice should be at least 50 percent covered with the cheese, and it's okay for some of the cheese to fall on the fish.
6. Bake the fish, uncovered, for 8 minutes, then turn the oven to a high broil and continue to cook for 6 to 8 minutes or until the cheese on the tomatoes begins to brown. Serve two pieces of fish together, with rice on the side.

• SERVES 2.

Nutrition Facts

SERVING SIZE—2 FILLETS   FAT (PER SERVING)—6G
TOTAL SERVINGS—2   CALORIES (PER SERVING)—370

•   •   •   •

SWISS MISS FAT-FREE CHOCOLATE FUDGE PUDDING

☆   ✌   ●   ✎   ☯   ✂   ☞

Hunt-Wesson first introduced a light variety of Swiss Miss Puddings in 1990, but three years later changed the formula to fat-free. This chocolaty clone of the rich pudding you find in the refrigerated section of the supermarket will satisfy your chocolate craving without contributing any of those nasty fat grams. You'll notice that the sweetened condensed milk helps to replace fat, and the cornstarch jumps in to keep the pudding thick and creamy. Add two types of chocolate and you've got an irresistible snack that tastes just like the real deal.

2½ cups fat-free milk
2 tablespoons unsweetened cocoa
    powder
3 tablespoons cornstarch
½ cup sweetened condensed skim
    milk

3 tablespoons Hershey's chocolate
    syrup
dash salt
½ teaspoon vanilla extract

1. In a saucepan, combine the fat-free milk with the cocoa powder and cornstarch and whisk thoroughly until the powders are dissolved.
2. Add the condensed milk, chocolate syrup, and salt to the saucepan. Set the pan over medium/low heat. Heat the mixture, stirring constantly, until it comes to a boil and then thickens. This will take about 6 minutes.

3. Remove the pan from the heat and let it sit, covered, for 5 minutes. Then add the vanilla.
4. Transfer the pudding to serving cups, cover each with plastic wrap, and chill for at least 2 to 3 hours before serving.

- SERVES 4.

TIDBITS

Cover the pudding tightly when chilling and eat it within a few days or it may begin to thin.

Nutrition Facts

SERVING SIZE—¾ CUP   FAT (PER SERVING)—0G

TOTAL SERVINGS—4   CALORIES (PER SERVING)—170

• • • •

SWISS MISS FAT-FREE TAPIOCA PUDDING

☆   ✌   💣   ✏   ☯   ✂   ☞

When the first instant hot cocoa mix was developed in the fifties, it was available only to the airlines in individual portions for passengers and was called Brown Swiss. This mix was so popular that the company packaged it for sale in the grocery stores and changed the name to Swiss Miss. In the seventies, the first Swiss Miss Puddings were introduced and quickly became the leader of dairy case puddings. When the fat-free versions of the puddings were introduced some 23 years later, they, too, would become a popular favorite.

No sugar needs to be added to this recipe that recreates one of the best-tasting brands of fat-free pudding on the market. The condensed milk is enough to sweeten the pudding; plus it provides a creamy consistency, which, along with the cornstarch, helps to replace the fat found in the full-fat version of this tasty tapioca treat. It's a simple recipe to make and you won't even "miss" the fat.

2 tablespoons cornstarch
2½ cups fat-free milk
½ cup sweetened condensed skim milk

dash salt
2½ tablespoons instant tapioca
½ teaspoon vanilla extract

1. Combine the cornstarch with the fat-free milk in a medium saucepan and whisk thoroughly to dissolve the cornstarch.
2. Add the condensed milk, salt, and tapioca to the pan. Stir until smooth and then set the pan aside for 5 minutes.
3. After 5 minutes, bring the mixture to a boil over medium/low

heat, stirring constantly until it thickens, then cover and remove from the heat. Let the pudding sit, covered, for 20 minutes.

4. Stir in the vanilla, then transfer the pudding to serving cups. Cover the cups with plastic wrap and let them chill for at least 2 to 3 hours before serving.

- SERVES 4.

TIDBITS

Cover the pudding tightly when chilling and eat it within a few days or it may begin to thin.

Nutrition Facts

SERVING SIZE—¾ CUP	FAT (PER SERVING)—0G
TOTAL SERVINGS—4	CALORIES (PER SERVING)—140

• • • •

T.G.I. FRIDAY'S JACK DANIEL'S GRILL SALMON

☆　　✌　　💣　　✏　　☯　　✂　　☞

The glaze that is brushed over this salmon is one of the most scrumptious sauces you will ever taste on fish, or just about any other meat. T.G.I. Friday's introduced the glaze in 1997 and it became the company's most successful new product launch. I was encouraged to figure out how to clone the stuff when the *Oprah Winfrey Show* requested a recreation of the glaze for an appearance. This recipe is the result of hard work, and darn accurate at that. Plus, when the glaze is brushed over salmon, it makes for a very healthy meal.

While the fat count here may seem high compared to other recipes in the book, don't be too concerned. That fat, which comes from the salmon, is called Omega-3 fatty acids, and it is a beneficial type of fat found in fish and nuts. Research has shown that Omega-3 fatty acids can actually prevent heart disease and lower cholesterol.

As for the sauce, you will find it is very versatile. You can brush it on almost any type of fish, as well as ribs, chicken, and beef. It also keeps very well for long periods of time if stored in the refrigerator in a sealed container.

GLAZE

1 head of garlic
1 tablespoon olive oil
2/3 cup water
1 cup pineapple juice
1/4 cup teriyaki sauce
1 tablespoon soy sauce
1 1/3 cups dark brown sugar

3 tablespoons lemon juice
3 tablespoons minced white
  onion
1 tablespoon Jack Daniel's whiskey
1 tablespoon crushed pineapple
1/4 teaspoon cayenne pepper

4 1/2-pound fresh Atlantic salmon
  fillets
fat-free butter-flavored spray or
  spread

salt
pepper

1. Preheat the oven to 325ºF.
2. To roast the garlic for the glaze, cut about 1/2-inch off the top of the garlic head. Cut the roots so that the garlic will sit flat. Remove most of the papery skin from the garlic, but leave enough so that the cloves stay together. Place the head of garlic in a small casserole dish or baking pan, drizzle the olive oil over it, and cover it with a lid or foil. Bake for 1 hour. Remove the garlic and let it cool until you can handle it.
3. Combine the water, pineapple juice, teriyaki sauce, soy sauce, and brown sugar in a medium saucepan over medium/high heat. Stir occasionally until the mixture boils, then reduce the heat until the mixture is just simmering.
4. Squeeze the sides of the head of garlic until the pasty roasted garlic is squeezed out. Measure 2 teaspoons into the saucepan and whisk to combine. Add the remaining glaze ingredients to the pan and stir.
5. Let the mixture simmer for 40 to 50 minutes or until the glaze has reduced by about one-third and is thick and syrupy. Make sure it doesn't boil over. When the glaze is done, cover the saucepan and set it aside until the fish is ready.
6. To cook the fish, preheat your barbecue or kitchen grill to medium/high heat. Remove any skin or bones from the fillets. Brush the entire surface of each fillet with a light coating of the

fat-free butter-flavored spread or spray. Lightly salt and pepper both sides of the fillets and place them on the hot grill at a slight angle, so that grill marks will be made at an angle on the fish. Cook each fillet for 2 to 4 minutes, then turn them over, placing them back on the grill at an angle once again. After 2 to 4 minutes, turn the fish over at a different angle so that the grill marks will criss-cross. Cook 2 to 4 minutes more, flip again, and cook until done. The entire cooking time should be somewhere between 8 to 15 minutes depending on the thickness of your fillets and the heat of the grill. Be careful not to burn the fish, and quickly move the fish away from any flare-ups.

7. When the fillets are done, remove them from the grill and spoon a generous portion of glaze over each one. Serve hot with a baked potato and vegetables, if desired.

• SERVES 4 AS AN ENTRÉE.

Nutrition Facts

SERVING SIZE—1 FILLET

TOTAL SERVINGS—4

FAT (PER SERVING)—16.5G

CALORIES (PER SERVING)—525

•   •   •   •

WEIGHT WATCHERS SMART ONES CHOCOLATE ÉCLAIR

☆　　　✌　　　💣　　　✐　　　☯　　　✂　　　☞

Weight Watchers was one of the first companies to introduce low-fat foods to the freezer section of your local supermarket. Those earlier items were mostly meals, such as dinners and lunch items. In 1980, the company began offering a selection of low-fat desserts, which quickly gained in popularity; probably because they didn't taste low-fat. But more recent favorites are these small chocolate-frosted, crème-filled eclairs, developed in 1993. The originals are bought and stored frozen, but they can be defrosted at room temperature within an hour and scarfed down, guilt-free.

The clone recipe here is designed so that you don't need a special pastry bag to make the shells, or to fill them with the delicious, custard-like combination of fat-free vanilla pudding and Dream Whip. It's an éclair recipe you won't find anywhere else, and it's guaranteed to satisfy your most fierce dessert craving.

FILLING

¼ cup instant vanilla pudding
　　(½ of a 3.4-ounce package)
⅔ cup fat-free milk

1 envelope Dream Whip
dash salt

SHELLS

1½ cups cake flour, sifted
¼ teaspoon baking powder
1½ cups water
2½ tablespoons butter

¼ teaspoon vanilla
1 tablespoon sugar
dash salt
4 egg whites, slightly beaten

GLAZE

¾ cup powdered sugar
2 tablespoons cocoa powder
dash salt

scant ½ teaspoon vanilla
4 to 5 teaspoons water

1. First make the filling by combining the pudding mix with the milk and beating with an electric mixer on low speed for about 30 seconds.

2. Add the envelope of Dream Whip and mix again on low speed for about 30 seconds.

3. Turn the mixer speed to high and continue beating the mixture for about 2 minutes until it's light and fluffy. Cover and chill for at least an hour (while you are making the shells).

4. Preheat the oven to 400°F.

5. To make the shells, mix the flour and baking powder together in a medium bowl and set aside.

6. Combine the water, butter, vanilla, sugar, and salt in a medium saucepan and bring the mixture to a boil over high heat.

7. Turn the heat down to low and add the flour and baking powder mixture all at once. Stir vigorously with a wooden spoon until the mixture forms a ball and pulls away from the side of the pan. Remove the pan from the heat and immediately transfer the mixture to a medium mixing bowl.

8. Add the 4 egg whites to the bowl. Beat the mixture with a wooden spoon to incorporate the egg whites until it becomes smooth and forms a paste.

9. Make a pastry bag by cutting the corner off a plastic storage bag. Cut about ¾-inch in from the corner to create a hole that is about 1 inch in diameter. Fill the bag with the dough while it is still warm—you don't want the dough to cool.

10. Pipe 4½-inch strips of dough onto an ungreased baking sheet. You should be able to make 9 strips of dough.

11. Bake for 20 to 25 minutes, then reduce the heat to 325°F and bake for an additional 30 to 35 minutes until the shells are light brown. Let cool.

12. Cut the tip off one end of each shell and scrape out the soft

doughy centers with a cocktail fork or handle end of a spoon.

13. When the inside of the shells have cooled completely, use another bag with a corner cut off (a little smaller hole this time) to fill each one with the chilled filling.

14. Make the chocolate glaze by combining the powdered sugar, cocoa, and salt in a medium bowl. Add the vanilla and 4 teaspoons of water and stir the mixture until it is smooth. If it is too thick, add an additional teaspoon of water.

15. Spread the glaze over the top of each éclair. Serve immediately, or you can freeze the éclairs. If frozen, the éclairs should thaw at room temperature for 1 hour before serving.

- MAKES 9 ÉCLAIRS.

Nutrition Facts

SERVING SIZE—1 ÉCLAIR	FAT (PER SERVING)—4G
TOTAL SERVINGS—9	CALORIES (PER SERVING)—160

•　•　•　•

BOSTON MARKET
CREAMED SPINACH

When Boston Market first opened in 1989, it was called Boston Chicken. That's because at that time chicken was the only meat served at the chain. But three years later, in 1992, the chain added meatloaf, turkey, and ham, and officially became Boston Market. Yes, a lot of signs had to be changed, at considerable expense.

This popular side dish, which contains three types of cheese, normally has 24 grams of fat per serving. So, for this clone recipe, we'll be using two fat-free cheeses along with regular Provolone, and we'll be able to re-create the taste of the real thing; but with only 25 percent of the fat in the original.

2 10-ounce packages chopped
    frozen spinach
2 tablespoons diced white
    onion
3 ounces provolone cheese, chopped

4 slices Kraft fat-free Swiss Cheese
    Singles, quartered
4 slices Kraft fat-free Mozzarella
    Singles, quartered
1 ½ teaspoons white vinegar
¼ heaping teaspoon salt

1. Thaw the spinach and place it in a medium saucepan over medium/low heat with the onion. Heat for 7 to 10 minutes or until the liquid begins to bubble. Drain.
2. Add the remaining ingredients to the saucepan and heat for an additional 5 to 7 minutes or until smooth and creamy.

- SERVES 4.

Nutritional Facts *(per serving)*

SERVING SIZE—½ CUP   TOTAL SERVINGS—4

	LITE	ORIGINAL
CALORIES	180	300
FAT	6G	24G

•   •   •   •

CALIFORNIA PIZZA KITCHEN SEDONA WHITE CORN TORTILLA SOUP

When you get a steaming bowl of good tortilla soup plopped in front of you, it's tough to stop slurping until you hit bottom. California Pizza Kitchen has just such a soup, but the oil and fried tortilla chips put it a bit too far on the fat side. Never fear; we can make this delicious white corn tortilla soup taste just as good as the original without most of the oil and fat. Fat-free chicken broth stands in well for the regular stuff, and baked corn tortilla chips give the soup its traditional taste and texture. You'll want to use a hand blender for this one, if you've got one. If not, a regular blender or food processor will work fine to puree the soup so that it has the smooth consistency of the original but with only a minuscule two grams of fat per serving.

1 teaspoon olive oil
1/4 cup minced white onion
2 cloves garlic, minced
3 cups frozen white corn, thawed
3 medium tomatoes, chopped
    (about 3 cups)
1 cup tomato sauce
2 tablespoons granulated sugar
1 teaspoon ground cumin

1 teaspoon salt
1/4 teaspoon crushed red pepper
    flakes
1/8 teaspoon white pepper
1/2 teaspoon chili powder
2 14 1/2-ounce cans fat-free chicken
    broth (4 cups)
1 1/2 cups crumbled baked corn
    tortilla chips

½ cup crumbled baked tortilla chips   I tablespoon minced
½ cup fat-free shredded cheddar   cilantro
  cheese

1. Preheat I teaspoon of oil in a large saucepan over medium heat.
2. Sauté the onion and garlic in the oil for a couple minutes or until the onions begin to turn translucent.
3. Add half of the corn and the remaining ingredients to the saucepan, then bring mixture to a boil. Reduce heat and simmer for 20 minutes.
4. Using an electric handheld blender, puree the soup until it is smooth. You may also puree the soup with a standard blender or food processor in batches.
5. Add the remaining corn to the soup, and simmer for an additional 20 minutes or until the soup is thick.
6. If desired, add some of the crumbled baked tortilla chips, cheddar cheese, and cilantro as a garnish and serve hot.

• SERVES 4.

Nutrition Facts *(per serving)*

SERVING SIZE—I ½ CUPS   TOTAL SERVINGS—4

	LOW-FAT	ORIGINAL
CALORIES (APPROX.)	260	305
FAT (APPROX.)	2G	I4G

• • • •

CHILI'S
BONELESS BUFFALO WINGS

☆　　✌　　💣　　✎　　☯　　✂　　☞

Not only does this conversion for Chili's new appetizer give us the zesty flavor of traditional Buffalo chicken wings without the bones or fatty skin, but I've come up with a way to bake the chicken, rather than fry it, so that we eliminate even more of those pesky fat grams. These "wings" are actually nuggets sliced from chicken breast fillets that have been breaded and fried and smothered with the same type of spicy wing sauce used on typical wings, but without the butter. If you like Buffalo wings, you'll love this reduced-fat clone, which can be served up with some celery sticks and fat-free bleu cheese dressing on the side for dipping. Party down.

1 cup all-purpose flour
2 teaspoons salt
1/4 teaspoon ground black pepper
1/4 teaspoon cayenne pepper
1/4 teaspoon paprika
1/4 cup egg substitute
1 cup reduced-fat (2%) milk

2 skinless chicken breast fillets
oil cooking spray
1/4 cup Frank's or Crystal Louisiana
　　hot sauce
2 tablespoons fat-free butter-flavored
　　spread
2 tablespoons water

ON THE SIDE
fat-free bleu cheese dressing
　　(for dipping)

celery sticks

1. Preheat oven to 475ºF.
2. Combine flour, salt, peppers, and paprika in a medium bowl.
3. Whisk egg and milk together in a small bowl.
4. Slice each chicken breast into 5 or 6 pieces.
5. Working with one or two pieces of chicken at a time, dip each piece into the egg mixture, then into the breading blend; then repeat the process so that each piece of chicken is double-coated.
6. Coat a baking sheet with a generous portion of the oil cooking spray. Arrange the chicken on the baking sheet and then spray a light coating over the top of each piece.
7. Bake the chicken for 10 to 12 minutes or until it begins to brown. Crank the heat up to broil, and continue to cook the chicken for 2 to 4 more minutes or until the surface begins to become golden brown and crispy.
8. As the chicken cooks, combine the hot sauce, butter-flavored spread, and water in a small saucepan over medium/low heat. Cook just until the mixture begins to bubble, then remove the sauce from the heat and cover it until it's needed.
9. When the chicken pieces are cooked, remove them from the oven and let them cool for a couple minutes. Place the chicken into a covered container such as Tupperware or a large jar with a lid. Pour the sauce over the chicken in the container, cover, and then shake gently until each piece of chicken is coated with sauce. Pour the chicken onto a plate and serve the dish with fat-free bleu cheese dressing and sliced celery sticks on the side.

- SERVES 4 AS AN APPETIZER.

Nutrition Facts (per serving)
SERVING SIZE—3 PIECES   TOTAL SERVINGS—4

	LOW-FAT	ORIGINAL
CALORIES (APPROX.)	200	280
FAT (APPROX.)	5.5G	15G

• • • •

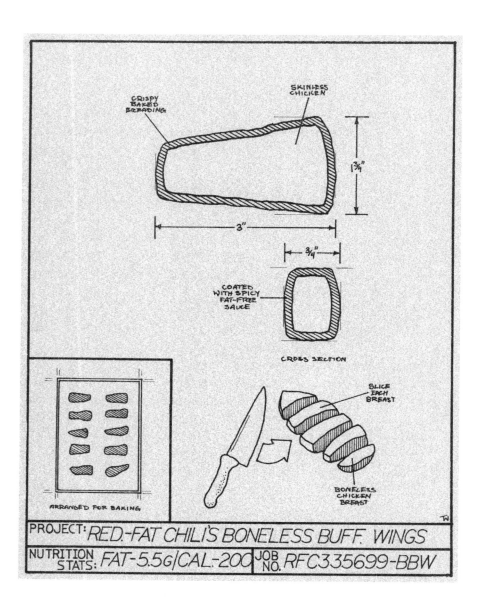

CRISPY BAKED BREADING

SKINLESS CHICKEN

1¾"

3"

¾"

COATED WITH SPICY FAT-FREE SAUCE

CROSS SECTION

ARRANGED FOR BAKING

SLICE EACH BREAST

BONELESS CHICKEN BREAST

PROJECT: RED.-FAT CHILI'S BONELESS BUFF. WINGS

NUTRITION STATS: FAT-5.5G/CAL.-200

JOB NO. RFC335699-BBW

CHILI'S
FAJITA SALAD

☆   ✌   💣   ✎   ☯   ✂   ☞

This big salad of mixed greens, fajita steak, pico de gallo, black beans, bell peppers, corn and guacamole comes slathered with two types of salad dressings plus fried tortilla chips, making the restaurant version a fat-filled fiesta.

When made from scratch with this secret Top Secret Recipes formula, the two dressings are made fat-free, knocking the fat grams down to around a third of what you munch down in the original. There are several components here in this conversion, but this recipe makes four of the huge entrée-size salads, and the results are worth the effort. This recipe clones the steak version of the salad, but you can also replace the beef with chicken.

MARINADE
⅔ cup water
1 tablespoon vegetable oil
2 tablespoons soy sauce
1 large clove garlic, pressed
1 tablespoon granulated sugar
1 teaspoon liquid smoke

1 teaspoon chili powder
½ teaspoon salt
½ teaspoon cayenne pepper
½ teaspoon ground black
    pepper
½ teaspoon onion powder

4 sirloin steaks (approximately
    4 ounces each)

FAT-FREE CHIPOTLE RANCH DRESSING
¼ cup fat-free mayonnaise
¼ cup fat-free sour cream
3 tablespoons buttermilk

1 tablespoon water
1 ½ teaspoons white vinegar
¼ teaspoon plus ⅛ teaspoon salt

⅛ teaspoon dried parsley
⅛ teaspoon onion powder
dash dried dillweed

dash garlic powder
dash ground black pepper

FAT-FREE SANTA FE DRESSING
⅓ cup fat-free Catalina dressing
1 tablespoon stone ground mustard
1 tablespoon water
½ teaspoon lemon juice

½ teaspoon white vinegar
¼ teaspoon cumin
¼ teaspoon cayenne pepper
⅛ teaspoon ground black pepper
⅛ teaspoon dried thyme

PICO DE GALLO
2 medium tomatoes, chopped
½ cup chopped Spanish onion
1 jalapeño, seeded and diced (about
    2 tablespoons)

2 teaspoons finely chopped cilantro
⅛ teaspoon salt

SOUTHWESTERN GARNISH
1 cup frozen corn, thawed
⅔ cup canned black beans, drained
    and rinsed

¼ cup diced red bell pepper
¼ cup diced green bell pepper
⅛ teaspoon salt

MIXED GREENS
1 head iceberg lettuce, chopped
1 head romaine lettuce, chopped

1 carrot, shredded
1 cup shredded red cabbage

2 cups crumbled baked corn tortilla
    chips

1 cup guacamole

1. Prepare the marinade by combining all of the ingredients in a small bowl. Stir well. Add meat to marinade, cover, and chill for at least 4 hours. Marinating overnight is even better.
2. While meat marinates, prepare the dressings and garnishes. Combine the ingredients for each of the dressings in separate small bowls. Stir well, then cover and chill. Hope you have some more small, clean bowls, because you're going to need a few

more for the garnishes. Combine the ingredients for each of the garnishes in separate bowls, then cover and chill these as well.

3. If you have some more room in the fridge, you may want to prepare your greens now by combining the lettuces with the carrot and cabbage in a large salad bowl. Cover this bowl and chill it until you are ready to assemble the salads. You may choose to save this step until you are ready to grill the meat.
4. When the meat has marinated, preheat your barbecue grill to high heat.
5. Grill the steaks for 5 to 7 minutes per side or until done.
6. While the meat is grilling, prepare the salad by tossing the mixed greens with the Santa Fe dressing in a large bowl.
7. Spoon approximately ⅛ of the greens onto each of four plates.
8. Sprinkle ¼ of the pico de gallo onto the greens on each plate, followed by ¼ of the Southwestern garnish.
9. Spoon ¼ of the remaining greens onto the salad on each plate.
10. Sprinkle ¼ of the tortilla chips over the greens on each plate.
11. Drizzle the ranch dressing over the salads with a sweeping motion. If you have an empty squirt bottle, such as an empty mustard or honey bottle, fill that with the dressing and use it to drizzle the dressing across the salad.
12. When the meat is done grilling, slice each steak into bite-size strips and arrange it over the top of each salad.
13. Spoon the guacamole onto the top of each of the sliced steaks and serve.

- SERVES 4 AS AN ENTRÉE.

Nutrition Facts *(per serving)*

SERVING SIZE—1 SALAD   TOTAL SERVINGS—4

	LOW-FAT	ORIGINAL
CALORIES (APPROX.)	591	784
FAT (APPROX.)	15G	45G

• • • •

CHILI'S
SOUTHWESTERN EGGROLLS

☆　✌　💣　✏　☯　✂　☞

Spend some time on the message boards at the Top Secret Recipes Web site (*www.topsecretrecipes.com*), and you'll find out that this is one of the most requested conversion recipes. Here now is our reduced-fat version of the tastiest appetizer on Chili's menu. Unlike the real thing that's fried, this amazing clone is baked. Inside is a delicious mixture of corn, green onions, black beans, spinach, jalapeño peppers, reduced-fat Monterey Jack cheese, and spices. Once these babies come out of the oven hot and crispy, just slice 'em in half and serve 'em surrounding a killer low-fat version of the tasty avocado ranch dressing. It's a taste bud party, and your tongue's invited!

I skinless chicken breast fillet
salt
ground black pepper
I teaspoon vegetable oil
2 tablespoons minced red bell
　　pepper
2 tablespoons minced green onion
⅓ cup frozen corn
¼ cup canned black beans, rinsed
　　and drained
2 tablespoons frozen spinach,
　　thawed and drained

2 tablespoons diced, canned jalapeño
　　peppers
½ tablespoon minced fresh parsley
½ teaspoon cumin
½ teaspoon chili powder
¼ teaspoon salt
dash cayenne pepper
¾ cup shredded reduced-
　　fat (2%) Monterey Jack cheese
5 7-inch flour tortillas

LOW-FAT AVOCADO-RANCH DIPPING SAUCE

¼ cup smashed, fresh avocado
   (about ½ avocado)
¼ cup fat-free mayonnaise
¼ cup fat-free sour cream
1 tablespoon buttermilk
1 ½ teaspoons white vinegar

⅛ teaspoon salt
⅛ teaspoon dried parsley
⅛ teaspoon onion powder
dash dried dillweed
dash garlic powder
dash ground black pepper

oil cooking spray

GARNISH

2 tablespoons chopped tomato

1 tablespoon chopped onion

1. Preheat barbecue grill to high heat.
2. Rub the chicken breast with some vegetable oil, then grill it on the barbecue for 4 to 5 minutes per side or until done. Lightly salt and pepper each side of the chicken while it cooks. Set chicken aside until it cools down enough to handle.
3. Preheat 1 teaspoon of vegetable oil in a medium-size skillet over medium/high heat.
4. Add the red pepper and green onion to the pan and sauté for a couple minutes until tender.
5. Dice the cooked chicken into small cubes and add it to the pan. Add the corn, black beans, spinach, jalapeño peppers, parsley, cumin, chili powder, salt, and cayenne pepper to the pan. Cook for another 4 minutes. Stir well so that the spinach begins to fall apart and is incorporated into the mixture.
6. Remove the pan from the heat and add the cheese. Stir the mixture until the cheese is melted.
7. Wrap the tortillas in a moist cloth and microwave on high temperature for 1 ½ minutes or until hot.
8. Spoon approximately ⅕ of the mixture into the center of a tortilla. Fold in the ends and then roll the tortilla over the mixture. Roll the tortilla very tightly, then pierce it with a toothpick to hold it together. Repeat with the remaining ingredients until you have five eggrolls. Cover the plate with plastic wrap and

chill for an hour or two. You may chill the eggrolls overnight if you wish.

9. When you are ready to cook the eggrolls, preheat the oven to 425⁰Fs.

10. Prepare the low-fat avocado-ranch dipping sauce by combining all of the ingredients in a small bowl. Cover and chill this until needed.

11. Spray the entire surface of each of the eggrolls with the oil cooking spray. Arrange the eggrolls on a baking sheet and bake for 17 to 20 minutes or until surface browns and becomes crispy. Turn the eggrolls over about halfway through cooking time.

12. Let the eggrolls cool for a few minutes and then slice each one diagonally lengthwise and arrange on a plate around a small bowl of the dipping sauce. Garnish the dipping sauce with the chopped tomato and onion.

• SERVES 3 OR 4 AS AN APPETIZER.

Nutrition Facts *(per serving)*

SERVING SIZE—3 HALVES   TOTAL SERVINGS—3.3

	LOW-FAT	ORIGINAL
CALORIES (APPROX.)	480	725
FAT (APPROX.)	12G	42G

• • • •

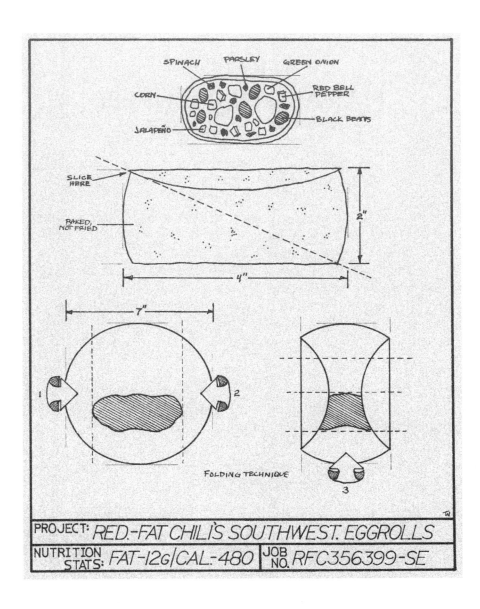

SPINACH PARSLEY GREEN ONION
CORN RED BELL PEPPER
JALAPEÑO BLACK BEANS

SLICE HERE
BAKED, NOT FRIED
2"
4"

7"
1 2
FOLDING TECHNIQUE
3

PROJECT: RED.-FAT CHILI'S SOUTHWEST. EGGROLLS

NUTRITION STATS: FAT-12g/CAL.-480

JOB NO. RFC356399-SE

KFC
MACARONI & CHEESE

In 1991, the world's largest chicken chain introduced a new logo to better reflect the addition of non–fried chicken products. Kentucky Fried Chicken morphed into KFC.

One of the chain's classic side dishes is the tasty macaroni and cheese, which has been on the menu for years. Using the light version of Velveeta cheese and some reduced-fat cheddar, we easily duplicate the taste while cutting the fat grams in half here in our cheesy conversion.

6 cups water
2 cups elbow macaroni
4 ounces Velveeta Light
    cheese

½ cup reduced-fat shredded cheddar
    cheese (2% fat)
2 tablespoons fat-free milk
¼ teaspoon salt

1. Bring water to a boil over high heat in a medium saucepan. Add the elbow macaroni to the water and cook it for 10 to 12 minutes or until tender, stirring occasionally.
2. While the macaroni is boiling, prepare the cheese sauce by combining the remaining ingredients in a small saucepan and cooking over low heat. Stir often as the cheese melts into a smooth consistency.
3. When the macaroni is done, turn off the heat, then use a colander or sieve to strain off the water. Pour the macaroni back into the pan without the water.

4. Pour the cheese sauce over the macaroni and stir until it is well coated. Serve immediately.

- SERVES 6 AS A SIDE DISH.

Nutrition Facts *(per serving)*

SERVING SIZE—5.4 OUNCES   TOTAL SERVINGS—6

	LOW-FAT	ORIGINAL
CALORIES	95	180
FAT	4G	8G

• • • •

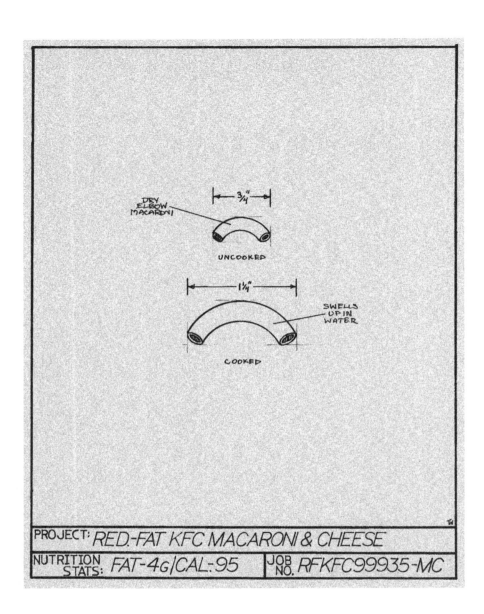

DRY
ELBOW
MACARONI

3/4"

UNCOOKED

1 1/4"

SWELLS
UP IN
WATER

COOKED

PROJECT: *RED.-FAT KFC MACARONI & CHEESE*

NUTRITION STATS: *FAT-4g/CAL.-95*   JOB NO. *RFKFC99935-MC*

OLIVE GARDEN FETTUCINE ALFREDO

☆   ✌   ●   ✎   ◉   ✂   ☞

This is a classic Italian dish, but with cheese and cream and butter in the traditional version, you can get a whopping seventy grams of fat in a single plateful. For this conversion, we'll replace those fatty ingredients with substitutes such as evaporated skim milk, fat-free milk, Butter Buds, and a great cheeselike substance made from straining yogurt with a coffee filter.

To easily prepare this useful ingredient, we'll use a technique that I picked up from watching Graham Kerr, the once–galloping gourmet. Graham loves to use this yogurt cheese in many of his low-fat dishes that require a creamy white sauce, traditionally made with fatty foodstuffs. This fat-free substitute is made by straining the whey from the yogurt with a coffee filter. You simply place a filter into a large strainer or metal steamer basket in a covered saucepan. Pour the yogurt into the filter, and let this sit covered overnight in the refrigerator. As the hours tick by, the whey slowly drips from the yogurt, leaving a thick, creamy substance in the filter. The liquid in the bottom of the pan is chucked out, and you measure the yogurt cheese left in the coffee filter for the recipe.

Using this technique, we can shave something like forty-nine grams of fat off the traditional recipe for fettucine alfredo presented at the country's largest Italian restaurant chain. This recipe makes two way-huge dinner-size entrées like they serve at the restaurant, though you might rather divide this up as four more modestly portioned servings.

1 cup strained yogurt (see above)
2 tablespoons cornstarch
1 cup evaporated skim milk
1/2 teaspoon olive oil
1 large clove garlic, minced
1/2 cup grated Parmesan cheese
1/2 cup fat-free milk

1 tablespoon Butter Buds Sprinkles
1/4 teaspoon salt
1/8 teaspoon ground black
    pepper
4 to 5 quarts water
12-ounce box fettucine pasta

1. Combine the strained yogurt with the cornstarch in a medium bowl. Stir until smooth. Add the evaporated skim milk. Set aside.
2. Heat the oil in a medium saucepan over medium heat. When the oil is hot, add the garlic and sauté for about a minute. Don't cook the garlic long enough that it begins to brown.
3. Add the yogurt mixture to the saucepan and stir. Add remaining ingredients, except the water and pasta, to the saucepan and continue to heat over medium/low heat. If it begins to boil, turn heat to low and simmer, stirring often.
4. As the sauce heats, bring 5 to 6 quarts of water to a rolling boil in a large pot or saucepan. Add the pasta to the boiling water and stir. Return water to a boil, and cook uncovered for 12 to 15 minutes or until pasta is mostly tender but slightly tough (al dente). Strain.
5. Toss pasta and sauce together in a large bowl and serve.

- SERVES 2 AS A LARGE, RESTAURANT-SIZE PORTION (OR SERVES 4 AS A STANDARD-SIZE ENTRÉE).

Nutrition Facts (per serving)
SERVING SIZE—4 CUPS   TOTAL SERVINGS—2

	LOW-FAT	ORIGINAL
CALORIES (APPROX.)	1035	1236
FAT (APPROX.)	18G	67G

• • • •

OLIVE GARDEN
ZUPPA TOSCANA

It's the white, creamy broth in the original version of this delicious soup that adds unnecessary fat grams. By replacing the fat-filled dairy ingredients from the original with fat-free milk and chicken broth, and by using lean Italian turkey sausage, we can whack around fifteen grams off the original version.

½ pound hot Italian lean turkey
    sausage (2 large links)
3 cups fat-free chicken broth
3 cups fat-free milk
2 tablespoons minced onion
1 tablespoon Hormel Real Bacon
    Pieces

¼ teaspoon salt
dash of crushed red pepper
    flakes
1 medium russet potato
2 cups chopped kale

1. Grill or sauté the sausage until cooked.
2. Combine the chicken broth, milk, onion, bacon pieces, salt, and pepper flakes in a medium saucepan over medium/high heat.
3. Quarter the potato lengthwise, then cut into ¼-inch slices. Add to the saucepan. When mixture begins to boil, reduce heat and simmer for 30 minutes.
4. Cut the sausage at an angle into ¼-inch-thick slices. Add the sausage to the saucepan. Simmer for 1 hour or until potato slices begin to soften.
5. Add the kale to the soup and simmer for an additional 10 to 15 minutes or until potatoes are soft.

• SERVES 3.

Nutrition Facts *(per serving)*

SERVING SIZE—1 ½ CUPS   TOTAL SERVINGS—3

	LOW-FAT	ORIGINAL
CALORIES (APPROX.)	196	275
FAT (APPROX.)	4.5G	19G

•   •   •   •

OLIVE GARDEN
PASTA E FAGIOLI

☆   ✌   ●   ✎   ◕   ✂   ☞

One of the most popular and hard-to-pronounce items on the Olive Garden menu is found in the soup column. But it's more like a thick chili than a soup, really, with all those beans and veggies and ground beef in there. The reduced-fat grams in this clone are especially important when we consider that this dish makes an excellent meal by itself, and you may want to eat more than the 1½ cups serving size measured for the nutrition stats.

We'll keep the added fat to a minimum by sautéing the veggies in what little fat is not drained off from browning the super-lean ground beef. The soup will fill your mouth with so much flavor that it won't matter that we don't add any additional fat. You'll have a hard time distinguishing between this version and the original. Try it out, and you'll see what I mean.

This recipe makes about eight 1½-cup servings, so if you can't eat it all within a few days, it freezes well.

1 pound super-lean ground beef
 (7 percent fat)
1 small onion, diced (1 cup)
1 large carrot, julienned (1 cup)
3 stalks celery, chopped (1 cup)
2 cloves garlic, minced
2 14.5-ounce cans diced tomatoes
1 15-ounce can red kidney beans
 (with liquid)
1 15-ounce can great northern beans
 (with liquid)

1 15-ounce can tomato
 sauce
1 12-ounce can V-8 juice
1 tablespoon white vinegar
1½ teaspoons salt
1 teaspoon dried oregano
1 teaspoon dried basil
½ teaspoon pepper
½ teaspoon dried thyme
½ pound (½ package)
 ditali pasta

1. Brown the ground beef in a very large saucepan or soup pot over medium heat. Drain off the fat.
2. Add the onion, carrot, celery, and garlic and simmer for 10 minutes.
3. Add the remaining ingredients, except the pasta, and simmer for 1 hour.
4. About 50 minutes into the simmer time, cook pasta in 1½ to 2 quarts of boiling water over high heat. Cook for 10 minutes or just until pasta is *al dente*, or slightly tough. Drain.
5. Add the pasta to the large pot of soup. Simmer for 5 minutes and serve.

• SERVES 8 AS AN APPETIZER.

TIDBITS

Ditali pasta is small ¼-inch tubes of pasta—short, little hollow cylinders. They may also go by the name salad-roni.

Nutritional Facts *(per serving)*
SERVING SIZE—1½ CUPS   TOTAL SERVINGS—8

	LITE	ORIGINAL
CALORIES (est.)	312	416
FAT (est.)	4G	17.5G

• • • •

OLIVE GARDEN TIRAMISU

☆ ✌ 💣 ✏ ☯ ✂ ☞

You have now come to the most dramatic low-fat conversion recipe in this book, and one of the most unique. If you love tiramisu, but long for a lower-fat version, you should totally dig this one.

The Olive Garden chain offers a very popular and delicious tiramisu that is produced outside the restaurants and then delivered fresh to each outlet. The layers of fluffy mascarpone cheese and lady fingers soaked in a solution of strong coffee and coffee liqueur is a delicious and memorable combination. But mascarpone cheese has 13 grams of fat per ounce, and there's nothing that tastes quite like it.

However, there is one way to get very close; and it's a special combination of Dream Whip, gelatin, and fat-free cream cheese never before created and revealed in a cookbook. Entenmann's fat-free pound cake, sliced and brushed with a coffee/liqueur, will substitute nicely for the lady fingers. Layer it all into a square dish and you've got a "must try" TSR low-fat conversion clone that you won't forget.

FLUFFY CHEESE

1 cup low-fat milk (1 percent fat)
1 envelope unflavored gelatin
3 envelopes Dream Whip Mix

4 ounces Philadelphia fat-free cream cheese, softened
½ cup sugar

CAKE

1 Entenmann's fat-free Golden Loaf, or use recipe on p. 49
1 tablespoon instant coffee

¼ cup plus 2 tablespoons hot water
1 tablespoon sugar
2 tablespoons Kahlua Coffee Liqueur

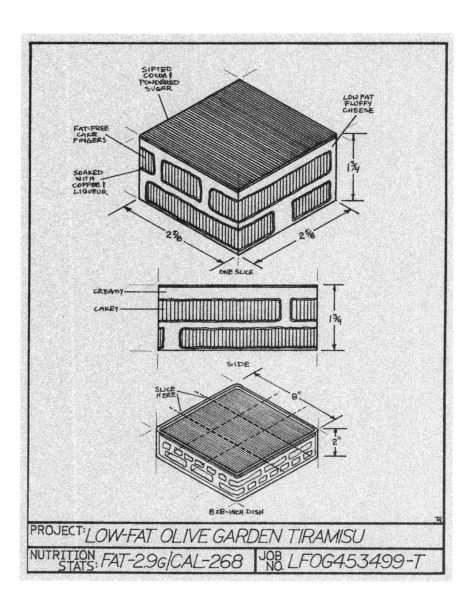

SIFTED COCOA & POWDERED SUGAR

LOW FAT FLOFFY CHEESE

FAT-FREE CAKE FINGERS

SOAKED WITH COFFEE & LIQUEUR

1¾

2⅝

2⅝

ONE SLICE

CREAMY

CAKEY

1¾

SIDE

SLICE HERE

8"

2"

8 X 8-INCH DISH

PROJECT: *LOW-FAT OLIVE GARDEN TIRAMISU*

NUTRITION STATS: *FAT-2.9g/CAL-268* JOB NO. *LFOG453499-T*

400

1. For the fluffy cheese, measure 1 cup of milk, remove 3 table-spoons, and set the rest aside. In a small bowl, combine the 3 tablespoons of milk with the gelatin. Let the mixture sit for 5 to 10 minutes, then microwave on half power for 2 minutes, or until the gelatin dissolves. Set this mixture aside to cool for 15 minutes.

2. Pour the remaining milk into a large mixing bowl. Add one envelope of Dream Whip at a time to the milk and beat after each addition for about 2 minutes until the mixture is light and fluffy.

3. In a separate bowl, beat together the softened cream cheese and the sugar. Add the gelatin/milk mixture and beat until smooth.

4. While beating the Dream Whip on high speed, add 1/3 of the cheese mixture at a time. Mix about 1 minute or until it is well-blended and smooth. Set aside while preparing the cake.

5. Cut the ends off the pound cake, then slice the remaining cake into 10 even slices. Discard the end pieces.

6. In a small bowl, mix the coffee with the hot water until the coffee dissolves. Add the sugar and stir until it dissolves as well. Add the Kahlua.

7. Cut each slice of cake into thirds (or in half, if using the recipe on p. 49), and arrange the slices on a wax paper–lined cookie sheet (rimmed to contain the liquid). Brush the coffee mixture generously over the top of each cake finger. Turn the fingers over and brush each once more with the coffee mixture.

8. To assemble the tiramisu, arrange the cake fingers side-by-side in an 8 x 8-inch baking dish. Leave about 1/4-inch between the cake fingers. Cover the fingers with half of the fluffy cheese mixture and spread carefully with a spatula until smooth and flat. Arrange the remaining cake fingers on the cheese mixture the same way as the first layers. Cover the cake with the remaining cheese mixture and smooth.

9. Put a couple teaspoons of cocoa powder into a sieve and tap it over the top of the tiramisu to dust it with a light, even coating

of the cocoa. Cover the tiramisu and chill it for at least 3 hours so that it sets up. When you're ready to serve, slice it into 9 even squares.

- SERVES 9.

Nutritional Facts *(per serving)*

SERVING SIZE—1 SLICE   TOTAL SERVINGS—9 SLICES

	LITE	ORIGINAL
CALORIES (est.)	268	475
FAT (est.)	2.9G	38G

•   •   •   •

OTIS SPUNKMEYER
CHOCOLATE CHIP MUFFINS

In Cayce, South Carolina, Otis Spunkmeyer muffins are manufactured with state-of-the-art robotic equipment that would make R2-D2 jealous. The amazing machines do everything from packaging 130 muffins per minute to sealing up the cartons ready for a quick shipment to stores across the country.

This custom Top Secret Recipes reduced-fat clone version uses unsweetened applesauce to keep the muffin moist and to help replace unnecessary fat.

¾ cup granulated sugar
⅔ cup unsweetened applesauce
¼ cup egg substitute
¼ cup vegetable oil
½ teaspoon salt
¾ teaspoon vanilla

1 teaspoon baking soda
½ cup low-fat buttermilk
2 cups all-purpose flour
2 teaspoons baking powder
½ cup mini chocolate chips

1. Preheat oven to 325°F.
2. In a large bowl, mix together sugar, applesauce, egg substitute, oil, salt, vanilla, and baking soda. Add buttermilk and blend well.
3. In a separate bowl, sift together the flour and baking powder. Add the dry ingredients to the wet, and mix well with an electric mixer. Add half of the chocolate chips to the batter, and fold them in by hand.
4. To bake the muffins, use a "Texas-size" muffin pan lined with large muffin cups. You may also bake the muffins without the

cups; just be sure to grease the pan well with cooking spray. (If you use a regular-size muffin pan, which also works fine, your cooking time will be a few minutes less and your yield will double.) Fill the cups halfway with batter.

5. Sprinkle the remaining chocolate chips over the tops of each cup of batter. That will be about $\frac{1}{2}$ tablespoon of chips per muffin (or a scant teaspoon of chips if you make the regular-size muffins).

6. Bake the muffins for 20 to 24 minutes or until brown on top (16 to 20 minutes for regular-size muffins). Remove the muffins from the oven and allow them to cool for about 30 minutes. Then put the muffins in a sealed container or resealable plastic bag.

• MAKES 8 "TEXAS-SIZE" MUFFINS (OR 16 REGULAR-SIZE MUFFINS).

Nutrition Facts *(per serving)*

SERVING SIZE—$\frac{1}{2}$ MUFFIN   TOTAL SERVINGS—16

	LOW-FAT	ORIGINAL
CALORIES	160	240
FAT	5.5G	13G

• • • •

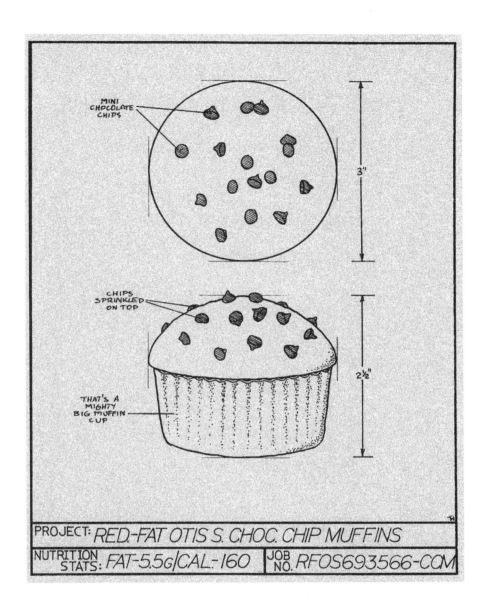

MINI
CHOCOLATE
CHIPS

3"

CHIPS
SPRINKLED
ON TOP

THAT'S A
MIGHTY
BIG MUFFIN
CUP

2½"

PROJECT: *RED-FAT OTIS S. CHOC. CHIP MUFFINS*

NUTRITION STATS: *FAT-5.5g/CAL-160*   JOB NO. *RFOS693566-COM*

OTIS SPUNKMEYER
WILD BLUEBERRY MUFFINS

After baking the big 'ol muffins, Otis Spunkmeyer freezes them so that they stay fresh on the way to the stores. Vendors thaw out the tasty baked goodies before displaying them on their shelves. Even after the muffins reach room temperature, they still have a very impressive shelf life of twenty-one days.

You can also freeze the muffins you make with this reduced-fat clone recipe. Just wait until they cool, then wrap the muffins in plastic wrap, and toss them in the freezer. And remember, the shelf life of your version without preservatives will be much less than that of the real McCoy, so dive into those muffins post haste.

1 cup dried blueberries	¾ teaspoon salt
¼ cup water	½ teaspoon vanilla
¾ cup plus 1 tablespoon granulated sugar	1 teaspoon baking soda
	½ cup low-fat buttermilk
⅔ cup unsweetened applesauce	2 cups all-purpose flour
¼ cup egg substitute	2 teaspoons baking powder
¼ cup vegetable oil	fat-free butter-flavored spray

1. Combine blueberries with ¼ cup water in a small, microwave-safe bowl. Zap blueberries in the microwave on 50% power for 2 minutes, stir, cover with plastic wrap, then set aside.
2. Preheat oven to 325ºFs.
3. In a large bowl, mix together ¾ cup of sugar, applesauce, egg substitute, oil, salt, vanilla, and baking soda. Add buttermilk and blend well.

4. In a separate bowl, sift together the flour and baking powder. Add the dry ingredients to the wet, and mix well with an electric mixer.
5. Add 1 tablespoon of sugar to the blueberries, then add them to the batter and fold in by hand with as few strokes as possible.
6. To bake the muffins, use a "Texas-size" muffin pan lined with large muffin cups. You may also bake the muffins without the cups; just be sure to grease the pan well with cooking spray. (If you use a regular-size muffin pan, which also works fine, your cooking time will be a few minutes less, and your yield will double.) Fill the cups halfway with batter.
7. Spray a couple of squirts of fat-free butter-flavored spray over the top of each portion of batter.
8. Bake the muffins for 20 to 24 minutes or until brown on top (16 to 20 minutes for regular-size muffins). Remove the muffins from the oven, and allow them to cool for about 30 minutes. Then put the muffins in a sealed container or resealable plastic bag.

- MAKES 8 "TEXAS-SIZE" MUFFINS (OR 16 REGULAR-SIZE MUFFINS).

Nutrition Facts *(per serving)*

SERVING SIZE—½ MUFFIN   TOTAL SERVINGS—16

	LOW-FAT	ORIGINAL
CALORIES	165	210
FAT	4G	11G

•   •   •   •

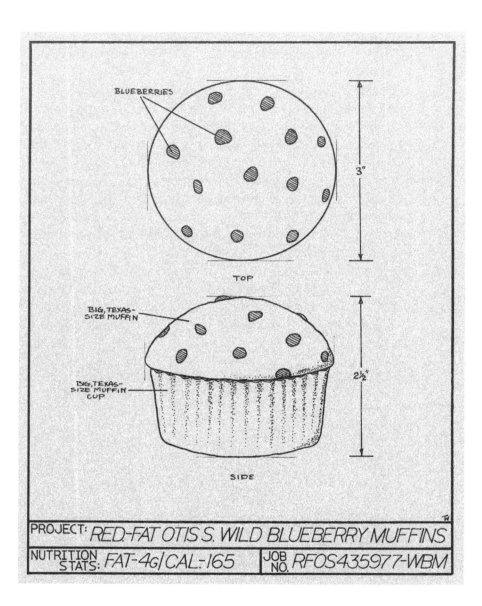

BLUEBERRIES

3"

TOP

BIG, TEXAS-
SIZE MUFFIN

BIG, TEXAS-
SIZE MUFFIN
CUP

2½"

SIDE

PROJECT: RED-FAT OTIS S. WILD BLUEBERRY MUFFINS

NUTRITION STATS: FAT-4g/CAL-165   JOB NO. RFOS435977-WBM

408

PANDA EXPRESS ORANGE-FLAVORED CHICKEN

☆ ✌ ● ✎ ☯ ✂ ☞

Andrew J. C. Cherng had lived in China, Taiwan, and Japan before he came to the United States to study mathematics at Baker University. After graduation in 1973, this brainiac used his extensive education and business savvy to open an Asian restaurant in Pasadena with his father, Master Chef Ming Tsai Cherng. Southern Californians went crazy for the Panda Inn and its cutting-edge menu that blended the styles of Szechwan and Mandarin cooking.

Today, the chain includes more than 320 units in thirty-two states and Japan and is famous for the addictive fried chicken dish with the tangy orange sauce. We can re-create this dish using a special baking technique to avoid the fat that's unavoidable when frying.

SAUCE

1 ½ cups water
2 tablespoons orange juice
1 cup packed dark brown sugar
⅓ cup rice vinegar
2½ tablespoons soy sauce
¼ cup plus 1 teaspoon lemon juice
1 teaspoon minced water chestnuts

½ teaspoon minced fresh ginger
¼ teaspoon minced garlic
1 rounded teaspoon chopped green onion
¼ teaspoon crushed red pepper flakes
5 teaspoons cornstarch
2 teaspoons arrowroot

CHICKEN

4 skinless chicken breast
    fillets
$\frac{1}{2}$ cup ice water

$\frac{1}{4}$ cup egg substitute
1 cup self-rising flour
$\frac{1}{4}$ teaspoon salt

vegetable oil cooking spray

1. Combine all of the sauce ingredients—except the corn-starch and arrowroot—in a small saucepan over high heat. Stir often while bringing mixture to a boil. When sauce reaches a boil, remove it from heat and allow it to cool a bit, uncovered.
2. Slice chicken breasts into bite-size chunks. Remove exactly 1 cup of the marinade from the pan and pour it over the chicken in a large resealable plastic bag or other container that allows the chicken to be completely covered with the marinade. Chicken should marinate for at least a couple hours. Cover remaining sauce and leave it to cool until the chicken is ready.
3. When chicken has marinated, preheat your oven to 475ºF.
4. Combine cornstarch with arrowroot in a small bowl, then add 3 tablespoons of water. Stir until cornstarch and arrow-root have dissolved. Pour this mixture into the sauce, and set the pan over high heat. When sauce begins to bubble and thicken, cover and remove from heat.
5. Beat the ice water and egg together in a medium bowl. In another medium bowl, combine the flour and salt.
6. Line a baking sheet with foil. Spray foil with a generous coat-ing of oil cooking spray.
7. First dip each piece of chicken into the flour, then into the egg mixture, and finally back into the flour. Arrange the coated chicken pieces on the baking sheet. When all of the chicken is positioned on the baking sheet, spray a coating of the oil cooking spray over the top of the chicken.
8. Bake the chicken for 4 to 6 minutes or until it begins to

brown on top. Turn the oven up to high broil for 2 to 3 minutes or until chicken has browned and has a crispy coating.

9. As the chicken cooks, reheat the sauce left covered on the stove. Stir it occasionally.

10. Pour the chicken into a large serving dish. Cover it with the thickened sauce. Stir gently until all of the pieces are well coated.

- SERVES 4.

Nutrition Facts *(per serving)*

SERVING SIZE—1 SLICED CHICKEN BREAST   TOTAL SERVINGS—4

	LOW-FAT	ORIGINAL
CALORIES (APPROX.)	400	580
FAT (APPROX.)	12G	30G

• • • •

WENDY'S
SINGLE WITH CHEESE

☆   ✌   ●   ✏   ☯   ✂   ☞

Over 5,000 Wendy's restaurants around the world serve the hamburger with the unique square patty that hangs over the edge of the bun. It's the burger that inspired the 1984 award-winning ad campaign that had a little old lady crying out, "Where's the beef?" With this secret recipe to create a lower-fat clone of the famous burger, the question is now, "Where's the fat?" By using super-lean ground beef, fat-free mayonnaise, and fat-free cheese, we have cut the fat to less than half of what is found in the original. Now you can have two cloned burgers for less than the fat found in one original.

1 plain hamburger bun
1/4 pound super-lean ground beef
    (7 percent fat)
salt
pepper
1 teaspoon ketchup
1/2 tablespoon fat-free mayonnaise

1 slice fat-free American
    cheese
1/2 teaspoon yellow mustard
1 lettuce leaf
2 to 3 separated onion slices
1 large tomato slice
3 dill pickle slices

1. Brown the faces of the bun in a large frying pan over medium heat. Keep the pan hot.
2. On wax paper, shape the ground beef into an approximately 4 x 4-inch square. You may find it easier to freeze the patty ahead of time, so that it doesn't fall apart when cooking. Don't defrost.
3. Cook the burger in the pan for 3 to 5 minutes per side, or until done. Salt and pepper both sides during the cooking.

4. Spread the ketchup and then the mayonnaise on the top bun.
5. Put the cooked patty on the bottom bun. On top of the meat, lay the slice of cheese.
6. Spread the mustard on the cheese, then place the lettuce, onion, tomato, and pickles on, in that order.
7. Complete the sandwich with the top bun and microwave the whole thing for 15 to 20 seconds to warm it up.

- SERVES 1.

Nutritional Facts (per serving)

SERVING SIZE—1 SANDWICH   TOTAL SERVINGS—1

	LITE	ORIGINAL
CALORIES (est.)	335	420
FAT (approx.)	10G	21G

• • • •

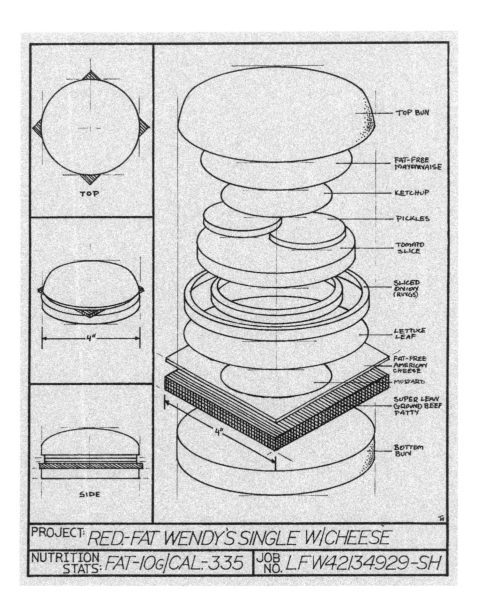

TOP

SIDE

TOP BUN

FAT-FREE MAYONNAISE

KETCHUP

PICKLES

TOMATO SLICE

SLICED ONION (RINGS)

LETTUCE LEAF

FAT-FREE AMERICAN CHEESE

MUSTARD

SUPER LEAN GROUND BEEF PATTY

BOTTOM BUN

4"

4"

PROJECT: *RED.-FAT WENDY'S SINGLE W/CHEESE*

NUTRITION STATS: *FAT-10g/CAL.-335*

JOB NO. *LFW42134929-SH*

WENDY'S FROSTY

Over 22 million gallons of this frozen chocolate dessert are served at Wendy's each year.

To make a version of this tasty treat at home that reduces the fat by around 75 percent, you will just need some fat-free vanilla ice cream, Nestlé Quik, and low-fat milk. Oh yeah, and a blender.

¾ cup low-fat milk (2 percent)
3 tablespoons Nestlé Quik

4 cups fat-free vanilla ice cream

1. Combine all of the ingredients in a blender. Blend on medium speed until creamy. Stir if necessary.
2. If too thin, freeze the mixture in the blender or in cups until thicker.

• MAKES 2 DRINKS.

Nutritional Facts (per serving)

SERVING SIZE—1 16-OUNCE DESSERT

TOTAL SERVINGS—2

	LITE	ORIGINAL
CALORIES	470	440
FAT	2G	11G

• • • •

WHITE CASTLE CHEESEBURGERS

☆ ✌ 💣 ✐ ☯ ✂ ☞

Some may call them "whitey one-bites." They're also known as "sliders," "gut busters," and "belly bombers." This 300-unit Midwestern hamburger chain celebrated its 75th anniversary in 1996 without much of a peep, and the company continues to stay impressively profitable despite its low-key marketing. The cooking technique is unique to the chain, because it involves steaming the ground beef patties. The minced onions are placed on the grill, with a beef patty on top. The steam from the grilling onions rises up through the five holes in each thin, square patty, allowing thorough cooking without having to flip the meat over.

Now you can use the same method, but with reduced-fat ingredients, to cook a reduced-fat version of one of the country's oldest burger creations.

1 pound super-lean ground beef (7 percent fat)	salt
16 dinner rolls	pepper
½ small onion, minced	16 slices fat-free American cheese

1. Prepare the patties by separating the ground beef into 16 1-ounce portions. On a sheet of wax paper, form the portions into square, very thin, 2½-inch patties. Using a small, circular object, such as a straw or the tip of a clean pen cap, create five holes in each patty. Make one hole in the center of the patty, and four holes surrounding the first one, with each about half

an inch in from each corner. Freeze these patties, still on the wax paper, until firm.

2. Toast the faces of the dinner rolls, either in a hot frying pan over medium heat, or under the oven broiler.

3. In a hot frying pan or skillet preheated over medium heat, arrange tablespoon-size piles of onions, 3 inches apart. Salt and pepper each pile of onions.

4. Spread the onions flat, and then place a frozen beef patty on each pile of onions. Salt each patty.

5. Cook each burger for 4 to 6 minutes. If you made the patties thin enough, steam from the onions will rise around the meat and through the holes in the patty, cooking the meat thoroughly without having to flip it.

6. To build each burger, turn the bottom half of a dinner roll over onto a patty, then hold it down as you scoop a spatula under the meat and onions, and turn the sandwich over onto a plate.

7. Cut a slice of American cheese into 2-inch-square portions and place a square onto the onions on the beef patty.

8. Complete the burger with the top half of the roll. Repeat with the remaining burgers, and serve hot.

- MAKES 16 BURGERS.

Nutritional Facts (per serving)

SERVING SIZE—2 BURGERS   TOTAL SERVINGS—8

	LITE	ORIGINAL
CALORIES	310	310
FAT	5G	17G

• • • •

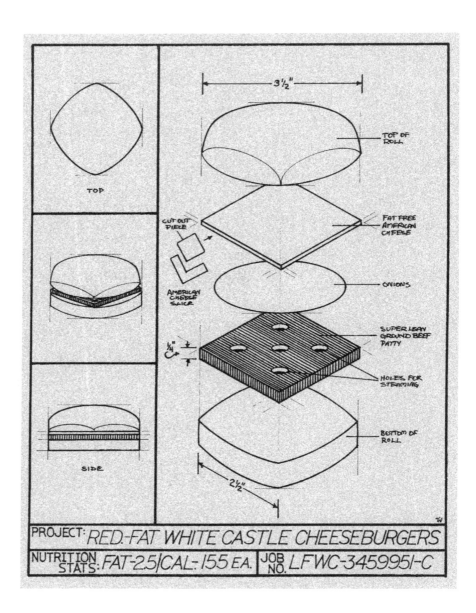

TOP

SIDE

3½"

TOP OF ROLL

CUT OUT PIECE

FAT FREE AMERICAN CHEESE

AMERICAN CHEESE SLICE

ONIONS

SUPER LEAN GROUND BEEF PATTY

HOLES FOR STEAMING

¼"

BOTTOM OF ROLL

2½"

PROJECT: *RED.-FAT WHITE CASTLE CHEESEBURGERS*

NUTRITION STATS: *FAT-2.5/CAL.-155 EA.*　**JOB NO.** *LFWC-345995l-C*

TRADEMARKS

A&W, 7UP, Squirt, and Hawaiian Punch are registered trademarks of Dr Pepper/Seven Up, Inc.

Almond Roca and Brown and Haley are registered trademarks of Brown and Haley, Inc.

Applebee's, Low Fat & Fabulous, and Tijuana 'Philly' Steak Sandwich are registered trademarks of Applebee's International, Inc.

Arby's is a registered trademark of Arby's Inc.

AriZona is a registered trademark of AriZona Beverage Co.

Auntie Anne's is a registered trademark of Auntie Anne's, Inc.

Baskin-Robbins is a registered trademark of Baskin-Robbins, Inc.

Bennigan's and Cookie Mountain Sundae are registered trademarks of Metromedia Co.

Big Boy is a registered trademark of Elias Brothers Restaurants, Inc.

Big Mac, Egg McMuffin, Filet-O-Fish, and McDonald's Breakfast Burrito are registered trademarks of McDonald's Corporation.

Bisquick is a registered trademark of General Mills Inc.

Blizzard, Orange Julius, Pineapple, Strawberry Julius, Dairy Queen and Smoothie are registered trademarks of American Dairy Queen Corp.

Boston Market, are registered trademarks of McDonald's Corporation

Burger King and Whopper are registered trademarks of Burger King Corp.

Butterscotch Krimpets, Peanut Butter Kandy Kakes, and Tastykake are registered trademarks of Tasty Baking Company.

California Pizza Kitchen is a registered trademark of California Pizza Kitchen, Inc.

Carl's Jr. and Charbroiled Santa Fe Chicken Sandwich are registered trademarks of Carl Karcher Enterprises, Inc.

Carl's Jr., Sante Fe Chicken, Western Bacon Cheeseburger, Six Dollar Burger are registered trademarks of Carl Karcher Enterprises.

Carnegie Deli is a registered trademark of Carnegie Delicatessen and Restaurant.

The Cheesecake Factory is a registered trademark of The Cheesecake Factory, Inc.

Chevys is a registered trademark of Chevys, Inc.

Chi-Chi's and Mexican Fried Ice Cream are registered trademarks of Family Restaurants, Inc.

Chick-fil-A is a registered trademark of Chick-fil-A, Inc.

Chili's and Chili's Guiltless Grill are registered trademarks of Brinker International.

Cinnabon, CinnabonStix, and Mochalatta Chill are registered trademarks of AFC Enterprises.

Coca-Cola is a registered trademark of The Coca-Cola Company.

Cracker Jack and Borden are registered trademarks of Borden, Inc.

Crunch 'n Munch is a registered trademark of ConAgra Brands Inc.

Dolly Madison, Zingers are registered trademarks of Interstate Brands Bakeries Corporation.

Double-Double and In-N-Out are registered trademarks of In-N-Out, Inc.

DoubleTree is a registered trademark of Hilton Hospitality, Inc.

Einstein Bros. and Eggs 4 Ways are registered trademarks of New World Restaurant Group Inc.

El Pollo Loco is a registered trademark of El Pollo Loco Inc.

Entenmann's and Entenmann's Light are registered trademarks of Entenmann's, Inc.

Fritos is a registered trademark of Frito-Lay Inc.

Girl Scout and Thin Mints are registered trademarks of Girl Scouts USA.

Girl Scout Cookies is a registered trademark of Girl Scouts USA.

Hershey's, PayDay, and Skor are registered trademarks of Hershey Foods Corporation.

Hidden Valley and Original Ranch are registered trademarks of HV Food Products Company.

HoneyBaked is a registered trademark of the HoneyBaked Ham Company.

Hostess Lights, Twinkie, and Hostess are registered trademarks of Interstate Brands, Inc.

Hot Dog on a Stick and Muscle Beach Lemonade are registered trademarks of HDOS Enterprises.

IHOP and International House of Pancakes are registered trademarks of International House of Pancakes, Inc.

Jamba Juice is a registered trademark of Jamba Juice Company.

Jimmy Dean is a registered trademark of Jimmy Dean Foods.

Keebler, Pecan Sandies, and Toffee Sandies are registered trademarks of Keebler Company.

KFC, Extra Crispy, Honey BBQ Wings, Taco Bell, and Border Sauce are registered trademarks of YUM! Brands Inc.

Krispy Kreme is a registered trademark of Krispy Kreme Inc.

Lipton and Brisk are registered trademarks of PepsiCo Inc.

Little Caesar's, Crazy Bread, and Crazy Sauce are registered trademarks of Little Caesar's Enterprises, Inc.

Little Debbie and Oatmeal Lights are registered trademarks of McKee Foods Corporation.

Lone Star Steakhouse & Saloon and Amarillo Cheese Fries are registered trademarks of Lone Star Steakhouse & Saloon, Inc.

Long John Silver's is a registered trademark of Jerrico, Inc.

M&M/Mars, Snickers, and Munch are registered trademarks of Mars, Inc.

Maid-Rite is a registered trademark of Maid-Rite Inc.

Marie Callender's is a registered trademark of Marie Callender's Pie Shops, Inc.

Mounds, Almond Joy, and Peter Paul are registered trademarks of Cadbury U.S.A., Inc.

Nabisco, Nutter Butter, Oreo, Double Stuff, Big Stuff, SnackWell's, Fudge Brownie Bars, HoneyMaid Grahams, Apple Raisin Snack Bars, Banana Snack Bars, and General Foods International Coffees are registered trademarks of Nabisco, Inc.

Nestlé, and 100 Grand Bar are registered trademarks of Nestlé USA, Inc.

Old Bay is a registered trademark of McCormick & Co. Inc.

The Olive Garden is a registered trademark of Darden Restaurants, Inc.

Outback Steakhouse and Bloomin' Onion, are registered trademarks of Outback Steakhouse, Inc.

Pal's and Sauceburger are registered trademarks of Pal's Sudden Service.

Panda Express is a registered trademark of Panda Management Company, Inc.

Peanut Butter Dream Bar and Mrs. Fields are registered trademarks of Mrs. Fields, Inc.

Pizza Hut and Stuffed Crust Pizza are trademarks of Pizza Hut, Inc.

Planters and Fiddle Faddle are registered trademarks of Planters, Inc.

Popeye's Famous Fried Chicken is a registered trademark of AFC Enterprises, Inc.

Ragu is a registered trademark of Unilever Bestfoods.

Reese's, Hershey, and York are registered trademarks of Hershey Foods Corporation.

Ruby Tuesday and Strawberry Tallcake are registered trademarks of Morrison Restaurants, Inc.

Ruth's Chris Steak House is a registered trademark of Ruth's Chris Steak House, Inc.

Sara Lee is a registered trademark of Sara Lee Corporation.

7-Eleven and Slurpee are registered trademarks of Southland Corporation.

Shoney's is a registered trademark of Shoney's, Inc.

Skyline is a registered trademark of Skyline Chili Inc.

Snapple is a registered trademark of Quaker Oats Company.

Sonic Drive-In is a registered trademark of Sonic Corp.

Starbucks and Frappuccino are registered trademarks of Starbucks Corporation.

Subway is a registered trademark of Doctor's Associates Inc.

Swiss Miss is a registered trademark of Hunt-Wesson Foods, Inc.

T.G.I. Friday's and Jack Daniel's Grill are registered trademarks of T.G.I. Friday's, Inc.

Tony Roma's A Place for Ribs, Carolina Honeys, and Red Hots are registered trademarks of NPC International, Inc.

INDEX